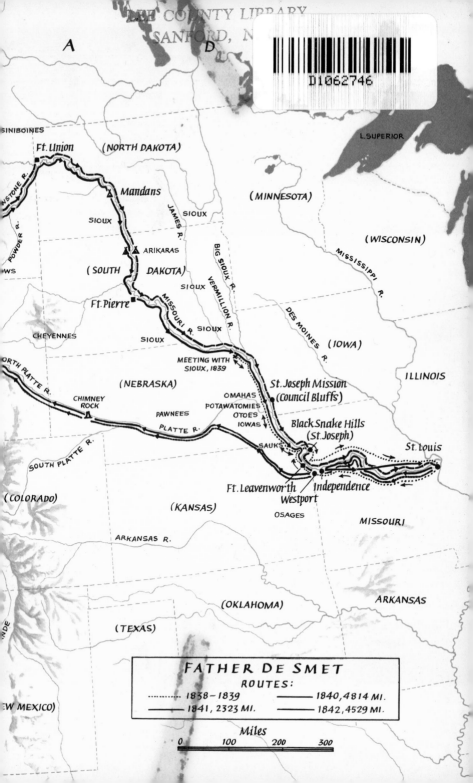

A

D

SINIBOINES
Ft. Union
(NORTH DAKOTA)
L.SUPERIOR

Mandans
SIOUX
SIOUX
(MINNESOTA)

JAMES R.

(WISCONSIN)

ARIKARAS
BIG SIOUX R.
VERMILLION R.

MISSISSIPPI R.

(SOUTH DAKOTA)
SIOUX

Ft. Pierre
MISSOURI R.
SIOUX

CHEYENNES
SIOUX
DES MOINES R.

(IOWA)

NORTH PLATTE R.
MEETING WITH SIOUX, 1839

ILLINOIS

CHIMNEY ROCK
(NEBRASKA)
OMAHAS
POTAWATOMIES
St. Joseph Mission (Council Bluffs)

PAWNEES
OTOES
IOWAS

Black Snake Hills (St. Joseph)

SOUTH PLATTE R.
PLATTE R.
SAUKS

St. Louis

(COLORADO)

Ft. Leavenworth
Westport
Independence

(KANSAS)
OSAGES

MISSOURI

ARKANSAS R.
(OKLAHOMA)

ARKANSAS

(TEXAS)

NDE

EW MEXICO)

FATHER DE SMET
ROUTES:
1838-1839 .... 1840, 4814 MI.

1841, 2323 MI. .... 1842, 4529 MI.

Miles

0   100   200   300

BLACK ROBE

By John Upton Terrell

BLACK ROBE

FURS BY ASTOR

JOURNEY INTO DARKNESS

PLUME ROUGE

SUNDAY IS THE DAY YOU REST

ADAM CARGO

THE LITTLE DARK MAN

For Younger Readers

THE UNITED STATES DEPARTMENT OF THE INTERIOR

THE UNITED STATES DEPARTMENT OF THE TREASURY

THE UNITED STATES DEPARTMENT OF STATE

THE KEY TO WASHINGTON

BLACK ROBE

The Life of Pierre-Jean De Smet
Missionary, Explorer & Pioneer

by John Upton Terrell

DOUBLEDAY & COMPANY, INC.

GARDEN CITY, NEW YORK

1964

First Edition

Library of Congress Catalog Card Number 64–19231
Copyright © 1964 by John Upton Terrell
All Rights Reserved
Printed in the United States of America

AUTHOR'S NOTE

Many eminent writers of western history have chosen to speak only briefly of the remarkable explorations and missionary accomplishments of Father De Smet. Some of the most prominent have completely ignored him. I cannot conceive of any reason which would justify this remissness.

For more than thirty years he was the most influential man in the western wilderness. These were the years when the era of the fur trade was drawing to a close and being supplanted by the era of mass migration and settlement—the years of transition, when the juggernaut of civilization smashed across the plains, deserts and mountains, and the call of the wild was lost in the ensuing uproar.

During this critical time no man was more trusted and revered by the Indians, and no man was a better friend to them. It is a great deal to say that during the worst of the Indian wars no other white man could have gone alone among the hostile tribes and remained alive. Yet, exactly that is said of Father De Smet by high-ranking Army officers, Indian agents, members of Congress, cabinet officers and other Washington officials, and numerous traders, all familiar with western conditions.

Four Presidents—Pierce, Buchanan, Lincoln and Johnson—sought his services, asking him to perform feats they knew no other person could accomplish, or would attempt. These Chief Executives understood that if any man could bring peace to the West it was the man the Indians called Black Robe.

If federal authorities had followed his advice, adopted his programs and carried them out, many of the bloodiest conflicts on the plains would not have taken place. They didn't listen to him. There was a force greater than the power he possessed. Its components were political corruption, unbridled venality and greed, and criminal negligence.

The richest source material about Father De Smet is to be found in the letters he wrote to his friends and family over a span of forty years. Nowhere else may be found guideposts and clues, lights and shadows, manifestations and avowals which so amply illustrate his inherent qualities, and provide such a reliable account of his adventures, his humanitarian deeds and his spiritual life.

It was Father De Smet's way—undoubtedly because of an insufficient supply of paper and ink in the wilderness, if not undependable mail service—to write long letters which, with very little editing, could be transformed into articles for magazines and newspapers, or adapted for inclusion in a book. This was frequently done, as well, with communications to his superiors in St. Louis and to the Father-General of the Jesuits in Rome. His books, therefore, are largely compilations of his correspondence, and are almost as valuable to the historian and biographer as the original letters.

The distinguished Hiram Martin Chittenden was the first historian to accord Father De Smet the high position in the history of the American West which he so rightfully deserves. In 1902, Chittenden published THE AMERICAN FUR TRADE IN THE FAR WEST (Francis P. Harper, New York). While doing research for this celebrated work he found himself "constantly running across the trail of a missionary-explorer named De Smet." The trail interlaced "the whole Northwest from St. Louis to the Strait of Juan de Fuca," and wherever encountered was "a tempting trail to follow."

Chittenden did follow the trail for several years in the company of a literary associate, Alfred Talbot Richardson, not only in the United States but in Europe. They collected every De Smet letter, article, scientific paper, religious treatise and essay—as well as numerous poems of dubious quality—they could uncover in their lengthy travels.

In 1905, they published THE LIFE, LETTERS AND TRAVELS OF FATHER PIERRE-JEAN DE SMET, S.J. (Francis P. Harper, New York). No attempt was made to write a definitive biography of him, for his papers and letters alone filled four large volumes.

It was a monumental contribution to American annals. For the first time Father De Smet's heroic accomplishments were brought to the attention of the general public. Yet—and I say again, inconceivably—most historians continued to pass him by. In this biography I have made an attempt to rectify this grievous omission.

Father De Smet's first book in English, LETTERS AND SKETCHES: WITH A NARRATIVE OF A YEAR'S RESIDENCE AMONG THE INDIAN TRIBES OF THE ROCKY MOUNTAINS, was published by M. Fithian, 61 N. Second Street, Philadelphia, in 1843. Dutch, German, French (2) and Italian editions appeared between 1844 and 1865.

OREGON MISSIONS AND TRAVELS OVER THE ROCKY MOUNTAINS IN 1845-46, was issued by Edward Dunigan, 151 Fulton Street, New York, in 1847. Two French editions and one in Flemish followed in 1848 and 1849. Arthur H. Clark & Company, Cleveland, published another American edition in 1906.

His WESTERN MISSIONS AND MISSIONARIES: A SERIES OF LETTERS, appeared first in 1863 under the imprint of James B. Kirker and Edward Dunigan & Brother, 599 Broadway, New York. Later editions were printed from the same plates by P. J. Kenedy, 5 Barclay Street, New York (no dates). This work also appeared in the French language.

NEW INDIAN SKETCHES was published by D. & J. Sadlier & Co., 31 Barclay Street, New York, in 1865. A second edition appeared under an 1885 copyright.

Father De Smet wrote numerous articles for the Belgian magazine, PRÉCIS HISTORIQUES, edited by Edward Terwecoran. In 1853, a selection of them was published in book form under the title, VOYAGE AU GRAND DESERT EN 1851, by J. Vandereydt, Bruxelles.

A number of his letters and sketches were reprinted in EARLY WESTERN TRAVELS, 1748–1846, 32 vols., edited by Reuben Gold Thwaites, and published by Arthur H. Clark & Co., Cleveland, 1904–7.

Shortly before his death Father De Smet authorized Father François Deynoodt, S.J., of Belgium, to prepare a complete edition of his writings and letters. The work appeared only in French. Six volumes were issued, one each year, between 1873 and 1878, by the Bruxelles houses of Victor Devaux et Cie, M. Closson et Cie, and F. Haenen, and the Paris publisher, H. Repos et Cie.

There are literally hundreds of histories, biographies and narratives available to one desirous of acquiring knowledge of the period 1838–69, in which Father De Smet made his epic journeys beyond the frontier. Whatever the locales of those which do not include him, it may be safely said that, at one time or another, he was there.

JOHN UPTON TERRELL

*To the memory
of the brave men whose voices
we still hear crying in the
wilderness*

BLACK ROBE

BLACK KORL

PROLOGUE

In the spring of 1864, Father De Smet went up the Missouri River by steamboat to Fort Berthold, in the new Dakota Territory, almost two thousand miles above St. Louis. He traveled as an emissary of peace for the United States Government. From the Red River of the North to the Columbia the frontier of the northern plains was aflame with Indian wars. Tribes fought each other in conflicts that had their roots in ancient causes, and they fought as allies against the swelling tide of white settlement and the venality of the federal bureaucracy.

The united Sioux, continuing the reign of destruction and murder they had begun two years before in Minnesota, were spreading their terror and their devastation far north and west along the upper Missouri, ranging on their bloody forays in all the vast territory between the Canadian border and the Platte, the Rivière à Jacques and the Yellowstone.

Blood darkened the summer sunlight, and the winds, stirring the flowers and the tall grasses and the cottonwood leaves, whispered of waiting death. Father De Smet found the Mandans, the Gros Ventres and the Arikaras, frequently belligerents in the past, grouped in the vicinity of Fort Berthold for their mutual protection against the Sioux scourge. He was received with cordiality and enthusiasm, for they, like Indians in all the Far West through which he had traveled for nearly two decades, had long revered him. They registered delight when he announced that he had come to reveal more about the Great Spirit to them, and to baptize their children, but they were aghast when he told them of his intention to go among the Sioux with a plea for

15

peace, of which he was the bearer, from the President, Mr. Lincoln.

In 1864, Father De Smet's fame as a wilderness missionary had long been established in both America and Europe. Now justification for that fame, the foundation of courage, determination, devotion to duty, political power and religious influence upon which it had been built, was incomparably illustrated.

On the afternoon of July 8, when Father De Smet was kneeling before the little altar he had erected in his room which the post trader, F. F. Girard, had provided for him, several horsemen appeared on the bluffs across the Missouri River from Fort Berthold. An alarm was sounded, accompanied by the wild screaming of women, the mad barking of dogs and the shrill cries of children. Indians raced for their weapons, and some climbed to the roofs of the biggest earthen lodges for a better view. Father De Smet, long used to uproars in Indian villages, completed his devotions. By the time he had emerged, the horsemen had been identified as Sioux, and the shouting and screaming and wild excitement had assumed the proportions of a general tumult.

As Father De Smet squinted into the dazzling afternoon sun, several chiefs and the white men of the trading post gathered about him. The riders across the river were steadily increasing in number. Out of the sky came long lines of naked warriors, and they formed a ragged colorful blanket that spread like a cloud shadow on the crest of the bluffs.

Three hundred Sioux braves sat on their ponies gazing across the valley of the Missouri at the lodges and tepees and stockades of Fort Berthold.

Father De Smet asked for quiet, and chiefs waved the Indians into silence. Even the dogs seemed to sense the tenseness of the moment, and stopped their barking. Father De Smet's calm announcement that he would cross the river and confer with the Sioux brought expressions of utter amazement into the faces of the men about him. Girard quickly advised against taking such a risk. He was emphatically supported by Pierre Garreau, the interpreter, and Gustave Cagnat, chief clerk of the post.

Soaring War Eagle, standing six inches above six feet in height, had a look of mingled fear and tragedy in his eyes as he implored Black Robe not to walk among men who were enemies of all peoples. Similar pleas came from White Parflèche, chief of the Arikaras, and Little Walker, the Mandans' chief. Black Robe, they declared, would be going to his death, for no man, either Indian or white, even a man who spoke with the Great Spirit, could go alone among the Sioux and survive. He would be tortured to death, his tongue would be torn from his mouth, his genitals slashed from his body, and he would be hacked to pieces by squaws, and his scalp would adorn a Sioux thigh.

Patiently Father De Smet explained that he had come north to talk with the Sioux, to give them Mr. Lincoln's message of peace, and he would carry out his mission. He started toward the river. Wailing and moaning arose among the women. A headman ran forward and touched the black robe, shaking his head in grief.

In a small skiff, Father De Smet paddled steadily across the river. For a time, the Sioux did not move, but as he neared the opposite bank several left their horses and ran toward the water.

Struck silent by their terrible fears, hundreds of Indian men, women and children, watched from Fort Berthold as Father De Smet stepped from the little craft and was suddenly lost in a horde of yelling Sioux, as if he had been swallowed by them.

For three hours the people at the fort continued their tragic vigil. They saw the smoke of campfires stand against the blaze of the falling sun on the hills across the river. Their dominant thought was reflected in eyes of terror and depthless sorrow.

The shadows had grown long below the bluffs when they saw the little skiff put out from the opposite shore. In it was one man, and he wore black. They dared not even to hope. It could not be true. It was a trick of some kind.

When they saw the broad, powerful figure of Father De Smet

step ashore, they burst toward him in a mad rush, crying out their joy, shouting their wonder and thankfulness, and not a few fell to their knees and crossed themselves.

Father De Smet had met with no difficulty, no trouble, no enmity. He had been welcomed, and he had been feasted—a fine rack of venison, kidneys and roots in suet, wild berries—and he had talked long and amicably with the headmen of the Sioux war party, and the message from Mr. Lincoln had been respectfully received.

The Sioux, Father De Smet told the anxious people of Fort Berthold, had not come to attack them. They had come there because they had heard that their good friend, Black Robe, had come up the river and desired to speak with them. Word of Black Robe's journey had spread throughout the Sioux Nations, even far north to the border of British territory where the Santees, who had committed the Minnesota massacres, were in hiding. The Santees had sent an invitation to Black Robe, asking him to come among them with his words from the American President, and Father De Smet had promised to go before the summer had ended.

No other white man—fur hunter, Indian trader, soldier, government agent, Man of God, or of any other calling—could have crossed the Missouri River at Fort Berthold that July day in 1864, and survived.

I

At dawn on the 10th of May 1838, the steamboat *Howard* made ready to cast off from the St. Louis waterfront for the upper Missouri. It was a routine departure, occurring frequently in the spring, but to one unfamiliar with such an event it might have appeared of immense historical importance.

Boat whistles, not only that of the *Howard* but of the many river craft at the long levee, shrieked repeatedly, men shouted and howled and fired guns in the air, horses neighed, mules bawled, dogs barked, as the stevedores hurried the last cargo aboard. For most of the *voyageurs*, the hunters and trappers going up the river, the tumult marked the end of days of carousing with Indian, Negro and half-breed sluts. Men staggered toward the waterfront, falling down, bleeding from smashed faces and heads. Those whose legs failed them were carried aboard and dropped on the deck like sacks of potatoes, and there they lay until revived by buckets of water dashed over them.

A thousand, perhaps two thousand, miles of unpredictable muddy current were ahead, weeks fighting the treachery of the great river, its boils and eddies, crumbling banks, snags and sand bars, perhaps in terrorizing storms, fierce heat, gale winds and numbing cold, and weeks of defending themselves against the arrows and gunshots that might come without warning, the inexplicable capriciousness and inconstancy of the Indian mind, qualities as inherent as the skin pigmentation and the physiognomic characteristics which distinguished the warrior from his white brother.

There would be no government, no law, no civil authorities on the upper river, no sheriffs, only a handful of troops at Fort

Leavenworth and a few powerless Indian agents. If the government was there in theory—it was the territory of a sovereign nation—it was not there in reality. If the laws were written, they were meaningless, for they were not enforced.

The law was the *bourgeois,* the partner, who reigned supreme in the trading post or was in command of the brigade in the wilderness. But if the *bourgeois* was the absolute authority, if he conducted his business with the discipline of a military post, he was little protection for the individual trapper, the *voyageur,* the *engagé,* the stupid *mangeur de lard.* The *bourgeois* might wear fine clothes, even a uniform of some sort, dine in splendor with linen napery and silver tableware, sleep with his squaw concubine between freshly laundered bedclothes, and he could beat a man, cast him out alone, rob him of his wages with dishonest bookkeeping, shoot him. Or he could, if he so desired, be kind, considerate, fair. He could be anything he wanted to be. Still, he had the responsibility of guarding the investment of the company for which he worked, and that job came first. Furs were more important than men, either red, white or black. Even horses ranked above them. The contracts which the men signed with the company said they had to go into the wilderness, but no contract said anything about their coming back.

Most white men reasoned that God could not be expected to protect them two or three thousand miles from the nearest church cross. All that stood between a man and an unmarked grave were his own superstitions, his own knowledge of ghosts, his own ability to sense the presence of danger, smell it in the wind, see it in the markings of the dust, hear it in the whispers of the grass.

As the steamboat *Howard* pulled out into the broad Mississippi, and the tumult and the shouting died away, Father De Smet sat on a crate on the afterdeck and gazed back at the retreating buildings of St. Louis. For some moments his eyes held to the spire and cross of the cathedral, which rose above the surrounding rooftops. He knew an inner excitement of a kind he had not experienced for years. He knew, too, a profound satisfaction, for he was, at last, on his way to the Indian Country. He was going with another priest and two lay Brothers to found a mission among the Potawatomies at the Council Bluffs.

Fifteen years had passed since he had first seen the shores of America from the deck of another ship, the little brig *Columbus,* on which he had traveled across the Atlantic from the Netherlands. Memories of that day, and of the exciting months preceding it, crowded back into his thoughts, as if stirred to new life by the voyage to the interior on which he was now embarking.

This was the life, the work, he had so long dreamed of living and doing. Even when he had been a student at Malines, he had known that he would devote himself to it. The exact road he would take had not then been determined, but he had known that it would one day open before him. The question had been settled suddenly during his last year at the seminary. It was in that year that Father Charles Nerinckx, who had been driven across the sea to America by the French Revolution, returned to Belgium in quest of funds and recruits.

Father Nerinckx had painted glowing pictures of the United States, of the great opportunities which awaited sincere young men willing to pledge their lives to cultivating the untilled religious fields of the New World. His fervency and his descriptions had inspired the young scholars of Malines. Yet, Father De Smet could recall very well that he had made his decision to volunteer only after long deliberation.

Sitting on the deck of the steamboat *Howard* he could remember vividly the arguments he had had with his parents, who were most devout but still were opposed to his making such a sacrifice. He could almost feel once more the pain he had suffered, not only that induced by the defiant stand he was forced to take against his father and mother, whom he deeply loved and respected, but that which came with the thought of leaving behind his many brothers and sisters, his good home, the old village and the land so deeply and indestructibly held in his heart. He had been nauseated by homesickness even before he had started.

Looking backward at the age of thirty-eight, he had good reasons to feel that he had literally followed the precept: *If thou wilt be perfect, go and sell that thou hast, and give to the poor, and thou shalt have treasure in heaven: and come and follow me.*

He could readily admit that he was far from perfect. He had, indeed, given to the poor, and he hoped that treasure awaited him in heaven. He had with all his heart and soul sought to follow the Master. As for selling what he had, he had been obliged to do that before he could sail on the *Columbus.* No money was forthcoming from his disapproving family, and he had been forced to pawn everything he owned to pay for his passage.

As the *Howard* churned its way into the brown flood of the Missouri, Father De Smet went forward to gaze at the mighty river. He had the sensation that he was starting out once more on another new highway of life, a highway that not only came out of the uncharted mountains and plains of a boundless wilderness, but out of the setting sun.

II

At the beginning of the nineteenth century, there were some houses in the Belgian village of Termonde on the Dendre which had been the quarters of soldiers and officials of the Dukes of Burgundy. There were newer houses, perhaps only one or two hundred years old, which had been built by the forebears of the families occupying them. Among these were the Buydens, the Duerincks, the Kolliers, the De Saegers and the De Smets.

There were buildings in which men and women tended looms, molded glass and pottery, made clothing, sold tools and drugs and shoes, practiced law and medicine, in which their great-great-great grandfathers and grandmothers had carried on the same work. History, heritage and tradition influenced and guided every new life in Termonde as they did the lives nearing their end. Indeed, it might have been said that most residents of the ancient place lived in the past as much as they did in the present. As for the future, it had a way of taking care of itself, and one hardly needed to consider it.

The Church of the Blessed Virgin Mary wore the scars of its years with dignity, reflecting its memories in grizzled cornices, worn stones, worm-eaten carvings, and big leather-bound tomes in which had been recorded an uncounted number of names of persons born in the parish, who took Communion there, and who had gone to their resting places in the adjacent cemetery.

Some entry was made in the records almost every day, so there was nothing of more than ordinary interest in the enrollment of two names in the baptismal register on January 30, 1801, except that they were the names of twins, a girl and boy.

Prêtre J. C. Ringoot wrote that he had "baptized Pierre-Jean, born this morning at about five o'clock, and Coleta Aldegunda, born at a quarter after five, twin children of Judocus De Smet of this parish and Joana Maria Buydens, of this parish, his wife. The sponsors were John Baptiste Kollier of Smerrebe and Coleta De Saeger of Botteliere."

The names of numerous other living De Smet children, cousins and half-brothers and half-sisters of Pierre-Jean and Coleta, were in the register. Their father had married twice. His first wife was Jeanne-Marie Duerinck, and she had six children. Pierre-Jean and Coleta were the fifth and sixth born to their mother. Three more, two boys and a girl, were to follow in the next four years.

When Pierre-Jean was very young, a priest at the church described him as an unusually well-formed youth, healthy and handsome. He rapidly developed into an athlete of no small ability, and this distinction and his robustness won him the sobriquet of Samson from his companions. Except for the nickname and her decided femininity and daintiness, the same description might have been applied to his twin sister.

Despite his proficiency in them, however, sports never held more than a small attraction for Pierre-Jean. From the time he attended his first classes as a child he displayed a consuming interest in books. Early in his teens he was skilled as a reader, not only of Flemish but of Latin and French. He was fourteen when he was sent to the old seminary of Malines. During the ensuing six years he was not only distinguished as a student, but he demonstrated qualities of intelligence, tact and understanding that would have complimented a fully matured man. Some of his instructors felt certain he was destined to become a great lawyer or diplomat. Others urged him to pursue a career as a teacher. He had his own dreams and aspirations, and although he talked little about them before his nineteenth year, an observant person might well have detected the nature of them. His increasing devoutness and interest in religious history were unmistakable signs.

From Termonde in the summer of 1821, the road on which he

had known he would one day set out led across the rich old fields of the Flemish Plain, through brawling Antwerp, over the dikes to the Rhine and smoky, bustling Rotterdam, across the pastoral lowlands, over the canals and through the curving streets of Amsterdam and along the North Sea coast to the isle of Texel.

With him were five other young men, all struggling to conceal their emotion, all wondering if they were making a grave mistake, all driven on by an irrepressible dream, all as badly scared as was he. It was the summer of 1821.*

They watched the low shore of Texel fade into the twilight one August evening, and forty days later, on September 21st, they went ashore from the brig *Columbus* on the waterfront of Philadelphia.

Passing through the streets of Philadelphia, they were astonished to see substantial commercial buildings and charming town houses, well-dressed people and liveried coachmen, and all the amenities of civilization. Pierre-Jean, no less than the others, had envisioned America as an untamed wilderness inhabited only by frontiersmen in buckskin and naked savages.

The erroneousness of this conception was further made clear by a sightseeing trip to Baltimore, Washington and Georgetown, on which they were taken by Father Charles Van Quickenborne, the Master of Jesuit Novices in the United States. They journeyed through a lovely land painted with fall colors, traversed by beautiful rivers, marked by magnificent woodlands, blue hills always ahead of them against the clear October sky. They passed through neat little villages, and they saw in the countryside fine mansions surrounded by expansive gardens, groves and pastures, estates that would have graced the holdings of European aristocrats.

The apprehension that he had come to study for the priesthood and to be a missionary among heathens in a land in which steamboats, turnpikes and scheduled stage lines were commonplace

---

* Pierre-Jean De Smet's companions were Felix Verreydt, Jodocus Van Assche, Pierre J. Verhaegen, Jean Smedts and Jean Elet.

was soon relieved, however, by the assurance that the true wilderness was not far away. It had been pushed westward over the Alleghenies, but beyond them it swept away for more than two thousand miles. After one crossed the Mississippi it reached out through plains, deserts and mountains, largely as it had been created, much of it still wrapped in mystery, and all of it the realm of the savage. He would see all the wild country, and wilder people, he could desire in time.

From Georgetown the six novices were taken to White Marsh, in Maryland on upper Chesapeake Bay, where the first Jesuit novitiate in the United States had been established more than a decade before. It consisted of several small buildings in a sad state of dilapidation, and as an institution was in a precarious condition because of a lack of funds. Hope for relief and rehabilitation had all but been abandoned by the elderly priests in residence there, and this situation was not improved during the next eighteen months as Pierre-Jean De Smet and the other novices applied themselves to their studies.

Early in 1823, Secretary of War John C. Calhoun made a suggestion to his good friend, the Right Reverend Louis W. Du Bourg, Bishop of Louisiana, which brought hope anew that the Jesuits would be enabled to enlarge their missionary work in the West. It was Calhoun's thought that the plight of the White Marsh fathers and novices might be greatly relieved if they were moved to Missouri. There was every prospect that St. Louis and the surrounding territory would steadily develop and prosper. The Church already held title to several parcels of land in the town and adjacent countryside. In addition to locating a novitiate there for the training of missionaries, a school could be established for Indian boys who eventually could serve as guides, interpreters and helpers to the priests sent into the wilderness. Arrangements could be made, said Calhoun, to obtain an annual government subsidy of $800 for the school.

Enthusiastically Bishop Du Bourg placed the plan before

Father Van Quickenborne. He eagerly accepted it, and quickly set about putting it into effect.

It was on April 11, 1823, that five priests and seven novices, led by Father Van Quickenborne, left White Marsh on the long journey to the newest part of the United States. They traveled with three wagons to Wheeling on the Ohio River. In the two largest wagons were the few sticks of furniture, crates of books, utensils and tools, and the trunks which contained the few worldly possessions of the little band. In a lighter wagon were their treasured religious articles, the altar pieces and sacred vestments, the images and emblems and crosses, and the boxes containing their sparse supply of foodstuffs.

There was no room in the wagons for the travelers, except the drivers, and all but three walked, often giving their shoulders to the wheels to aid the horses in rough and muddy reaches of road. Pierre-Jean De Smet wrote that they proceeded the entire distance to the Ohio River *"pedibus apostolorum,* staff in hand." They were passing through a land of Protestant communities in which many residents had never seen a living priest. In several places they were mistaken for a band of adventurers seeking their fortune, and they were approached by crooked land promoters and various other types of swindlers. The few Catholics they encountered sought to persuade them to remain and establish places of worship. Regretting they were unable to comply with such requests, they pressed onward.

The little money in Father Van Quickenborne's purse was badly depleted by the necessary purchase of two small flatboats. Lashing them together, they loaded their baggage, climbed aboard and pushed out into the strong spring current of the Ohio. At Louisville they were obliged to unload, portage around the falls, and send the boats through to calm water in command of a hired pilot. Once more on their way, they floated to Shawneetown, Illinois. Traveling any farther by water would have carried them sharply toward the south and southwest, always away from their destination, until they struck the Mississippi, and they would have had no means of breasting its current upstream to St. Louis. Their funds would not permit them to take passage on a steamboat for the balance of the journey, but Father Van Quickenborne managed to pay the cost of transporting their possessions on one. Sending them off, they started out once more on foot.

For several weeks they trudged through a rolling country bursting with spring, its few roads often impassable with deep mud, its vales and lowlands flooded. They could not afford to pay for lodging in the few inns found along their route, and they took refuge in barns and outbuildings of friendly farmers. Many nights they spent huddled about a campfire, wet, cold, and hungry.

It was a tattered, dirty, and very exhausted group that, on the 30th of May 1823, stood on the left bank of the Mississippi River and gazed across its broad shining waters to the rooftops and smoking chimneys of St. Louis.

The St. Louis of 1823 was hardly more than a ragged cluster of clapboard, stone and log buildings, but it was the trading center of a territory a hundred times as large as Belgium. Almost its entire economy was derived from a single source, the fur trade.

A few miles to the west the rolling wilderness hills gradually diminished, melting into widening prairies. Woodlands decreased, breaking apart into scattered islands, and at last only a few trees remained to trace the crooked courses of shallow streams across flat earth that touched the sky, the grass sea of the high plains, growing steadily more immense, sweeping onward for a thousand miles until they washed against the towering, impregnable wall of the western mountains.

There were a few spacious and carefully tended residences in St. Louis which denoted the presence of some persons of cultured taste and affluence. These were the homes of French families which for several decades or more had engaged in the fur trade, and which, although surrounded by a savage wilderness, had striven to preserve something of the gracious manner of living they would have known had they remained in the Old World or in New Orleans.

To a young man of proper and gentle rearing, however, the general grubbiness, the vulgarity, roistering, and undisguised wickedness of the town were both repelling and frightening. At the age of twenty-three, Pierre-Jean De Smet had known for only two years the world beyond the cloistered walls of the seminary at Malines and the safety of a well-ordered and comfortable Termonde home in which kindness and thoughtfulness were as scrupulously practiced as religious devotions. He had never known poverty, real hunger or abuse.

Now he saw a swiftly growing town at the gateway to its greatest days as the fur trade capital of North America. It swarmed with a heterogeneous population that kept it in a continual uproar. French-Canadian *voyageurs*, British, Scotch and Irish factors, *bourgeois*, partners, American traders and merchants, hunters from Virginia, Kentucky and Tennessee, river louts, steamboat hands, mountain men who lived and acted like Indians, the Indians themselves, both full-bloods and breeds of all fractions, prostitutes of varied colors, Negroes, soldiers and government officials, gamblers and thieves, degenerates and false prophets, all thronging the streets, the brothels, saloons, trading houses, cafés, shops and inns, camping on the river bank and living in ramshackle cabins and filthy hovels dug in the earth.

Yet, if he were repulsed by the iniquity, Pierre-Jean De Smet was not surprised to find it there. St. Louis was much as he had pictured it in his mind. It was, in fact, as he had expected all America to be.

III

The site selected for the first novitiate west of the Mississippi was on farmland some fifteen miles north of St. Louis near the tiny village of St. Ferdinand de Florissant, within walking distance of the Missouri River. It was a lovely place. Bordering rich loam fields were wide groves of black willows, sycamores, oaks and walnut and hazelnut trees. The houses of the village were widely spaced, surrounded by spacious grounds, gardens and orchards. The tree-shaded lanes bore the names of saints, given them half a century before by the first French settlers.

At the west end of St. Francis Street stood the white brick church of St. Ferdinand, completed only two years before the group from White Marsh arrived. The imposing two-and-one-half-story rectory had been built two years before the church. Nearby was the convent of the Sisters of Loretto, a sturdy brick building with dormer windows. For only a few months had Mother Rose Philippine Duchesne and the four Sisters who had come from France with her enjoyed the comfort of a safe home. Since 1818—five years before they greeted Father Van Quickenborne and his novices—they had lived, taught and suffered in both St. Ferdinand de Florissant and the frontier town of St. Charles, not infrequently menaced and frightened out of their wits by drunken Indians and trappers.

With the older priests voicing their approval and moral support, the seven young men set to work wielding saws, hammers and axes as if inspired by visions of the fruits their labors would produce. Although he had no more energy, and certainly no greater zeal, than his six companions, Pierre-Jean De Smet was stronger by far than any of them. He stood only seven inches above five feet, but this lack of height was compensated by an extraordinary physical power. His shoulders were broad, his limbs heavy and muscular. Father Van Quickenborne marveled at his brawny pupil's ability to hold up one end of a log alone while two or three others struggled to raise the opposite end. The good master also shook his head in despair, wondering if he would be able much longer to pay the food bills, when he observed how much "Samson" De Smet consumed at a single meal.

The first creation of the new novitiate was a crude log structure, but the young men gazed on it with inordinate pride. However, if the humble little building rewarded them with a feeling of accomplishment, it did little in the way of providing creature comforts. The novices had forsaken good homes and the promise of profitable professional or commercial careers. Now they found themselves crowded together in a low loft to sleep on pallets of straw. They washed their few clothes on the rocks of a brook with insufficient soap. They cooked their food on open fires or in ovens made of stones. For the most part their fare consisted of wild game obtained from professional hunters, potatoes, onions and rutabagas purchased from farmers near them, a little beef or pork, hominy and grits (eternally), an occasional chicken lean and tough from an arduous life in the open, and now and then an egg or two of which they had good reason to be suspicious. After laboring at building and farming during the day, they pursued their studies by the flickering light of tapers.

"It is at such times," Pierre-Jean De Smet wrote to his family, "that one feels the full weight of the sacrifice he makes in a good and holy cause."

The single room below the loft was divided by a curtain. On one side Father Van Quickenborne made his home. The other side was the chapel of the novitiate. The building continued apace, however, and soon two more small log cabins were completed. These were devoted to the Indian school and mission. One of them was furnished with crude benches. It was the first schoolroom of the kind established west of the Mississippi.

From the day the first Indian boys arrived at the mission school, Pierre-Jean happily added the duty of instructing them to his many other obligations. It was the work he loved most. He displayed an inexhaustible patience with the six wild little fellows with eyes like obsidian, wild, indeed, as the foxes of the forest from which they came, and he strongly disagreed with the prediction of Father Van Quickenborne that the school would be an acknowledged failure within a year.

The sagacity of the master, however, was soon demonstrated. Four of the Indian boys slipped out of their blankets late one night and vanished. Pierre-Jean was soon on their trail, and he caught up to them as the first streaks of dawn marked the sky. Having become confused, they were huddled in a hollow about a small campfire.

The boys had not fled because they disliked school. They did, in fact, enjoy their lessons. But working in the fields, cutting firewood, carrying water and helping with the cooking were chores they would not do. Such "squaw work" injured their pride. Pierre-Jean and his colleagues, thereafter, were forced to work with their pupils whenever there was manual labor to be done in order to show them the necessity and nobility of it.

Even this system was only partially successful. After two years of struggling with a dozen pupils who vanished whenever moved by the urge to regain the complete freedom they had always known, Pierre-Jean was obliged to admit that Father Quickenborne was right. No great or permanent results would be accomplished among the indolent, restless people of the adjacent forest that would compensate for sacrificing all the energies and resources of the little mission and the novitiate.

He came to accept—though not without deep regret—Father Van Quickenborne's conviction that more solid and lasting good might be done among the swiftly increasing white population of St. Louis and the surrounding territory, on both sides of the Mississippi. Missionary work among the Indians need not be abandoned, merely continued to a minimum extent. It was the moral and spiritual obligation of the Jesuits to provide not only churches and secondary schools but a university in which the arts and sciences could be taught on the highest academic levels.

If Pierre-Jean De Smet was resigned to accepting the dictum of his superior, he was privately unenthusiastic about it, and he did not look forward to participating in it. His dream prevailed unshattered and unadulterated. In a free hour he would sit on the bank of the great river that poured its turbid muddy torrent into the Mississippi, and he would look into the west, his thoughts carrying his vision far beyond the actual reach of his sight, into the world of his imagination.

He had studied every available history, searched every book for knowledge of the country through which the Missouri flowed on its long course from the western mountains, knowledge of the red people, the scores of tribes whose names he heard cross the lips of the mountain men and the fur hunters with whom he spoke, thirsting for understanding of their ways, their customs, their minds, and always praying that he would one day soon— once he had been ordained—be sent among them.

On the way home from their epic journey across the continent, Lewis and Clark met the vanguard of American traders ascending the Missouri River. As he read the history of the West, Pierre-Jean De Smet realized the significance of the event. It marked the beginning of a new era, an era which was becoming more significant with the passage of each succeeding year. Thoughtfully he wondered how and when it would end, and what part he would play in that ending.

Four years after arriving in St. Louis, in 1827, Pierre-Jean De Smet became Father De Smet. His ordination made it possible for him to be sent as a full-fledged missionary in the Indian Country, and he hoped fervently each day for orders to go.

He would have suffered deep disappointment and discouragement if he could have looked into the future and learned that another ten years must pass before the assignment he wanted more than any other in life would come to him.

IV

Bishop Du Bourg had founded St. Louis Academy under the twin handicaps of insufficient funds and inadequate housing in 1818. Although the funds had not increased much, a room or two had been added by the end of two years, and the name was changed to the more imposing St. Louis College.

No less than Father Van Quickenborne had Bishop Du Bourg hoped that ways and means might be found to establish a general university in the rapidly growing city of St. Louis. The opportunity came suddenly in 1827. Funds were on hand for the erection of a new building, but even without it the Bishop undoubtedly would have carried on, for he had at his disposal seven thoroughly competent and trained young teachers and several older priests.

It was in 1827 that the novices who had come from White Marsh to St. Ferdinand de Florissant were ordained. The Indian school they had founded was a failure, and their varied and excellent talents would have been wasted on it. Bishop Du Bourg directed them to join the small and harried staff of St. Louis College, which henceforth would be St. Louis University. *

Young, brilliant Father Verhaegen became the new university's first president. He took pleasure in awarding a prominent and responsible faculty post—that of directing the departments of languages, history and philosophy—to his boyhood companion and colleague, Father De Smet. This work, of course, would have to be carried on in addition to other duties already assigned to Father De Smet.

* The first university west of the Mississippi River, it received a charter in 1832.

It had been found that he was particularly good at organizing new programs and dealing with such persons as builders and contractors. He got along very well with carpenters, masons and suppliers, and he was especially adept at keeping costs to a minimum. Father De Smet could have been kept busy doing nothing more than establishing and building churches, schools and convents—and securing money to pay for them, an occupation for which he also had a remarkable talent—in communities of western Illinois and Missouri. So in addition to being the chief businessman and procurator, Father De Smet was obliged to find the time to conduct daily classes, and the faces before him were those of sons of midwestern farmers and merchants, traders and shippers, not those of the red youths with the look of distance in their eyes, which he would have much preferred to see.

More than once he remarked that he had never attempted to understand the mysterious ways in which the activities of the Society of Jesus were fashioned and directed, feeling that such an understanding was in all probability beyond the capability of his mind. Yet, he did not complain, being a loyal and dutiful member, to a greater extent than might have been reasonably expected of him in the face of such a severe disappointment—such as grumbling under his breath—and his opinions of the efficiency and intelligence of those who commanded him were never permitted to escape beyond the confines of his private thoughts.

Although the Indian school at St. Ferdinand de Florissant was closed, the Indian mission and the novitiate were continued and enlarged. When the mission had been founded it was a dependency of the province of Maryland, but in 1831 it was awarded independence and ordered to support itself. Shortly afterward the Provisional Council of Baltimore had proposed that all Indian missions in the United States be placed under the jurisdiction of the Jesuits, and the plan had received favorable action in Rome.

The move added to the responsibilities of the priests in the western country, but it also opened fully the door to the Far West for the Jesuits. All missionary work in that immense territory, still so little known, was theirs to command and to carry out.

Once again Father De Smet's hope of going into the wilderness soared to a new height. Then suddenly illness struck. The physician he consulted in St. Louis could attribute his ailment to no single organ. His heavy, powerful body—he weighed more than two hundred pounds—was afflicted with an unprecedented weariness, and his appetite had for the first time in his life failed him. He was nervous, and unable to sleep.

In addition to root tonics, which it was hoped would help to revive his spirit and strengthen his blood, but which usually had the effect of getting him tipsy, the doctor prescribed a long rest and a complete change of environment. Father Verhaegen promptly arranged to have him given a leave from active service in St. Louis, and sent him off to Europe. In order that he would not think of himself as being relegated to pasture and of no more use to the Society, he was ordered to perform some business missions in Europe for the Church, to seek recruits for the Missouri novitiate, and to solicit new equipment and funds. The requests made of him might well have dismayed a healthy man. Yet, the assignments did little in the way of allaying his immeasurable disappointment. He suspected that Father Verhaegen and his other colleagues believed they would not see him again on the American frontier, but he had no intention of permitting such a thing to occur.

He would return, if God let him recover his strength and his spirit. To give emphasis to his determination, he took out his final naturalization papers, and on September 23, 1833, became a citizen of the United States.

As the year 1833 was ending he arrived in Termonde in obviously bad health. Uninterrupted rest in his old home, the ministrations of the De Smet physician and of members of his family, and good Belgian cooking, however, had soon started him on the road to recovery. But he did not spend his days in complete indolence. Within a short time he had succeeded in recruiting three novices and acquiring a valuable set of scientific instruments for St. Louis University. For the second feat he was rewarded with a commendation in the form of a resolution. "Whereas," it said over the signatures of Fathers Verhaegen and James Van de Velde, the secretary, "the board and faculty of St. Louis University are highly indebted to the liberality and exertions of the Rev. P. J. De Smet, for the splendid apparatus of physical and chemical instruments received at the university on the 7th of March, 1834."

Father De Smet wept a bit with the joy of being able to serve even during his indisposition. By the end of 1834, although not yet fully himself, he felt sufficiently mended to attempt the journey back to America. The decision was a serious mistake. Despite objections from friends and family, he embarked from Antwerp, but before his ship had passed through the North Sea he had become violently ill and almost too weak to stand. He was forced to land at Deal, in England, where he was told by a physician that he could not survive an ocean crossing. He took a stage to Margate, a steamer to London, a stage to Dover, crossed the English Channel to Calais, and passing by stage through Dunkirk and Lille, reached Termonde.

He realized now the folly of attempting to return before his health had been without question fully restored, and he turned once more to occupying himself with soliciting money and equipment for the university, the Missouri Mission, and the cathedral in St. Louis. During the next two years, traveling through Belgium, Holland and France, he obtained worthwhile contributions, thousands of books, and many fine church pictures, some of them oils of high value. His acquisitions, and three more candidates for the novitiate at Florissant, were with him when, in the fall of 1837, he boarded an American packet at Havre for New York.

The crossing took thirty days. He traveled by rail and canal to Pittsburgh, thence by steamboat to St. Louis.

He was joyously welcomed by Father Verhaegen and the university faculty. Once his superiors had assured themselves that he had returned as the robust, congenial, energetic, buoyant, good-humored Father De Smet they had known for so many years before his illness, they disclosed the plan which they had hoped he would be able to carry out.

He was to be sent to found a mission among the Potawatomies.

At last, after more than fifteen years of hard labor, study, and serving willingly at whatever duty was assigned to him, he was on his way to the field he had so often prayed he would reach, the work which was closest to his heart.

V

Besides the Potawatomies, there were in the general vicinity of the Council Bluffs the remnants of several other tribes which had been driven or transferred there from their original homes east of the Mississippi. It was considered a promising area for a mission, and Father De Smet looked forward with eagerness to reaching it. Orders, however, prevented him from going straight through. He had been instructed to leave the *Howard* at the Kickapoo village, near Fort Leavenworth, and report on conditions there. He would continue on in time to meet the steamboat *Wilmington* at the fort. Father Felix Verreydt and two lay Brothers would travel up from St. Louis on it, and they would go on together to their ultimate destination at the Council Bluffs.

Reaching the Kickapoo village, Father De Smet noted that the soil in the area "seemed to me very rich, the woods . . . superb and the prairie smiling and beautiful." The head chief, Pashihi "appeared much attached to us . . . He is a man full of wit and good sense."

Pashihi told Father De Smet of a vision in which the ancient Mahetaconia (Black Gowns) who formerly visited his tribe—when the Kickapoos dwelt in the woodlands east of the Mississippi, and the Jesuits reached them from Canada—had appeared to him. They had reproached him for the "hardness of heart of his nation and their perversity in stubbornly refusing to receive and follow the law of Christ." That, Pashihi maintained, was the reason why the Great Spirit had abandoned them "to all sorts of irregularities and to the impositions of a false prophet, Keokuk, and that none of them should escape his wrath in the other world."

39

Even though he was on his first official mission to the Indians, Father De Smet was fully aware of their propensity to speak what they believed their guests would like to hear. There were many shrewd and intelligent Indian leaders, and they often were the possessors of great imaginations. They also were gifted as liars and propagandists, and they applied these dubious talents with motives aforethought. Their expressed adoration of the white man's God, and their seeming eagerness to adhere to the Christian doctrines, were not always founded upon sincerity. More often these words and attitudes belonged in the category of adroit salesmanship, which seldom failed to bring from the Black Robes useful gifts and trinkets as well as honor and attention.

Understanding the Indian nature as well as he did, Father De Smet always appeared to be without suspicion. If he realized that his leg was being pulled—which, of course, he did often—he chose to ignore the matter, and to indicate that he attributed to those deceiving him only the noblest and most honorable intentions.

It was on his first journey up the Missouri in 1838 that he began the journals and wrote the first of the long letters that were to enhance his fame as the greatest of all western wilderness missionaries. He was to continue his writings almost to the day of his death, complementing them with detailed descriptions of the country, the flora and fauna, the costumes of the countless peoples, their customs, dances, social habits, hunts and wars, all of which comprised a rich storehouse of knowledge, a major contribution to the history of the West and Northwest.

He left the Kickapoos on May 25, 1838, and rode alone to Fort Leavenworth. There he learned to his dismay that the *Wilmington* had departed two hours before his arrival. "Arming myself with a good switch, I applied it to the sides of my poor Rozinante." After galloping seven miles in half an hour, he sighted the steamboat. It had stopped to take on wood. He received a joyous welcome from his anxious colleagues.

When the *Wilmington* tied up to the bank late that afternoon for the night, the passengers, most of whom had long before thrown off the evil effects of their St. Louis debauches, amused themselves by putting up small coins on sticks at which the Indians visiting the boat would shoot with bows and arrows. "One especially," wrote Father De Smet, "only seven or eight years old, handled his bow and arrows with admirable dexterity, for though the distance was considerable he never missed, and he always went promptly to put the little piece of money into his poor mother's hands. I rejoiced in his good success: he was the only one who had a chaplet and medal about his neck, and I learned that he had been baptized by Father Van Quickenborne."

Father Van Quickenborne had been the first Jesuit to cross the Mississippi after the cession of Louisiana to the United States. He had died at St. Charles, Missouri, in August 1837, only a few weeks before his devoted friend and former pupil, Father De Smet, had returned from Europe.

The *Wilmington* stopped for two hours at the Black Snake Hills, and Father De Smet thought the place "one of the finest on the Missouri for the erection of a city."* There he had a long talk with Joseph Robidoux, who operated a trading post and a fine farm. Robidoux, who had previously lived in Florissant, showed him "a great deal of affection and kindness, and expressed a wish to build a little chapel there, if his father can manage to get some French families to come and settle near them."

At one place, while traveling through the country of the Sauks, the river bank for more than a quarter of a mile was occupied by large groups of Indian men, women and children, accompanied by an army of howling and barking dogs. They had come to see the steamboat pass. When the *Wilmington* stopped, several chiefs went aboard. They knew two of Father De Smet's companions, Father Felix and Brother Mazelli, who had made a

* Site of the city of St. Joseph, Missouri.

previous trip up the river, and "they saluted us in a most affectionate manner, wished us a fortunate voyage and promised to come and see us soon."

A stop of several hours was made at a large village of the Iowas. Father De Smet held a council with White Cloud, the Iowa chief, and "made him a little present of tobacco, which he accepted with much pleasure."

White Cloud remarked that his people were dissatisfied with the Protestant missionary who had been sent to them, and he expressed the wish to have a Black Robe assigned to his tribe. Father De Smet was to hear and report numerous complaints of this nature. The basis of them was not a belief held by the Indians that the Protestants and Catholics worshiped different Gods. The Indians understood that all white men, regardless of their religious affiliations, paid obeisance to only one Supreme Spirit. It was the differences in methods, customs and ceremonies of the two churches that provided the grounds for their criticisms and influenced their affections.

Generally the Indians showed a preference for the Black Robes. The sublime and exalted forms of Catholic worship appealed to the imagination of the Indian, and he was attracted by the rituals and ceremonies of the Mass and other services. Abstract preaching made no impression on him.

Moreover, the Black Robes came to the Indians without secular or temporal ties. They were first and last men of the cloth, and they devoted their lives solely to serving their God. The Black Robes were without worldly possessions, and they sought none. No suspicion could be entertained that they desired to acquire land or wealth to enhance their own personal positions or to assure their own security. They had no families which they must support from the returns of their church work, or from some business or farm. They had only the problem of sustaining themselves, obtaining adequate lodging and enough food and clothing to permit the uninterrupted pursuit of their calling. In such respects the Black Robes stood separate and distinct from all other men, and this stirred the admiration of the Indian and inspired his confidence in them.

Father De Smet found the Iowas "very poor and very drunken." They "sell everything they have to obtain the unlucky stuff, the great scourge of the Indians."

As the *Wilmington* continued to fight its way up the river, Father De Smet became increasingly awed by the incalculable power and the magnificence of the Missouri. He wrote of the vertical cliffs "several hundred feet high, the caverns, the forests and the immense prairies which follow one another in prodigious variety on its shores; its bed, strewn with numberless islands one, two, three and even four leagues in length,† and filled with every kind of game."

Snags raked and scraped the boat's bottom, and frequently the *Wilmington* became stuck on sand bars. Generally the only way it could be freed was by lifting it over the obstruction, an extremely dangerous and difficult operation. Two heavy spars were set in the water before the bow and the boat was made fast to them. Then the engine was started at full speed, the stern was raised and the boat shoved forward two or three yards. The same method was repeated until the bar had been crossed. Sometimes a whole day was consumed in lifting and shoving the craft over a single bar.

In places wide forests had been swallowed by the river, which often broke out of its banks and tore through the surrounding countryside, creating a new course. The early traders had given to one area of this kind the name Devil's Rake. In it gigantic trees lifted naked and menacing limbs from the water on all sides. The limbs thrashed in the current, throwing up a foam with a furious hissing sound. Not infrequently in struggling to gain a passage through such impediments a steamboat's boiler would explode, killing crew and passengers.

After the *Wilmington* had passed the Iowas the weather be-

† Three to twelve miles.

came unseasonably hot. "The warm muddy water of the Missouri was our only drink," Father De Smet said, "and myriads of mosquitoes, fleas, and other insects were our traveling companions."

The violence of the Missouri struck fear in the hearts of brave men. "I fear the sea, I will admit," Father De Smet wrote, "but all the storms and other unpleasant things I have experienced in four different voyages did not inspire so much terror in me as the navigation of the somber, treacherous and muddy Missouri.

"Steam navigation on the Missouri is one of the most dangerous things a man can undertake. The current of this river is the swiftest; high pressure is therefore required to overcome it, and hence the continual danger to which the traveler is exposed of finding himself overturned, and even, as happens only too often, of having his limbs shattered and hurled here and there . . . Add the sand bars with which the river is filled, and upon which one is always being cast, and the innumerable snags and sawyers upon which boats are often wrecked; all these things brought us several times within a finger's breadth of our destruction."

Father De Smet's fears, however, were not so great when it came to going ashore alone to explore. He went at every opportunity. When the *Wilmington* became stranded on a large sand bar ten miles below the mouth of the Platte River, he went eagerly along the bank and was interested to find "a great number of petrifactions . . . among them fine specimens of the polyp, tubipores, encrini, trachitae, columner asteria, etc. . . ."

The Otoes dwelt along the Platte River near its confluence with the Missouri. He described them as "poor and miserable; steal when they can and get drunk when they have a chance. They are the only Indians I know of who, in their misfortunes and reverses, lay the blame upon the Great Spirit. . . ."

Particularly distressing to him was the manner in which the Otoe children were neglected: "Their hair seems never to have undergone the operation of a brush, so that their heads look like masses of cobwebs. Many have eye trouble, and their faces and all their limbs look as if water had never touched them. The younger ones are generally naked." Most of the children and young people had never seen a Black Robe, and ran away screaming in fright when Father De Smet appeared among them. The dogs were no less terrorized by the sight of him and by his strange smell, which had nothing in common with the odors emanating from their masters. "The dogs in these villages (all belonging to the wolf family)" he wrote with irritation, "are the greatest torments to a stranger; the barking of one brings all the others together, of all sizes; they form a chorus, utter piercing yelps and roars and follow you in all directions."

The Otoe village consisted of a number of earthen buildings, in each of which at least ten families lived, and many tents of tanned buffalo hides. Some of the buildings were large enough to lodge as many as a hundred and fifty persons. Father De Smet thought the largest structure resembled a temple: "the rafters which support the sods [roof] rest upon a score of pillars or posts; a hole arranged in the top lets in light and gives an outlet to the smoke."

He was appalled by the appearance of the women. They presented a picture of the "utmost misery. Some were blind, others one-eyed, and all extremely filthy and disgusting to look at. They were clothed in petticoats of deerskin, reaching to the knees, jackets, leggings and shoes of the same material, all as dirty and black as if they had been their towels for the last century."

Father De Smet made no attempt to conceal his aggravation at the men, who appeared to pass the days eating, sleeping, smoking and gambling, and who "subsist the greater part of the time on a small quantity of dried meat and a mush made of roasted and pounded corn. But this temperance and frugality are the result of necessity, not of choice, for when they have an abundance you will see them thrust their whole hands into the pot and eat incessantly like starving wolves until they are ready to split; then they lie down and go to sleep. All their wealth consists of a few horses which graze at large in the uncultivated prairie."

Energetic and industrious missionary that he was, Father De Smet was made melancholy by the sight of the "desolate villages surrounded by such fine country and such fertile virgin soil. The Indian at his birth is wrapped in rags; he grows up in buffalo skins; he is raised in idleness, and industry has no attractions for him; he never tries to improve his condition, and in fact were one of them to aspire to higher enjoyments and to raise his fortune by his efforts and activity, he would soon find himself the object of universal hatred and envy, and whatever he had gathered together would speedily be pillaged or sacked."

Father De Smet's experience in the Otoe village might well have turned back to civilization a man of less determination and physical stamina. Soon after he arrived he was invited to a meal, and he told of the incident in this way: "I was introduced into the largest cabin, that of the first chief; his queen [offered] me a cushion, shining with grease, upon a still more greasy mat, and made me the sign to be seated. She then presented me a rudely made wooden dish (for everything here is done with the hatchet and knife) and a pot spoon of the same material, which seemed not to have been washed since the day of their manufacture. Then she served me with a stew of her own compounding and a pie of a gray color and sufficiently disgusting in appearance. To refuse a savage who offers you food in his own cabin would be considered a grave affront. 'Well, well,' I said to myself, 'you are not in Belgium; let us begin our apprenticeship in earnest, and so long as we are in the woods, howl heartily with the wolves.' A dozen or more dogs, sitting on their hams in front of me, with their eyes fastened on my dish, seemed really to envy me my happiness as I approached my spoon to it, and to be offering their aid and assistance in case of need. But it was not necessary to have recourse to my canine company; I had a good appetite and the stew was excellent, a buffalo tongue with a good gravy of bear fat, mixed with flour from the wild sweet potato. I thanked my hostess, and handed her dish back much cleaner than I had received it."

Their arrival at the Council Bluffs on May 31, 1838, brought a pronounced feeling of discouragement to Father De Smet and his associates. They had been told in St. Louis that the Potawatomies were eagerly looking forward to having Black Robes in their country. It took Father De Smet no time at all to discover that the reverse was true.

Some two thousand Potawatomies, garbed in their finest trappings and profusely painted, were on hand to meet the *Wilmington*. Father De Smet was greatly impressed by the sight of them, and he thought them the best-looking savages in America. However, the Potawatomies were not there to greet the Black Robes. They virtually ignored them. "We were far from finding here the four or five hundred fervent Catholics we had been told of at the College of St. Louis," he said in dejection. "Of the 2000 Potawatomies who were at the landing, not a single one seemed to have the slightest knowledge of our arrival among them, and they all showed themselves cold or at least indifferent toward us. Out of some thirty families of French half-breeds, two only came to shake hands with us. . . ."

VI

The old fort stood on a rise overlooking the broad sweep of the Missouri. Abandoned for several years, it was in a state of deterioration. Its stockade had fallen, or had been torn down for firewood by passing trappers, and its walls and roof were decayed and marked by gaping holes. A family of badgers were the only residents. Nearby were three old Indian cabins, unoccupied and suffering from long neglect.

This was the Jesuit mission to the Potawatomies in 1838.*

Although it was United States property, Colonel Stephen W. Kearney, the renowned soldier of the plains, had arranged to have it turned over to Father De Smet. With great energy and zeal, he and his companions had soon made enough repairs to halt the intrusion of wind and rain, had dispossessed the badger family, and had erected an altar. On Corpus Christi Day, Father De Smet climbed a ladder to affix a cross to the roof. Watching with pride from the ground, Father Felix declared that when the cross was raised he saw the devil clap his tail between his legs and take flight over the big hills.

The three vermin-infested cabins were the mission residences. They had been a gift from Caldwell, the aged half-breed chief of the Potawatomies, whom Father De Smet thought to be a "very worthy honest man; he is well disposed toward us and ready to assist us."

The Indians soon had begun to take more interest in the Black Robes than they had shown at first, and each day some of them visited the church. It was obvious, however, that they were

* It stood within the present limits of the city of Council Bluffs, Iowa.

48

prompted more by curiosity than any desire to attend a religious ceremony.

The French half-breeds, nearly two hundred of them—some of the families contained eight or ten youngsters—had soon commenced to show affability but not much enthusiasm, although a number of them were inclined to have their children receive instruction. Father De Smet found them all "very ignorant of the truths of religion; they cannot even make the sign of the cross nor say a Pater or an Ave. This, I suppose, is the cause of their great reserve toward us. They change wives as often as the gentlemen of St. Louis change their coats."

The church had been constructed under the protection of the Blessed Virgin and St. Joseph, so the mission came to be known by two names. Father De Smet called it St. Joseph's Mission, but others spoke of it as St. Mary's.

The Potawatomies were widely scattered, and to facilitate the task of keeping in touch with remote bands, a few months after St. Joseph's had been prepared Father De Smet sent his assistants to establish a branch west of the Missouri. They selected Sugar Creek, a tributary of the Osage River. A large group of Potawatomies had recently moved to the area from east of the Mississippi. As the location was nearly two hundred miles by land from St. Joseph's, regularly attending it was quite impossible, and Father De Smet arranged to have another priest sent up from St. Louis on temporary duty there. Father De Smet and Father Felix took it upon themselves to visit all camps within a twenty-five-mile radius of St. Joseph's at least once a week, really a monumental schedule and one that kept them in the saddle much of the time.

In a remarkable understatement, Father De Smet wrote his superiors in St. Louis that there were "great obstacles to be overcome in converting an Indian nation." Yet, his words were significant, for they represented the greatest extent he ever permitted his complaints to reach. As if he feared it might be thought he was too discouraged and dissatisfied to carry on his work successfully, he explained: "In these remote regions, we necessarily meet with numerous privations; but the Lord never lets himself be outdone in generosity; he repays a hundredfold the slightest sacrifice made for him; and if our privations are great, our consolations are much greater. I thank Divine Providence daily for having put me in these countries."

The first summer had not ended at St. Joseph's when he found reasons to be genuinely encouraged. In addition to the church, a school had been built. It necessarily was small, and could accommodate only thirty pupils, but each day that classes were held it was filled with shy Indian children whose shiny dark eyes revealed their eagerness to learn of the Great Spirit who spoke through the lips of the Black Robes. By August, one hundred and eighteen Potawatomies of all ages had been instructed and baptized.

"The day of the glorious Assumption of the most holy Virgin Mary will not soon be forgotten among the Potawatomies," Father De Smet recorded with gratification.

The church in which the service was celebrated he termed "one of the poorest in America," but on that day twelve young neophytes, who three months before had had no idea of the law of God, sang Mass in a manner he called "truly edifying." Father Felix preached a brilliant sermon through a French-Indian interpreter. The sacrament was conferred upon twenty adults, one of whom was the wife of Caldwell. She was a woman Father De Smet found very charitable, with religious zeal, and she stood high in the esteem of her nation. He mentioned his hope that her conversion would inspire others to seek reception into the Church. Following Mass he officiated at the marriages of four Indian couples, feeling that he had struck a strong blow against polygamy.

The council fires were lighted wherever Father De Smet rode on his missions. The speeches of the chiefs and noted warriors were long and involved and often colored by extreme fancies. Like all Indians, the Potawatomies loved nothing so much as to tell tales of their former days of glory, to recount their great deeds in war and in the hunt, and expound through long nights on the legends of their creation. Father De Smet never revealed that he grew weary of listening. Nor did he ever display impatience with the medicine men. If he privately condemned them, he never disclosed his prejudice, and he did not show disrespect for them. Rather, he took every opportunity to counter their influence by recitations of God's supreme power and by telling stirring Biblical tales that contained the action and the drama he understood the Indians liked so well.

The sick and the injured and the dying came to St. Joseph's, seeking both medical attention and spiritual solace, and the Black Robes ministered to them as best they could. They had little white man's medicine in bottles, few medical supplies, and they were neither physicians nor surgeons. They learned much from actual practice, however, and if they were successful they felt a small miracle had been performed, and if they failed they asked God to forgive their stupidity.

"I visit the Indians in their wigwams," Father De Smet wrote a Belgian friend, "either as a missionary, if they are disposed to listen to me, or as a physician to see their sick. When I find a little child in great danger, and I perceive the parents have no desire to hear the word of God, I spread out my *vials*. I recommend my medicine strongly. I first bathe the child with a little camphor; then taking some baptismal water, I baptize it without their suspecting it . . . and thus I have opened the gate of heaven to a great number, notwithstanding the wiles of hell to hinder them from entering."

One morning Father De Smet arose to find three men waiting to see him. They were big, handsome, coppery men, and he knew from their costumes and feathers that they were chiefs, but not Potawatomies. He was surprised—and not a little elated—to learn through his interpreter that they were Pawnees, and that they had ridden far for the sole purpose of holding council with him. He welcomed them to his cabin and set food before them, and as they breakfasted he was aware that they were observing him closely, analyzing him and attempting to see "behind his eyes." At last they revealed the purpose of their mission. They had come to request that he visit their villages, and they wanted a Black Robe to live among them and teach them of the white man's Great Spirit.†

Father De Smet expressed delight at the invitation, and promised to do all he could to fulfill the request. If he could not come himself, he told them, he would make an effort to have another priest sent up from St. Louis. The Pawnee chiefs spent a day and a night in Father De Smet's cabin. After their departure he wrote enthusiastically to Father Verhaegen about the opportunity to establish a church for them. The chiefs had noticed, he said, the sign of the cross which he had made before and after praying, and at the beginning and conclusion of meals, and had indicated that when they returned home they would teach all Pawnees to make the same sign. They interpreted it as being "something agreeable to the Great Spirit."

"The use of liquor is prohibited in this tribe," Father De Smet added, "and when anyone tries to bring them any they answer that they are crazy enough already . . . They also have a singular custom; they eat the vermin off one another, and render the same service to those who come to visit them."

It was at this time that Father De Smet's reputation as a wise and trustworthy man began to spread through the Indian Country. Such word traveled fast in the wilderness, perhaps even faster than adverse news, for of that there was a plenitude.

White men—trappers, traders, Army officers and government officials—never ceased their attempts to ascertain the reasons, the forces, which created the Indians' indestructible friendship, trust and reverence for him. It is doubtful if any one of them understood all the reasons—at least there is no record that any one of

† The Pawnee Country was along the Platte River, and the main villages of the tribe were in the vicinity of the present cities of Fremont and Columbus, Nebraska.

them did—but all of them understood one thing: he possessed a power, mysterious and God-given, to walk alone where no other white man dared to trod, to win confidence and bring peace at a time when any other white man going in his footsteps would have found only distrust and probably bloodshed.

If this cannot be satisfactorily and completely analyzed, perhaps there are some clues which partially explain it.

He was a man of powerful physique, vigorous and active. These were qualities admired by the Indians. Yet, there were in the Indian Country countless men, both red and white, of much greater stature. But there was in his short, heavy body and its features much more than great physical strength.

His eyes were intensely blue. They were eyes that changed quickly, as an occasion demanded. They could be calm and serene. They could be instantly filled with gaiety and delight. As instantly could they be fixed and cold. Yet, never under any circumstances were they unfriendly.

There was no hesitancy in his manner, in any move he made. It was as if he knew exactly what he wanted to do, and did it. He spoke in the same way, forthrightly and with assurance, and in a strong, deep voice.

In the touch of his large, strong, calloused hands there were kindness and goodness. He was never known to raise them in violence.

No man enjoyed more a humorous story or a good joke, even if they were about himself. He was extremely fond of jest and merriment, and he readily joined in them with Indian friends. He recounted with admirable humor awkward experiences he had undergone, all to the great appreciation of his listeners.

He would listen with obvious rapture to an Indian chorus, watch with unconcealed pleasure the complicated ceremonial dances, keeping time, with a foot or a hand, with the rhythmic beat of the drums.

It is improbable that any man—white, red or black—who knew him ever doubted his sincerity, or did not understand that his buoyancy, cheerfulness and optimism shared his heart with the deepest sentiments of tenderness and affection. He could be easily moved to tears. "It is my nature," he said, "to rejoice with those who rejoice and weep with those who weep."

If he sympathized with the Indians in the wrongs they suffered, he was fully aware of their faults and limitations. If he was an affectionate and true friend, he was also a practical one. He hated their revolting uncleanliness, abhorred their cruelties, and suffered at the thought of their idolatry and paganism. He did not conceal these feelings, but he sought to halt the practices only through persuasion, only by efforts to convince them they were wrong and that no good could result from them, never with outright condemnation or physical force.

Perhaps three characteristics above all made Father De Smet the most respected and revered white man who ever lived among the savage Indians of America, which made them delight in honoring him, and which made them travel far to hear his words and seek his advice and counsel.

There was in his manner, his gestures, his ways something that inspired confidence and trust. There was in his broad, open, rugged, weathered face something that reflected a depthless honesty. There was in his eyes something that manifested an unqualified goodness and an absolute fearlessness.

No sooner had the three Pawnee chiefs departed than a contingent of some forty Omahas, among them the chiefs Kaiggechinke and Ohio, arrived at the mission.‡

The Omahas began their visit by dancing the calumet, their ceremony of friendship. Father De Smet thought it "really worth seeing," but that describing it was very difficult, because it seemed to be based on complete confusion.

"They yell and strike their mouths, at the same time performing leaps in all directions, now on one foot, now on the other, always at the sound of the drum and in perfect time, pell-mell,

‡ Their home was on the right bank of the Missouri, about twenty miles below the present city of Sioux City, Iowa.

without order, turning to the right and left, in every direction and in every shape, all at once."

He escorted the chiefs into the mission chapel, and was pleased to see the interest they displayed "in the explanation I gave them of the cross, the altar and the images of the passion of our Lord. . . ." In solemn council the Omahas also requested Father De Smet to visit them. They presented him with a fine beaverskin, and he responded with the gift of a tobacco bag. He also gave them some "chaplets for the children and to each one a fair copper cross, which they received with great gratitude. . . ."

Father De Smet lamented that there were so few Jesuits available for work among the Indians. So many good opportunities to help them had to be rejected.

"Ah! if there were more of us!" he told his superiors. He had heard that the government was creating a new Indian Territory. The southern boundary of it would be the Red River of the South, and the eastern boundary would be the states of Arkansas and Missouri and the Missouri River. Living in this area already were the Poncas, Otoes, Kansas, Osages, Kickapoos, Potawatomies, Delawares, Shawanoes, Sauks, Quapaws, Creeks, Cherokees and Choctaws. There was no established western boundary, for westward there was no problem of white settlement, but only the great empty plains ranged by the fur hunters, and presumably no one knew enough of the geography or the people out there to draw a suitable boundary line—it was simply wild Indian Country.

He wrote of the "sad remnants of once powerful nations," and of the "mournful monuments of their misfortunes and decadence" which had been inflicted upon them by the westward push of white men. Of those tribes who would be forced to live in the new Indian Territory, he said: "Here today are 100,000 of them upon the borders of the vast and uninhabitable prairies; hunting cannot suffice for their subsistence; they are unused to labor. . . ." He felt that if the number of Jesuit missionaries could be increased, and they could be distributed equably, permanent good might be accomplished and the total extinction of the Indians might be prevented.

"There are besides," he said, "many other nations on both sides of the mountains called Rocky Mountains: they number several hundreds of thousands; some of these tribes, which are numerous, have already invited us to come and settle among them. . . ."

At St. Joseph's, Father De Smet had no fear of any Indians, except those crazed by liquor, and he went freely and without a feeling of danger into each village. He carried no gun. The mission had other neighbors, however, which were to be feared.

He noted: "It is not uncommon to meet bears in our neighborhood, but this animal will seldom attack a man first, though he will defend himself when wounded. Wolves come very often to our very doors; quite lately they have carried off all our chickens. They are of all kinds; prairie wolves [coyotes], small and timid; black mountain wolves, large and dangerous. We are obliged to be continually on our guard against these bad neighbors, and so I never go out without a good knife, a tomahawk or a sword cane." There were many types of snakes about the mission, including the rattler, and "field, forest and cabin swarm with mice, which gnaw and devour the few fruits that we possess." Butterflies were large and beautiful, and "the night moths are of all colors and of a prodigious size; they are no less than eight inches in length. We also live in the midst of horseflies and mosquitoes; they come upon us by thousands and give us no rest day or night."

Father De Smet gained such a thorough knowledge of the Potawatomies' religious beliefs and their creeds that he was able to recognize subtle similarities between them and the Christian religion. He spent hours conversing on the subject with a chief named Potogojecs, a man of exceptional wisdom and intelligence.

"Many among us," Potogojecs told him, "believe that there are two Great Spirits who govern the universe, but who are constantly at war with each other. One is called Kohemnito, that is, the Great Spirit, the other Mohemnito, or the Wicked Spirit" [God and the Devil].

The Potawatomies frequently came to sing for Father De Smet, and he found that their songs "always have some bearing on their religious opinions." He thought the music beautiful, and he spent many enjoyable evenings listening to the fine voices of the warriors who were grouped in the light of a large campfire.

"The costume of the men," he wrote, "consists of a colored shirt; a woolen blanket, white, red or blue; a pair of leggings or gaiters, of red or blue cloth, adorned with silk ribbons of various colors; an *azeeun*, or small piece of blue cloth passed between the legs; slippers of tanned deerskin, adorned with beads and silk ribbons; a bead necklace or silver crescent . . . with four or five bracelets of silver on each arm. Earrings are common . . . They always carry a big knife in a sheath . . . the head is decorated with a band of tanned hide, which holds back the hair and has feathers stuck in it. . . . The hair is worn very long. Every Indian has two braids; one of them hangs over his face and the other down behind; they are generally adorned with little silver trinkets or with silk ribbons or feathers. They use various colors to paint their faces."

Father De Smet's description of a Pawnee princess whom he saw at a trading post in Bellevue, a short distance below the Council Bluffs, is a classic among historical writings about the West. Her name was Pack-Up-And-Get, and she was the daughter of Big Axe.

"Mademoiselle," he said of her, "wore for coiffure, when she made her appearance in the great council lodge, the principal feather of the right wing of a female goose and a *bandeau* of blue beads interlaced with small cords. Her shirt of crimson curtain cloth was fastened at the neck with a deer's foot and pizzle, and adorned with seven silver spangles. . . . The draperies of this garment descended gracefully to the loins, covering her blue petticoat, which hung to her knees. Her leggings or gaiters were decorated with figures, worked in porcupine quills and embroidered with sky-blue silk. A blue-red blanket was thrown negligently over the princess' shoulders.

"Her Royal Grandeur's moccasins were adorned with little beads of assorted colors, ingeniously worked in the form of toads [*crapeaux*]. She had employed a great profusion of vermilion to add to the natural pink of her complexion, while Spanish brown and Venetian red had been mingled to paint her hair where it was parted in front. This long growth, the princess' natural ornament, did not cover her shoulders, but it was plaited and tied together on the back of her head, as to display a real and positive phrenological bump.

"The princess had been prodigal in her toilet of that perfume so much admired by the Indians, the essence of the skunk, the odor of which is unsupportable to civilized noses, and which announced her approach to the assembly, even before her form appeared. . . .

"A black and blue spot above the left eyebrow, which the princess had received from the mule of her father, as she was attaching a bundle on his back, appeared to render her countenance the more interesting."

Winter closed the country in December 1838, and the trees lifted dark bare arms from the white hills, as if beseeching heaven to let warmth and sun save them from perishing. The Missouri River was choked with ice, and traffic on it was impossible. The buffalo herds had drifted south weeks before. The birds had long been gone. Indian ponies, like the deer and elk, pawed into the snow to get at the frozen grass, and the wolves cut them down at the hamstrings, gorged themselves, and howled with bloody fangs at the moon. All else in the world was silent. The Indians huddled in their lodges, surviving on the dried meat and root flour and bear grease they had stored against the time of want and stillness on earth. The winds moaned with the wolves as the blizzards swept down from the north, biting at the little church and the cabins of the mission on the hill, and the Fathers struggled to drive out the cold with inadequate wood fires in inefficient stone fireplaces.

Father De Smet spent long hours at his rough board desk writing in his small neat script letters and reports and articles that could not be dispatched for weeks. The last post from the Potawatomie Country went down the river with the last steamboat, unless some trappers happened to be descending at a later date, not a usual occurrence. The military sent an occasional winter express overland from St. Louis to Fort Leavenworth, but above that station there were none, and once the river was closed and the snow had fallen the upper river country might as well have been on another planet, as far as communications were concerned.

But Father De Smet wrote industriously, using both sides of a sheet of paper to achieve the greatest usage of his small supply. He had so much to say, so much to tell the world, so much he wanted to leave as part of the legacy of his life.

VII

It was during the winter of 1838–39 that Father De Smet began the campaign against the liquor traffic in the Indian Country which he was to wage with undiminishing vigor as long as he was a missionary in the wilderness. With the advent of spring he sent out the first of his letters and papers which not only told of the horrors of the evil commerce, and of how it had destroyed the economy and the lives of the Indians, but which severely condemned the federal government, the Indian Department, and all officials for permitting it to continue.

His voice and his pen were powerful, but they spoke no words which had not been heard in years gone by. From the beginning of the sixteenth century, when the first fishermen from Europe began to trade for furs among the Indians of eastern Canada, the red man had suffered the curse of the white man's liquor.

In more than three hundred years, neither kings, parliaments, Presidents nor honorable individuals had been able to halt the diabolical practice. Not even Indian leaders had been able to stop the flood of liquor, and the destruction of their people. After the birth of the United States, successive administrations talked much about preventing whiskey from reaching the Indians, but did little or nothing to bring about that desirable end. The Congress had no more than assembled in the new city of Washington when it passed an act which authorized the President "to take such measures, from time to time, as to him may appear expedient to prevent or restrain the vending or distributing of spiritous liquors among all or any . . . of the Indian tribes."

It was a weak, vacillating measure. If it put Congress on the side of righteousness and good sense, it did nothing more. All action was left to the discretion of the President, and every President had more important things to worry about. For the next twelve years no President used his powers to halt the trade in alcohol. It was a fact, of course, that the sale of corn whiskey to traders brought welcome revenue to western farmers, and only a careless politician would have ignored the growing strength of the western electorate by depleting income. It was also a fact that British fur traders trafficked in alcohol, and it was deemed unfair to deny the same privileges to Americans who must compete with them.

The horrors, the crimes, the terrible butchery and suffering that took place on the frontier in ensuing years, however, moved Congress to give brief attention to the problem once more, and in 1815 it forbade the setting up of a still in the Indian Country under pain of a fine of $5000. If Congress had deliberately set out to pass a law which would have little or no effect on the situation, it could not have done better. No one worried about distilling whiskey in the Indian Country. It was too easy to bring it in.

There the matter stood, with whiskey and rum pouring into the region of the Great Lakes, which John Jacob Astor controlled, and later being taken up the Missouri River by the boatload, where he also dominated that trade. Congress at last got around to saying that the use of whiskey in the Indian trade was illegal, but even this sterner law had no effect. Astor had retired from the trade when Father De Smet first went up the Missouri, but the American Fur Company he had founded continued operations under other leaders, and the liquor traffic continued as it had in the past. The federal government, infiltrated with dishonest, grafting bureaucrats, failed to enforce its own statutes.

If Father De Smet was not a new voice, he portrayed, through the medium of his literary ability, the wickedness of the abominable trade in a more forceful manner than any of its previous enemies. However, many of his most scathing and unvarnished denunciations were not published until years after they had been written. He was subject to censorship by church officials.

The noted historian of the fur trade, Hiram Martin Chittenden, stated that Father De Smet's attacks "were carefully pruned by his superiors of whatever savored too much of hostile criticism of the government." Father De Smet said that he wrote the Indian Department on the subject, but these letters have never been found. But much of the other material he wrote about the liquor trade survived.

To the Father-General in St. Louis he communicated his fear that liquor, "which brings in its train war, famine and pestilence, all together," would soon be the ruin not only of his favored Potawatomies, but all other tribes along the river and in the western mountains unless it could be halted by force of law and, if necessary, arms.

"The country is overrun with vagabond Americans," he said, "and the government, which alone could put a stop to this abominable traffic, in spite of the severity of its laws, pays no attention to the matter.

"The Potawatomies, by their treaty with the government, receive $50,000 per annum; this payment having been omitted last year, they received double in 1839. Such a sum, well placed, would procure for the savages victuals and goods in abundance, and would render them happy in regard to temporal things. But alas! all this money goes for liquor. As long as it lasts they neither work nor hunt; and they now have enough to keep them going from New Year's Day to the end of December.

"They quarrel and fight from morning to night; their bodies become veritable furnaces, full of foul humors, which cause them all sorts of maladies. Their love for liquor is really inconceivable. . . . It is a regular tarantula to them; as soon as they are bitten by it, all their blood flames in their veins, and they are crazy for more. . . . More! More! is their war cry, until, as the flames consume them, they fall over . . . and when the fumes of drink evaporate from their brains their first and only cry is 'Whiskey! Whiskey! Whiskey!' as if it was a matter of life and death.

"The other day I counted nine bitten-off noses in a single group of Indians. In their rage, this little member is the principal object of their attack; and a drunken Indian who deprives a comrade of his nose, boasts of it as much as a brave soldier of having carried off a flag from the enemy.

"When they are sober, no one would recognize them; they are mild, civil, quiet and attentive; but there is no safety in the presence of a drunken savage. Several times our lives have been in the greatest danger; but fortunately by gentle and moderate words we have managed to appease the rage of these barbarous drunkards, who were breathing only blood."

If the liquor trade with the Indians had been a new problem, men like Father De Smet might have been more patient with the failure of the government to solve it, but it had been inherited by the first administration of the United States, and it had faced every succeeding administration. Washington files literally bulged with reports and pleas from officers in the field to take strong remedial action, and these appeals continued to pour in as Father De Smet penned his own indictments at St. Joseph's Mission.

Superintendent of Indian Affairs Thomas L. McKenney, a decent man, lamented in an official report: "There are many honorable and high-minded citizens in this [fur] trade, but expediency overcomes their objections and reconciles them for the sake of the profits of the trade." The famed William Clark, while Indian Superintendent at St. Louis, told his department: ". . . the laws in relation to that subject are but little regarded by the civil authority . . ." Colonel Josiah Snelling protested to the Secretary of War: "The neighborhood of the trading houses where whiskey is sold presents a disgusting scene of drunkenness, debauchery and misery; it is the fruitful source of all our difficulties, and of nearly all the murders committed in the Indian Country . . . I have daily opportunity of seeing the road strewn with the bodies of men, women and children, in the last stages of brutal intoxication. It is true there are laws in this territory to restrain the sale of whiskey, but they are not regarded . . ."

Father De Smet did not delude himself into believing that he could, anymore than the sincere men who had preceded him, bring about the elimination of the hideous conditions. He was too worldly and too practical for that, and he understood only too well that justice for the Indians was not a matter with which either the general public or the government was concerned. The most he could do was to strive unceasingly to educate the Indians among whom he served, seek to teach them to see the folly of their ways, and get off his written protests to Washington and the superiors of his church.

Following the arrival of a steamboat which brought liquor to the Potawatomies, he wrote in a letter to a Mother Superior in Belgium: "Already fourteen among them are cut to pieces in the most barbarous manner, and are dead. A father seized his own child by the legs and crushed it, in the presence of its mother, by dashing it against the post of his lodge. Two others most cruelly murdered an Indian woman, a neighbor of ours, and mother of four children. We live in the midst of the most disgusting scenes . . . I wrote an energetic letter to the government against these abominable traffickers."

Father De Smet kept a journal of what he called "the most remarkable events which take place about us." It was an amazing diary, reflecting what he termed "abominations of the place." During a twenty-day period it told of twelve murders, one poisoning, four drownings, several stabbings and a number of fights during which half a dozen noses were bitten off, all attributable to liquor.

On May 30, 1839, the journal said: "Arrival of steamer Wilmington . . . A war of extermination appears preparing . . . Fifty large cannons have been landed, ready charged with the most murderous grapeshot, each containing thirty gallons of whiskey, brandy, rum or alcohol. The boat was not yet out of sight when the skirmishes commenced. After the fourth, fifth and sixth discharges, the confusion became great and appalling. In all directions, men, women and children were seen tottering and falling; the war whoop, the merry Indian's song, cries, savage roarings, formed a chorus. Quarrel succeeded quarrel. Blows followed blows. The club, the tomahawk, spears, butcher knives, brandished together in the air. Strange! astonishing! only one man, in this dreadful affray, was drowned in the Missouri, another severely stabbed, and several noses lost."

On September 15th, he wrote: "Colonel Kearney arrived at Bellevue with 200 dragoons. Held council with the Iowas. Took four prisoners among the most distinguished for depredations on their white neighbors and missionaries. Preparations were made to whip them. The colonel reluctantly pardoned them at the intercession of their new agent, Mr. Hamilton, and after having consulted with experienced gentlemen living in this neighborhood."

Father De Smet neglected to note that he was one of the "experienced gentlemen." He was influential in saving the Indians from punishment, feeling that it was a miscarriage of justice, for they had been made drunk by white men supplying them with drink in violation of the law.

Between May and September, he wrote of seventy-four violent deaths. Hardly any wonder he told a friend: "You may easily gather that our prospects are not so very bright and flattering, surrounded as we are by so many evils and obstacles, which all our efforts to the contrary are not able to stem."

Looking back on the work done by himself and his assistants in the past two years, however, he found some grounds for satisfaction, and he said stubbornly: "We have not lost courage . . . our endeavors have not been altogether fruitless and unavailing. We performed the ceremonies of marriage for twenty-three couples who have so far remained very steady . . . We baptized in all 242, among whom were upward of eighty adults . . . Forty have been admitted already to the Lord's Supper. Some I must own have slackened . . ."

Loneliness and homesickness added to the burdens of mind and body as Father De Smet drove himself to perform his duties. After sending out, over a period of months, scores of letters, he wrote plaintively to an old friend in the clergy: "I have written to fathers and brothers whom I cherish the most in the world, at St. Louis and roundabout. Well, I have received in return, aside from your letter, *five lines*. Ah! how gladly would I attribute this afflicting delay to the negligence of the postal authorities.

"Here in this veritable corner of the world, remote from our brothers and friends, surrounded with all sorts of miseries, poor as hairless rats, constantly witnessing the most revolting scenes, which are at the same time irremediable, in the midst of strangers and infidels, I will tell you plainly, every letter that we receive makes a great feast day for us."

VIII

On April 20, 1839, word had sped from village to village near the Council Bluffs that the first steamboat of the season from St. Louis was approaching. During the last months of the winter a scarcity of game had reduced many Potawatomies to a diet of acorns and roots. Joyously they moved toward the landing to get the supplies from the government which they knew would be aboard the steamer.

No less relief was displayed at St. Joseph's Mission, for there the larder was almost empty, and that end had been averted only by supplementing the few remaining staples with the same type of unpalatable food on which the Indians were subsisting. Father De Smet had been for several weeks without shoes, his last pair having disintegrated like snow in a spring thaw. Without delay, and thinking of his suffering feet as much as his stomach, he followed two handcarts drawn by his assistants toward the river.

Upon reaching the crowded landing he heard news that sickened him. Hardly a mile away, the boat had struck a sawyer, which tore a great hole in its hull, and was sinking. His feet aching with the bruises which his thin moccasins could not prevent, he hurried along the bank. The stricken craft was in a perilous position. It rested on the river bottom, listing dangerously, while the crew, passengers and Indians worked furiously at salvaging what cargo they could. Father De Smet gave himself vigorously to the task. On board the boat were a season's food supplies for the mission, ornaments for the church, a tabernacle, a bell, and clothes for himself and his ragged colleagues.

When the work of saving all possible cargo had been completed, the people of the Council Bluffs faced a sad reckoning. The loss was estimated at more than $40,000. All provisions for the Indians had been lost, swept away in the raging current. Of the goods consigned to the mission, only a few articles had been saved: a plough, a saw, a pair of boots and some wine.

Bravely Father De Smet wrote in a letter to the Mother Superior of the orphanage of Termonde: "Providence was still favorable to us. With the help of the plough, we were enabled to plant a large field of corn; it was the season for furrowing. We are using the saw to build a better house and enlarge our church, already too small. With my boots I can walk in the woods and prairies without fear of being bitten by the serpents which throng there. And the wine permits us to offer to God every day the most holy sacrifice of the Mass, a privilege that has been denied us during a long time.

"We therefore returned with courage and resignation to the acorns and roots."

For two years the Potawatomies had lived in terrible dread of the menacing Sioux, who were threatening to exterminate them. With the coming of the spring of 1839, they believed the hour for the Sioux to attack had come, and they sought the advice of Father De Smet. Several councils were held—during which time the Sioux murdered two Potawatomies—and the final meeting on the grave situation was an important event in the history of the West. It was then that Father De Smet agreed to make the first of his many famous journeys into the wilderness as an emissary of peace.

The next boat to come up the river after the disastrous wreck was the *St. Peters,* owned by the American Fur Company. It reached the Council Bluffs without serious mishap, and Father De Smet arranged for his passage on it to the Sioux Country. The departure took place on April 29th. He was delighted to find on board Jean Nicholas Nicollet, a distinguished explorer and a friend of his for many years. Nicollet, a native of Savoy, had come to the United States in 1832 to study physical geography.

He had explored the basins of the Red, Arkansas and Missouri Rivers, and in 1836 had reached the sources of the Mississippi. Nicollet was the leader of a party en route to the far upper reaches of the Missouri. He immediately arranged to leave a number of scientific instruments in charge of Father De Smet so that during the coming summer observations could be conducted in the vicinity of the Council Bluffs.

A member of Nicollet's company was the German botanist, Charles A. Geyer. On a day when the *St. Peters* was held up by sand bars exposed by low water, Geyer invited Father De Smet to accompany him on a walk ashore. They followed a game path to the crest of a high hill and began their descent by a different route.

"I followed him, thinking I could go where he had gone," Father De Smet recorded, "but almost the first step I took, the slippery earth gave way under my feet, and I made a third of the descent at railroad speed* . . . partly on my hindquarters without regard of my breeches, which felt this treatment deeply, I reached *terra firma* in safety."

In the country of the Omahas, Father De Smet walked across a prairie three miles in width, "full of onions of the size of a marble and very excellent for eating." On another shore walk he found "a great deal of asparagus the size of your thumb, which supplied the passengers for four days."

"Everywhere," he noted, "there was abundance of strawberries, blackberries, gooseberries and plums, nuts of various kinds, cherries and grapes . . . the fruit of the blackthorn also appeared to be quite plentiful." He hoped that he might return when all these delicacies were ripe.

He was now entering for the first time the immense sweeps of the northern plains, and he extolled the grandeur and beauty of the immense country, speaking admiringly of the great distances, and the far promontories which, "when the mists of evening

* Perhaps a frightening twenty miles an hour in 1839.

descend upon the landscape, make the impression of lofty mountains seen at a distance . . . The windings of the river present lovely views every moment, but the regular succession of bluffs and bottoms give such a sameness to the country that unless one were familiar with the region he could never tell in which one of a dozen precisely similar spots he found himself. The Author of nature seems to have chosen to divert himself by repeating over and over the first forms that he applied to this charming and fertile land."

In his letter to the Mother Superior at Termonde, he said: "I thought of you . . . when I found myself in those beautiful *parterres*. I imagined once for an instant that you were there, with your children. I heard your exclamations: '*Potten, potten, kinderen! Wel, wel! . . . Dat zijn schoone bloemen! Wie zoude Komt hier, moeder; hier heb ik eene schoone.*'† Indeed it was truly the most beautiful view one could fancy. When the bell called us back to the steamer, I quitted those little parks of wild flowers with much difficulty. I gathered a great number of plants which I preserved in my herbal . . . I will tell you nothing of our encounters with the wolves and serpents; that would dispel the charm."

In the Omaha Country, Father De Smet's boat passed two graves of historic significance. The first was that of Blackbird, the notorious Omaha chief who used poison in a struggle to maintain his supreme rule. Twenty-five miles farther upstream the travelers saw the grave of Sergeant Charles Floyd of the Lewis and Clark expedition, the first American soldier to die on the upper Missouri. Almost within sight of each other were two tombs which might be said to have marked the close of one period whose beginning was lost in indefinable antiquity, and the dawn of another whose end could not be surmised . . . the exit of one race of man and the entrance of another into the world of the West.

† "Children, get some vases! Well, well! Those are pretty flowers! Who would have thought it? Just look! Mother, here is a pretty one."

No one came from the main village of the Omahas to see the *St. Peters* pass, and there was a good reason for the unusual behavior. Two years before, the same boat had carried smallpox into the upper Missouri country.

It was a tragedy that could easily have been averted. Officials of the American Fur Company were passengers on the boat when several cases of the disease were discovered. They had ample time to turn it back, but, of course, that would have meant a severe loss in trade. They might have unloaded the cargo, fumigated it, and sent it on up the river in keelboats. They did neither. Instead, they stupidly attempted to keep Indians from coming near the boat. If they had commanded the sun not to rise they would have known as much success. The Indians knew the boat carried supplies for them, and they suspected that the efforts to keep them away from it were part of a scheme to cheat them. They swarmed about it, and virtually everything they touched sealed their doom.

On went the *St. Peters,* spreading the scourge. Hundreds of Indians died each day. It was impossible for those not stricken to bury the bodies, and they were thrown over cliffs and into gulleys, and at most villages a terrible stench filled the air for miles about.

"Of 1200 members of the tribe of the Mandans," wrote Father De Smet, "only seven families escaped the contagion.‡ About eighty warriors of this little nation committed suicide . . ."

On each side of the river for five hundred miles, between Fort Pierre and the Yellowstone, tents stood but no smoke rose from them; no sounds but "the croaking of the raven and the howling of the wolf broke the fearful silence." Father De Smet said that twenty-five or thirty thousand Indians died in a few weeks.§

‡ Hiram Martin Chittenden, distinguished historian of the American fur trade, says thirty persons survived.
§ This is excessive. Actual losses could not, of course, be determined. However, judging from the number of Indians still alive after the plague had run its course, the total mortality among the river tribes probably amounted to 15,000 men, women and children.

In the first week of May 1839, Father De Smet's boat entered the Sioux country, and he made preparations to leave it at an opportune place. The presence of large herds of buffalo was taken as a favorable sign, for in all probability the Sioux would be drawn to them on a spring hunt. The herds were drifting northward, and frequently the bloated bodies of calves, which had been drowned while crossing the river, floated by the *St. Peters.*

On May 11, the boat stopped at the Sioux trading post near the mouth of the Vermilion River, and Father De Smet learned that a large number of Yankton Sioux were in the area. He said farewell to his friends Nicollet and Geyer with regret, expressing the wish that he could have gone on with them, "so as to visit the numerous nations of the mountains."

A message dispatched from the post with an interpreter brought the desired results, and within two days Father De Smet had received an invitation to a feast and council from the Yanktons. Although they were one of the smallest Sioux tribes, he felt that they would serve his purpose and would relay his plea for peace to the other Sioux nations.

Obeying instructions, he rode with an interpreter to the designated meeting place on the Vermilion River. He was gratified to learn that the Yanktons knew of him, and that even though they had never seen him they held him in respect.

Escorted into a "grand lodge" made of buffalo hides, he found the chiefs and head warriors "seated in a circle . . . Each one rested his chin on his knees, the legs drawn close up to the body." His corpulence prevented him from assuming a similar position, and "I therefore seated myself like a tailor on his table, with my legs crossed. Everyone received a big piece of venison in a wooden trencher."

Father De Smet was informed by his interpreter that if he could not finish his portion, it would be polite to take the remainder with him to eat at a later time. He set aside the larger part of the immense slab of meat, estimating that he would have enough to satisfy his hunger for at least two days. When the feast ended, he did as the others to show his appreciation of the good food . . . rubbed his belly with both hands in a sign of satisfaction.

It was now time for him to address his hosts, and being given the signal to speak, he at once approached the subject of his mission. He had come, he said, to ask for "a durable peace between the Sioux and the Potawatomies, their neighbors." He cited numerous false reports which had caused relations to become strained between the two nations, and he pointed out the futility of attacking a people so much weaker than the Sioux. Nothing was to be gained by such a war, for the Potawatomies had nothing in the way of booty that would be useful to the Sioux. Certainly the Sioux, masters of the largest Indian domain on earth, a realm whose bounds were beyond comprehension and which was filled with the bounties bestowed by the Great Spirit on a noble people, could not want more territory. They could not ride over what they then ruled in a dozen moons. The Sioux would be wasting their time in attacking such a poor and helpless people, a people who wished only to live in peace and asked nothing of the powerful Sioux.

Father De Smet's success is best recounted in his own brief report: "I persuaded the Sioux to make some presents to the children of such of our Potawatomies as they had killed, which is called *covering the dead,* and to come and smoke with them the calumet of peace. The feast and the council were terminated with the most perfect cordiality."

Having won a diplomatic victory, Father De Smet took advantage of the opportunity to give the Yankton leaders "an instruction on the Apostles' Creed." When he had finished, a number of children were brought from the camp, and at the request of their fathers were baptized by him. After that the Indians honored him with a calumet dance. He returned to the trading post with a feeling of profound consolation, and he fell upon his knees to thank God for giving him the strength and the knowledge to make him successful in his first mission of peace in the wilderness.

Father De Smet did not linger in the Sioux Country. He arranged with two *voyageurs* attached to the trading post to take him down the river to the Council Bluffs. "My vessel this time," he wrote, "was a tree hollowed out, which is called a canoe, ten feet in length and one and a half in width. I could just seat myself in it. Before this, I had crossed the river in this sort of craft, but never without fear, it being evidently very dangerous; now I had 360 miles to descend on the most perilous and impetuous of rivers, and it was necessary, for I had no other way."¶

His pilots were skilled veterans "who, paddling on the right and left, darted with the fleetness of an arrow through the numerous sawyers with which the river was filled, the frail bark which the slightest shock would overturn." The swiftness with which they traveled was shown in his statement that "in three days, sailing from four o'clock in the morning until sunset, we had passed over 120 leagues. Two nights only I slept in the open air, having no bed but my buffalo robe, and no pillow but my traveling bag. Yet I can assure you that my slumbers were as peaceable and profound as I ever enjoyed in my life. A good appetite, for the air on the water is fresh, prepared us for three excellent meals each day. My companions were well provided with bread, butter, coffee and sugar; game was also abundant, and we had but to select. I never saw so many ducks, geese, bustards, swans and wild turkeys . . .

"We made our evening soup with the muddy water of the Missouri, which gave the meat the singular appearance of having been seasoned with mud.

"At our last encampment . . . a noble stag [elk] approached us, stamping with his feet . . . a little more and we might have

¶ The estimate of the distance is high, probably by 60 to 70 miles. The peril was, indeed, great in such a small craft, for the river might rise or fall several feet in a few hours, creating dangerous boils and eddies, luring inexperienced canoemen into false channels.

had our skulls broken in by this enraged animal. It aroused the pilot, who, seizing the gun . . . discharged it about two inches from my ear."

Father De Smet reached the Council Bluffs about the middle of May, and found that Father Felix had conducted the mission's affairs efficiently during his absence. On the day he returned, a young French Creole and his Indian wife appeared. He was astonished to learn that they had traveled on horses from beyond the Rocky Mountains. They asked his blessing and to be instructed in the religion of the Black Robes.

He talked with the couple for some time, hearing from the young woman a story that, although gruesome and "heart-rending," whetted his growing desire to go as a missionary among the tribes of the Far West.

The squaw was a Ute, and she told Father De Smet that the soil of her native country was one of the most "ungrateful; they had no [big] game at all." If the Utes "hazard leaving their country," she said, "their more numerous neighbors kill them without mercy. They are without clothes, without habitations, and roam like wild animals in the prairies [deserts?], where they live on roots, grasshoppers and large ants. They crush the last-named insects between two stones, and make a species of cake with them . . . This poor Indian woman, aged about twenty-five, *had never eaten meat.*° Her astonishment was excessive when she first saw chicken, pigs, cows and oxen . . . As soon as she is sufficiently instructed to receive baptism, I will name her Isabella . . ."

Thankful to be safely back in his cabin at St. Joseph's, Father De Smet found, nevertheless, that his dissatisfaction in being confined to the territory of the Potawatomies was assuming annoying proportions. He believed he could be of greater service farther out in the western wilderness, where the Indians had not

---

° Presumably until after she had left home with her Creole husband. The italics are Father De Smet's.

75

yet been so greatly degraded by the evil machinations of the traders.

Moreover, white settlers were advancing rapidly across Iowa, and farms already had been established on the Nisnabotna River at its confluence with the Missouri, only a few miles to the south of the Council Bluffs. The pressure of civilization grew greater with the passage of each day, and he understood that it would soon pass beyond the Council Bluffs, and towns would rise "as if by magic" where the Indian villages then stood. The Indians would once more be forced to retreat westward, perhaps far to the southwest in the so-called Indian Territory. That probably would not last long, either. Land that supposedly was set aside for the Indian one day was being furrowed by white men the next day.

As the summer of 1839 gave way to the clear brilliant days and nights of the fall, Father De Smet experienced a restlessness of a kind he had never known before, a strange urge to move on, as the Indians moved on, perhaps into oblivion, and even more peculiar was his feeling that an event would soon occur that would take him away forever from the little mission and church he had built with such great love and pride and hope on the hill overlooking the Missouri River in the land of the suffering Potawatomies.

The event occurred September 18, 1839. On that day there appeared at St. Joseph's Mission two Catholic Iroquois Indians, Pierre Gaucher and Young Ignace,† but they had not come from upper New York or from Canada. For twenty-three years they had lived among the Flathead and Nez Percé tribes on the western slopes of the Rocky Mountains. They had traveled over the mountains to the Yellowstone with a party of trappers who were en route to St. Louis. By canoe they had come down the Yellowstone and Missouri Rivers. Hearing that Black Robes lived near the Council Bluffs, they had left the company to visit them.

† The name *Ignace* was common among the Iroquois.

It was with a growing inner excitement that Father De Smet wrote in his journal: "I have never seen any savages so fervent in religion. By their instructions and examples they have given all that nation [the Flatheads] a great desire to have themselves baptized. All that tribe strictly observed Sunday and assembled several times a week to pray and sing canticles.

"The sole object of these good Iroquois was to obtain a priest to come and finish what they had so happily commenced."

When Pierre Gaucher and Young Ignace left St. Joseph's they carried letters of recommendation from Father De Smet to Bishop Joseph Rosati in St. Louis. They departed, said Father De Smet, thinking "nothing of adding three hundred leagues to the thousand they had already accomplished, in the hope that their request would be granted."

Father De Smet felt that the opportunity for which he had hoped so long had now presented itself, but he was greatly agitated by the question of how to avail himself of it. The two Iroquois would reach St. Louis by mid-October, and Bishop Rosati would take action on their request. There were few travelers moving down the river, and fewer ascending it. Even if he had dispatched a letter with the Iroquois to the bishop, requesting his own assignment to the Flatheads and asking permission to come to St. Louis to discuss the matter, there were no means by which he could have been assured of a reply before April of the coming year. The river would soon be closed to all possible travel, and obtaining the services of a reliable overland messenger was not only difficult but very expensive. Few men would face the hazards of a lone winter journey through the Indian Country.

Father De Smet at last decided that bold action on his part was necessary if he were to have any chance of obtaining the coveted assignment. He needn't have made any excuse to his colleagues, for they fully understood and sympathized with his feelings. Nevertheless, he expressed the opinion that by going to St. Louis he could make certain that the supplies and articles most urgently needed at the mission were aboard the first boat to come up the river in the spring.

It was the middle of November when Father De Smet mounted a mule and set off alone on the 600-mile ride to St. Louis. For the next five weeks he traveled in the saddle and in a wagon on a route which took him down the Missouri Valley to Fort Leavenworth, then by trail and rutted roads eastward and southeastward to St. Louis.

IX

The two Iroquois, Pierre Gaucher and Young Ignace were not the first emissaries to travel several thousand miles through the western wilderness for the purpose of inducing the Black Robes to establish a church among the Flatheads. Three previous missions had set out on the same quest, and all had met with failure.

It was shortly after the expedition of Lewis and Clark that traders from both Canada and the United States led brigades of trappers into the valley of the Columbia River. The factors and partners of these companies were usually British, Scotch and Yankee Protestants, but the *voyageurs* and *engagés*—many of them half-breeds—were Roman Catholics. On their heels came wandering Iroquois hunters, most of them also Catholics. It was from these two peoples, the rank and file of the fur brigades and the Iroquois, that the Indians of the Far West first heard of the priests.

The Flatheads and the Nez Percés, occupying immense domains in the heavily forested mountains of the Pacific slope, in territory that was to become part of western Montana and Idaho, were deeply impressed by the rites of the half-breeds, Iroquois, and French-Canadians, and the symbols and gestures they made in their devotions. The susceptibility of these remote tribes to religious influences is one of the anomalies of Indian history.

Régis Brugière, who had a French-Canadian father, and Ignace Shonowane, a full-blood, were the first two members of the Iroquois known to reach the lower Columbia. They had come from the region of Lake Huron with a party of twenty-four Iroquois hunters. This group, and those of the same nationality who followed them in the next few years, were sober, serious

79

and left no doubt that they believed the teachings of the Black Robes to represent the only true religion.

Profoundly concerned about their own spiritual state, the Flatheads and Nez Percés gradually turned to the Iroquois for guidance, and they adopted the rites and customs of the Church performed by them. They came to believe what the stern and stoical Iroquois maintained—that the Indian religion was false and the Flatheads and Nez Percés were in danger of being thrown into hell. Salvation could be achieved only by embracing the Catholic faith.

The wish to have a real priest instruct them increased through a score of years until it had become an obsession. At last, in the spring of 1831, a deputation of four Indians was named to go East in an effort to obtain one.

The Iroquois advised going to eastern Canada, but the Flatheads had good reasons for choosing St. Louis. Trading caravans traveled from the mountains both by water and by land to St. Louis each year, and by accompanying one the emissaries would have protection in passing through the countries of Indians who were known enemies or whose attitudes toward them could not be reliably predicted. Moreover, it had been from St. Louis that Lewis and Clark, whom both the Flatheads and the Nez Percés still revered, had come, and they had heard that General Clark still dwelt there. They felt that if they could have council with him their request would have a better chance of succeeding. His heart would be open.

Whether the four Indians who made the long journey in 1831 were Flatheads or Nez Percés, history does not record. There is evidence to show that two were from one tribe and two from the other. They reached St. Louis in the fall, and were welcomed by General Clark. Their presence and the nature of their petition were noted in the newspapers, reprinted in other areas, and soon had stirred excitement among religious organizations throughout the United States.

All four of the delegates became seriously ill in St. Louis. Two of them died after requesting and receiving absolution from a Black Robe. Their burial was recorded in the books of the old Catholic cathedral in St. Louis. The surviving two went [probably] by steamboat to Westport in the spring of 1832, and there joined a caravan going to the annual rendezvous of the fur hunters, which that year was held in Pierre's Hole, just west of the Tetons and on the border of the Flathead Country.

The Jesuits of St. Louis had neither the money nor the personnel which would permit them to send missionaries west of the mountains, and the more affluent Methodist Church was the first to respond to the Indians' request, which, incidentally, had not been made directly to it. The Methodists dispatched the missionaries Jason and Daniel Lee, but they chose not to stop among the Flatheads and went on to the Willamette Valley. In 1835, the Presbyterians sent out Marcus Whitman and Samuel Parker to investigate the field. It was in this same year that the Flatheads sent another representative to the Black Robes. He was Old Ignace, and he took with him two of his sons.

Traveling with a trading caravan, they reached St. Louis late in the fall and were welcomed by Bishop Rosati, who baptized the two young men. Unfortunately, the Jesuits were still not in a position to take action. Besides being poor, they had received very few recruits since the opening of the Missouri novitiate, and these and the few priests present were needed by the churches of the diocese and to teach at St. Louis University. Old Ignace and his sons returned home in disappointment.

In 1836, the Protestants, Dr. Whitman and the Reverend H. H. Spalding and their wives, went out from St. Louis, but they passed up the Flatheads. Dr. Whitman established a mission among the Cayuses near the Walla Walla River, and Dr. Spalding elected to work among the Nez Percés at Lapwai.

Still determined to have a Black Robe among them, the Flatheads, in 1837, sent a third commission East. Old Ignace was once more the leader, and he had with him three Flatheads and one Nez Percé chief. They traveled eastward with a party of white hunters. At Ash Hollow on the North Platte River they were attacked by Sioux. Old Ignace and his four companions were killed.

Pierre Gaucher and Young Ignace, who conferred with Father De Smet at St. Joseph's Mission in the fall of 1839, represented the fourth attempt by the Flatheads to have a Catholic mission established in their country.

Father De Smet arrived in St. Louis none too soon to offer himself for the assignment. Bishop Rosati had promised Pierre Gaucher and Young Ignace that a priest, possibly two, would be sent to their tribe in the spring of 1840.

Although it was midwinter, Pierre Gaucher left at once, alone, on the long journey home to give his people the good news. Young Ignace remained in St. Louis so that he might serve as a guide for the Father, or Fathers, who would leave in the spring.*

---

* Pierre Gaucher's journey from St. Louis to the Flathead Country was one of the most remarkable in western history. Traveling alone on foot he crossed the plains and mountains during the winter, reaching the Bitter Root Valley, his home, in April 1840. His word that a Black Robe was, at last, without doubt, coming out was received by the Flatheads with great excitement and joy.

X

Bishop Rosati had made every effort to send two priests to the Flatheads, but once again had found himself defeated by a lack of both funds and manpower. Father De Smet would have to go alone.

Accompanied only by Young Ignace, he started on March 27, 1840. From St. Louis he traveled by steamboat to Westport, a distance of approximately four hundred miles. Settlers were moving in hordes up the great river, and the boat was crowded far beyond its capacity with passengers and freight. Father De Smet believed the people on board came "from every state of the Union; I may even say from the various nations of the earth, white, black, yellow and red, with shadings of all these colors. The boat was like a little floating Babel . . ."

As it had done on his previous journeys through it, by water and by land, the beauty of the lower Missouri Valley entranced him. Although only the beginning of April, the spring was in full flower, and he made rapturous notes on the "oaks, and walnuts of a dozen different species; the sassafras and the *acacia triacanthus,* whose flowers load the air with their delicious perfume; the maple, which is the first to clothe itself with the livery of spring; and the sycamore, king of the western forest, which erects itself in the most gracious forms, with vast spreading branches, covered with a brilliant white bark, and adds a distinctive note of grandeur to the imposing beauty of the woods. I have seen them fifteen and a half [feet] in diameter. The cottonwood, *populus deltoides,* is another giant . . . the *bignonia radicans* seems to prefer it to all others, climbs to its very top and lets loose a profusion of great flame-colored trumpet-shaped blossoms . . . The dogwood and the redbud fill the gap twixt tree and shrub. . . ."

Ten days were required to reach Westport, on the frontier of Missouri, and there for more than three weeks Father De Smet was obliged to bide his time while the American Fur Company caravan with which he would travel west was being organized and readied. In command was the veteran Andrew Drips, a man of many adventures in the western mountains, who had been a fur trader among the Indians since 1820. The destination of the expedition was the upper Green River (now western Wyoming), where the annual rendezvous of the fur brigades was to be held. Carrying foodstuffs, equipment, trade goods and ammunition on the outward trek, the half-dozen wagons and several score pack animals would return over the same trail of nearly two thousand miles heavily loaded with the furs taken throughout the Far West during the preceding fall and winter by roving bands of trappers. Some forty hunters, packers and scouts would accompany the outbound company.

The start was made at dawn on the morning of April 30. During the next few days, as the train wound through the rolling country, Father De Smet's spirits soared. He was off at last on the great adventure to the western mountains, traveling toward a land that in most respects was still as clean as God had created it, toward peoples not yet despoiled and afflicted by the terrible diseases and crimes of the white man. Here was a boundless earthly garden in which the fruits of his spiritual labors could well be rich and rewarding. He was a contented man as he rode his horse along a trail that vanished ahead of him in the sky.

Most of the members of the company were raw-boned white men with hard bodies and steel muscles, faces like scorched leather and the look of distance in their sharp eyes. They wore smoke-blackened buckskin, and their hair was long, that of some reaching to the shoulders in a shaggy mane, and on others braided in the manner of Indians. At their belts were skinning knives, pistols, ammunition pouches, and little leather bags in which they carried their few personal belongings . . . perhaps a piece of mirror, a razor, tobacco, needles and thread. Night and day they were never without the rifles, which seemed to be as much a part of them as their limbs; indeed, they considered them more important assets.

The scouts said game was scarce, an assertion difficult for Father De Smet to believe, for his hunter supplied his tent "abundantly with ducks, snipe, prairie chickens, cranes, pigeons, badgers, deer and antelope."

The only persons met on the trail during the first days was a group of Kansas Indians on the way to Westport to dispose of some peltries. They lived on "the Kansas River, and their territory begins sixty miles west of the state of Missouri, and their villages are at a distance of eighty miles. Their language, customs and manners are the same as those of the Osages.

"In peace and war, these two nations unite their interests, and form, so to speak, a single nation of some 1700 souls. They live in villages, wherein their huts, which may be made of bark, like the wigwams of the Potawatomies, or of rushes, like those of the Osages, or of earth like the *akozos* of the Pawnees and Otoes, are placed at random and without order . . . The door is so low that one can enter only by crawling; it consists merely of a dried skin hung up."

Six days out of Westport, Father De Smet knew the first chills and sweats of a fever that was to plague him intermittently for weeks to come. Several of the men with the train advised him to turn back, but he stubbornly refused, announcing his determination to see the nations of the mountains unless death intervened.

On the days when his fever raged he followed the caravan as best he could, "sticking on my horse as long as I had the strength; after that I would go and lie in a cart on the boxes, where I was jolted about like a malefactor." Often the wagons had to cross deep ravines, into which they were lowered with ropes, and at such times Father De Smet would be thrown "into the most singular positions; now my feet would be in the air, now I would find myself hidden like a thief between boxes and bundles, cold as an icicle or covered with sweat and burning like a stove. . . . During three days when my fever was at its highest, I had no water but what was stagnant and dirty."

For eighteen days they had followed the general route of the Oregon Trail to the Platte River, and now they turned westward along the right bank of the Platte, which the traders looked upon as one of the most wonderful and useless rivers of the West. The mouth of the Platte, six hundred and fifty miles above St. Louis, was considered the dividing line, the "equator," between the upper and lower Missouri. Both the north and south branches of the Platte rose high in the western mountains. The North Platte was the longer, flowing more than six hundred miles to its junction with the south branch. The Platte Valley and the north branch provided one of the most direct and feasible routes toward the Northwest. There the caravans found the water, wood and grass they must have available at all times on the long trek between Westport and their tramontane destinations.

The short-grass country, rising like an endless yellow and brown carpet ever higher toward the west, began soon after the Platte was reached, traversed by the twisting green vein of the shallow river valley. It evoked admiration in Father De Smet: "Think of the big ponds you have seen in the parks of European noblemen, dotted with little wooded islands. The Platte offers you these by thousands, and of all shapes. I have seen groups of these islands that one might easily take, from a distance, for fleets under sail; garlanded with verdure and festooned with flowers . . . the trees which the isles chiefly produce are the species of white poplar commonly called cottonwoods; the savages cut them down in winter and the bark serves for fodder for their horses.

"Antelope are very plentiful . . . I have often seen several hundred in sight at one time. It is the most agile animal of the prairies. Hunters make use of a trick to come near him:* they run at him full gallop, and the animal is off like a flash, leaving the horseman far behind; but soon it stops to look at him, being a very curious creature; meanwhile, the hunter dismounts and lays himself flat on the ground; here he makes all kinds of flourishes with his arms and legs, now and then waving his handkerchief, or a red cap. . . . The antelope draws slowly near, to watch and investigate him; and as soon as it is within gunshot, the hunter fires and lays it low. Often one will get as many as six before the band scatters."

The heart of the buffalo plains, which reached from Canada to the Gulf of Mexico, often provided the stirring sight of immense herds drifting northward under the hot sun of the spring. In places the ground was covered over large areas "with buffalo bones and skulls arranged in circles or half-moons and painted with various devices. It is in the midst of these skulls that the Pawnees are wont to practice their superstitious divinations, when they go forth to war or to the chase," he wrote.

He thought the prairie dogs appeared "to have a kind of civil government established in their society," and he took particular interest in "the solitary burial places of the Pawnees . . . These tombs were adorned with buffalo skulls painted red; the body is put in a sitting position, into a little cabin made of reeds and branches of trees, strongly interwoven to keep the wolves out. The face is daubed with vermilion, the body is covered with its finest war ornaments, and beside it one sees provisions of every kind, dried meat, tobacco, powder and lead, gun, bow and arrows. For several years the families will come back every spring to renew these provisions. Their idea is that the soul hovers for a long time about the spot where the body reposes before taking its flight to the land of souls."

Wolves were numerous in the region, and Father De Smet was

* Writing chiefly in French, Father De Smet naturally used feminine and masculine pronouns, and his translators often let them stand instead of employing the neuter pronoun *it* of the English language.

informed that "they kill every year a third of the buffalo calves; often when they are in strong bands, they will even attack full-grown bulls or cows, hurling themselves all together upon a single buffalo, pulling him down very skillfully and devouring him."

Always interested in statistics, Father De Smet wondered how many buffalo inhabited the western plains. To the question, a half-breed scout smiled and gazed at the heavens, replying: "How many stars?" But Father De Smet succeeded in securing some figures. The American Fur Company had estimated it would bring some sixty-seven thousand hides into St. Louis that year, and a scout opined that, judging by the number of Indians known to live in the main buffalo country, more than a hundred thousand more would be killed for food, tepees, clothing, sleeping robes and saddle covers that summer. In reality, however, this was only a small fraction of the total number of buffalo.

Obviously Father De Smet had read Washington Irving's *Astoria*, which had been published in 1836, for he quoted descriptive passages, and he agreed in several respects with Irving's sad predictions for the future of "the great American desert," but his own analysis was far more shrewd than Irving's. Like most educated travelers of his generation, he reasoned that climatic and geographical conditions were too unfavorable to permit the development of an extensive civilization west of the ninety-ninth meridian, yet he qualified this opinion with the astute observation: "There are perhaps some places, more fortunately situated on the banks of rivers, where agriculture could be successfully practiced; others might be converted into grazing lands as fertile as those of the East. . . ."

Father De Smet anticipated the days of the "wild West" which were to follow the Civil War. "Some day perhaps," he said of the Great Plains, "it may be the cradle of a new people, composed of the savage old races and of . . . adventurers, of the fugitive and the banished, thrust out from the bosom of society, a heterogeneous and menacing population, which the American

Union is piling up like a sinister cloud upon its frontiers, increasing continually its strength and its irritation by transporting whole tribes of Indians from their birthplace on the banks of the Mississippi, into the place of exile assigned them among these western solitudes. These savages bring with them an implacable hatred of the whites, who, they say, have driven them from their own country, far from the burial place of their fathers, that they may take unjust possession of their heritage. If some of these tribes should some day form into hordes like the nomadic peoples, half shepherd, half warrior, who range the plateaus of Asia with their herds, is it not to be feared that in time others may organize themselves into bands of robbers and assassins . . . the desert for the scene of their brigandage, and inaccessible rocks for a safe refuge for their lives and their booty?"

On May 28, the caravan forded the South Platte, and, continuing along the right bank of the North Platte, three days later came in sight of Chimney Rock, one of the most notable landmarks on the trail. They were now five hundred and seventy miles from Westport, and in a country of fantastic formations. Chimney Rock rose from the top of a high conical hill. Father De Smet recorded the height of the shaft itself as a hundred and fifty feet, and remarked that it could be seen for a distance of thirty miles. On each side of the trail the badlands reached away in varied shades of umber, turquoise, copper, red and gold, some of the hills and ridges presenting the appearance of "towers, castles and fortified cities." For the first time he saw the *grosse-corne,* the bighorn sheep, and in the same region there were large bands of wild horses.

The *Fourche à la Ramée* was crossed on the fourth of June, a small clear stream named for a trapper, Joseph Laramee, killed on it by Indians in 1821. The junction of the Laramie River and the North Platte was an important point on the trail. Six hundred and seventy miles from Westport, it marked the end of the Great Plains and the beginning of the mountain country. Here, too, the American Fur Company's route from Fort Pierre and the upper

Missouri River came into the main Oregon Trail. The confluence was a customary stopping place for caravans. Equipment and wagons were overhauled and cargoes were rearranged. A much needed respite from the strain of daily travel was enjoyed. For thirty-six days since leaving Westport, Father De Smet's company had pushed steadily ahead, no more than briefly deterred by fierce heat, numbing cold and severe storms. It had averaged eighteen miles a day, about a normal rate of travel for the distance.

Some forty lodges of Cheyennes were encamped on the Laramie. Father De Smet, who had never seen Indians of this large tribe, found them "polite, cleanly and decent in their manners. The men in general are of great stature, straight and vigorous; they have aquiline noses and strongly marked chins." The Cheyennes had once dwelt along the Red River of the North, but under pressure from the more powerful Sioux were driven toward the Southwest. Once it had been their way to live in permanent villages, but disastrous attacks made nomads of them. They were a virile people, superb horsemen, tenacious and courageous fighters. They owned immense herds of good horses, and traded profitably in them with both Indians and whites.

Father De Smet may have been the first Black Robe these Indians had ever seen, although it was possible that some of them, ranging far over the plains, may have encountered a priest somewhere in the Southwest in the company of Mexicans. The extremely cordial welcome they gave to Father De Smet suggested that such a thing had happened, perhaps many years before.

He was invited to a feast and accorded the ceremony of the calumet. A pipe was lighted and first given to the Great Spirit to smoke. It was held "toward the heavens, then toward the sun, the earth and the water; then the calumet goes the round of the lodge three times; it passes from hand to hand, and everyone takes half a dozen puffs." Father De Smet was a pipe smoker, but he preferred a blend without the severe bite of the wild mixture used by most Indians.

Following the ceremony a chief arose and embraced Father De Smet, telling him: "Black Robe, my heart was very glad when I learned who you were. Never has my lodge seen a greater day. As soon as I received the news of your coming, I had my big kettle filled to give you a feast in the midst of my warriors. Be welcome. I have had my three best dogs killed in your honor; they were very fat."

Father De Smet found the flesh of the chief's dogs "very delicate and extremely good; it much resembles that of a young pig. The portion bestowed on me was large; the two thighs and the paws, with five or six ribs; the law of the feast required me to eat it all, but it was too much for me. Finally I learned that one may get rid of his dish by passing it to another guest, with a present of tobacco."

Not a man to overlook such a fine opportunity, he delivered a speech of gratefulness in which he included the "principal points of religion." He explained the Ten Commandments and several articles of the Church creed, and he departed with the feeling that a zealous missionary might be very successful among the Cheyennes.

The first range of the Rockies was visible to the west as the expedition went on from the Laramie. Nights grew steadily colder, and snow could be seen on the peaks ahead, although the days were balmy and bright. On June 14th, they passed Red Buttes, and a few miles farther on saw the last of the North Platte, which they had followed for nearly five hundred miles. The stream turned toward the south, while the trail mounted the high angle between it and the Sweetwater River.

The Sweetwater, which Father De Smet spoke of as *Rivière de l'eau douce,* was appropriately named. It was a clear mountain stream in a country in which most streams were so heavily laden with alkali as to be undrinkable. Yet, the Sweetwater had not received its name because of its good water. It was named not *Eau Douce* but *Eau Sucre* by some early trappers when one of their pack mules, bearing their supply of sugar, fell into it and was lost.

In the valley of the Sweetwater, the expedition camped near Independence Rock, a famous point on the trail. Oval in shape, covering twenty-seven acres, and standing a hundred and fifty feet high, it was completely isolated and appeared to have been dropped there by some freakish caprice of nature. The names of many noted mountain men were inscribed on it. A party of American trappers had christened it when they stopped beside it on the Fourth of July in an uncertain year in the decade of the 1820s.

The Devil's Gate loomed ahead, a tremendous chasm through solid granite at the bottom of which flowed the gentle Sweetwater. The trail mounted a long ridge to avoid the impassable canyon, but Father De Smet had to make only a short side trip from the route to gain a remarkable view. Below him was the gorge. To the westward spread a magnificent valley, which appeared to be no less than a paradise for wild animals. Through the valley, which was ten to fifteen miles wide, the serpentine course of the stream was plainly visible due to the silver sheen of its surface and the ribbon of foliage that grew along its banks. Eastward was a valley of equal grandeur. A cordon of great mountains completely encircled the plains above the Devil's Gate. To the northeast were the Rattlesnake Hills. Eastward was the Caspar Range. On the southeast the Seminole and Ferris Ranges lifted their eminences to the clear sky, south and southwest were the Green Mountains, and to the west the horizon was closed by the towering Crooks' Peak.

On June 24th, pushing up the Sweetwater, they crossed a high plain that was covered with snow, and on the following day entered the South Pass.

The scouts told Father De Smet that they were then almost exactly halfway to Fort Vancouver on the Columbia River, nine hundred and fifty miles from Westport. Behind them waters flowed into the Missouri River, and before them into the Pacific Ocean.

This was the most celebrated pass in the entire course of the Continental Divide across the territory of the United States. Father De Smet noted that as he traveled through it, it was "almost imperceptible." Seven thousand five hundred feet above sea level, it opened before them in a comparatively smooth sweep, a broad open valley gentle in its slope.

The scouts were vague as to the discovery of the pass, but they repeated the popular story that it had been found by a small party of trappers detached in 1823 from the brigade led by the intrepid Andrew Henry. These men were known to have traveled southward from the Big Horn River† and through the Green River Valley in that year. Yet, it could be said that before the pass was actually discovered it had received its name. For years the mountain men had been looking for such a way through the Rockies, a so-called "southern pass," south of those traversed by Lewis and Clark, the "northern passes." When at last it was found, the name fell naturally upon it.

South Pass behind it, the caravan left the Oregon Trail and turned toward the northwest, passing through an arid rough country, and ahead could be seen the immense wall of the Wind River Mountains, which Father De Smet mistakenly estimated to be "twenty to twenty-four thousand feet above the Atlantic Ocean."‡ At the foot of the mountains was the valley of the upper Green River, rendezvous of the fur traders.

Father De Smet looked down upon it on the 30th of June, and he saw the smoke of hundreds of campfires rising against the blazing afternoon light, pony herds drifting like shadows along the glistening stream, and ragged islands of tepees dotting the brown valley floor.

† In Montana
‡ Highest peak of the range, Fremont, rises 13,785 feet.

XI

The Green River rendezvous was several hundred miles from the Flathead Country, and Father De Smet was both astonished and delighted to find awaiting him there a deputation of ten Flatheads. They had been sent to meet him soon after the return of Pierre Gaucher, and it was their plan to escort him to their homeland, a dangerous and difficult journey through high mountains.

He described their meeting as "not that of strangers, but of friends; it was like children running to meet their father after a long absence." The incident becomes all the more remarkable when it is realized that these Indians had never seen a priest, that their knowledge of the white man's religion consisted of fragmentary information imparted by the few Iroquois among them, and the Iroquois themselves had been out of touch with the Black Robes for many years.

Nor had the Flatheads any understanding of Father De Smet's nature, knew nothing of his personality, nothing of his appearance. Yet, from the beginning they showed a childlike love and respect for him, wept in his presence, and displayed a consuming desire to please him.*

"They told me all the little news of their nation," said Father De Smet, "their almost miraculous preservation in a fight between sixty of their warriors and two hundred Blackfeet, a fight

---

* Weeping was commonplace among numerous tribes of American Indians, and was not always a manifestation of sorrow or grief. Mention of Indians weeping is to be found throughout the chronicles of early explorers, both in the lands of the Spanish conquest and in the north. It was often employed to give emphasis to a matter, as an indication of sincerity, even as an expression of profound gratefulness, and many Indians could shed tears at will.

that lasted five days, and in which they had killed fifty of their enemies without losing a single man."

This battle had taken place after word had been received that a Black Robe was coming out from St. Louis. The Flatheads were inspired by the news. "We fought like brave men in the desire to see you," they told him. "The Great Spirit took pity on us, he helped us to remove dangers from the path that is to lead you to our camp. The Blackfeet will not trouble us for a while; they went away weeping. Our brothers are burning with impatience to see you."

The annual rendezvous, wherever held in the western mountains, was primarily for the purpose of delivering furs to the caravans from the Missouri and obtaining supplies, but it also was something of a fair and celebration. Bands of trappers, both Indian and white, came great distances with their catches to the appointed place, and once the chief business had been concluded there were games and sporting events, especially horse races, and there was unconfined debauchery. Numerous Indian squaws took advantage of the opportunity to obtain money and gifts by selling their charms. Drunkenness was the order of the day, and fights, sometimes with fatal results, often occurred.

For the first time in history, Father De Smet added a new element to a rendezvous, the air of a Chautauqua. He delivered sermons and lectures, held religious ceremonies, and sat with groups of Indians to discuss, in something of the manner of a roundtable, current events and various problems, both economic and social, of the moment.

He saw for the first time the Shoshones, or Snake Indians.†

† He gave them a third name, that of Root Diggers, but this is not correct. Possibly a few true Root Diggers were with the Snakes at the rendezvous, but the tribe dwelt in the desolate wastes south and west of the Great Salt Lake. The name of Root Diggers was generally applied to the Pah-Utes. Although the Snakes and Root Diggers were of the same linguistic family, *Shoshonean,* the Root Diggers were not to be compared with the Snakes for intelligence, courage, shrewdness or other qualities. The Snakes were mentally superior, a higher order of human being, and their martial prowess was comparable to that of the Blackfeet and Crows.

They were, he reported, present in "great numbers."‡ The Snakes lived in the upper valleys of the Green and Snake Rivers and the northern part of Bear River Valley. They were exclusively a nomadic tribe, traveling annually to the great plains to hunt buffalo and to the upper tributaries of the Columbia River when the salmon came up from the sea. Seldom openly hostile to the white men, they were, however, such inveterate beggars and thieves that they were almost an intolerable nuisance. They were traditional friends of the Nez Percés and Flatheads, but deadly enemies of the Blackfeet and Crows, to whose territories they were forced by necessity to go for buffalo hides and meat.

The Snakes put on a show at the rendezvous, and he told of them giving "a parade to greet the whites that were there. Three hundred of their warriors came up in good order and at full gallop into the midst of our camp. They were hideously painted, armed with their clubs, and covered all over with feathers, pearls [?], wolves' tails, teeth and claws of animals, outlandish adornments. . . . Those who had wounds received in war, and those who had killed the enemies of their tribe, displayed their scars ostentatiously and waved the scalps they had taken on the ends of poles, after the manner of standards.

"After riding a few times around the camp, uttering at intervals shouts of joy, they dismounted and all came to shake hands with the whites in sign of friendship."

The Snakes observed Father De Smet with unconcealed interest and curiosity. He stood as an enigma before them, and they were aware of the reverence shown for the sturdy man in the black gown by the Flathead delegation. The desire to satisfy their curiosity and to gain as much worldly knowledge as their enterprising neighbors—a wish to acquire religious instruction hardly would have influenced them, for they had known nothing whatever of men called Black Robes—impelled them to extend to him

‡ If three hundred were there, this would have been considered a great number by the trappers, and undoubtedly would have seemed so to Father De Smet.

a cordial invitation to a council. Never one to reject a chance to explain his presence and his mission in life, he readily accepted.

He found himself seated with some thirty of the highest ranking Snakes. "To begin," he said of the meeting, "their chief made a little circle on the ground, placed within it a small piece of burning cow dung, and lit his pipe from it. Then he offered the pipe to the Great Spirit, to the sun, to the earth and to the four cardinal points. All the others observed a most profound silence and sat motionless as statues. The calumet passed from hand to hand, and I noticed that each one had a different way of taking it. One turned the calumet around before putting it to his mouth; the next made a half-circle as he accepted it; another held the bowl in the air; a fourth lowered it to the ground, and so on."

In all his voluminous writings, Father De Smet never ridiculed the religious ceremonies of Indians, except on the occasion of his council with the Snakes at the Green River rendezvous in the year 1840. Quite naturally opposed to the incantations and rituals which he considered idolatrous and paganish, he studiously refrained from injuring the feelings of his hosts by openly criticizing or condemning them.

An unexplained and unusual attitude is displayed in the passage: "I am naturally inclined to laughter, and I must confess that on this occasion I had to make serious effort not to break out, as I watched the gravity observed by these poor savages in the midst of all these ridiculous affectations. These forms of smoking enter into their superstitious religious practices; each one has his own, from which he would never dare deviate all his life long, for fear of displeasing his manitous."

While Father De Smet was at Green River he observed the Snakes preparing for an expedition against the Blackfeet. "The evening before their departure, the chief, at the head of his soldiers, performed his farewell dance at every lodge; everywhere he received a piece of tobacco or some other present."

The Snake squaws implored their warriors to capture some Blackfoot women. When Father De Smet inquired what would happen to those taken prisoner, the interpreter told him: "They carry them [the captured women] to camp and turn them over to their wives, mothers and sisters. These women immediately butcher them with their hatchets and knives, vomiting upon the poor wretches in their frantic rage the most crushing and outrageous language. 'Oh, Blackfoot bitches,' they cry: 'If we could eat the hearts of all your young ones, and bathe in the blood of your cursed nation!'"

Far from being repulsed and silenced by such replies to his inquiries, Father De Smet continued unceasingly to gather all the information possible about the red people who lived west of the mountains. Diligently he attended to his notes: "The Sampeetches, Pah-Utes and Yam-pah-Utes are the nearest neighbors to the Snakes. There is not, very likely, in all the universe a more miserable, more degraded and poorer people. The French commonly call them *les Dignes de pitié*, or those who deserve to be pitied, and the name suits them admirably. The land they inhabit is a veritable waste. They lodge in crevices of the rocks, or in holes dug in the earth; they have no clothing; their only weapons are a bow, arrows and a pointed stick; they range the barren plains in search of ants and grasshoppers, on which they feed, and they think it a feast when they come upon a few tasteless roots or nauseous grains. . . . They eat the corpses of their kindred, and sometimes even their own children.

"Their number is unknown, for they are seldom seen more than two, three or four together. They are so timid that a stranger would have a good deal of trouble to approach them. . . ."

On Sunday, July 5th, the first Mass ever celebrated in the Rocky Mountains took place at the Green River rendezvous. Not only was it one of the great spiritual experiences of Father De Smet's life, but one which stirred his emotions so deeply that it was only with the greatest difficulty that he completed it.

Around him the immense hills and the peaks swept in all their grandeur against an immaculate sky, the peaks of a wilderness where no Black Robe had ever trod before, a wilderness where

98

the holy words had never before been given to the wind that moved across its unnamed valleys and forests. Feeling thankfulness and consolation he had never known, choking back his tears, he celebrated the Holy Sacrifice of Mass Sub Dio. The altar stood on a slight elevation, surrounded with boughs and garlands of flowers. He addressed the congregation in both French and English, and he spoke through an interpreter to the Indians. He thought it "was a spectacle truly moving for the heart of a missionary to behold an assembly composed of so many different nations. . . . The Canadians sang hymns in French and Latin, and the Indians in their native tongue. . . ."

When the service concluded, the French-Canadians promptly christened the site *La Prairie de la Messe,* and it was so designated at later rendezvous.

On July 6th, the bands of trappers, the caravans and the Indians began to depart, to be separated for another year. As Father De Smet prepared to leave with his Flathead friends, a fortunate event occurred. Before him appeared Jean Baptiste de Velder, a Fleming from Ghent who had once served as a grenadier for Napoleon. He had left Europe thirty years before, and had never returned. For the past fourteen years he had been a wandering trapper in the western wilderness. He generously offered his services as a guide and adviser, and expressed a willingness to go with Father De Smet wherever his travels might take him. Father De Smet was overjoyed to welcome his countryman. The veteran mountain man would be a most valuable companion. Although De Velder had almost forgotten the Flemish language, Father De Smet was delighted to learn that he had remembered his prayers and a hymn in Flemish, which he had learned as a child from his mother, and which he frequently recited.

In addition to De Velder and the deputation of ten Flatheads, a similar number of French-Canadians going on a trapping expedition in the Snake Country were in Father De Smet's escort when it left the rendezvous on the 6th of July. For three days the party ascended the left bank of Green River, then forded it and set out through the high country separating the waters of the Colorado River from those of the Columbia.

Father De Smet was surprised to find flax growing abundantly in some of the valleys, and he remarked that "it is just the same as the flax that is cultivated in Belgium, except that it is an annual; the same stalk, calix, seed and blue flower, closing by day and opening in the evening."

Once across the high ridges, the company made a sharp descent into Jackson's Little Hole on the headwaters of the Hoback River. As they moved downstream Father De Smet was in a part of America which had never been visited by a man of the cloth of any denomination. It was a land of superb alpine beauty. In every direction were great peaks, and to the west towered one of the most magnificent ranges on earth, the Tetons. Proceeding down the Hoback River, they followed a narrow game trail high on the shoulder of an immense ridge, where "every step threatened a fall. We followed it for seventeen miles, upon a mountainside at an angle of 45° over a torrent which rushed uproarously in cascades, hundreds of feet below our route. The defile was so narrow, and the mountains on either hand so high, that the sun could scarcely penetrate it for an hour or two of the day. Pine forests like those of Norway, balsam firs, ordinary poplars, cedars, mulberry trees and many other varieties cover the sides of these mountains."

The company reached the confluence of the Hoback and Snake Rivers on July 10th. Melting snows had swelled the Snake into a raging torrent. The Indians and French-Canadians had no hesitation in starting across on their horses, but Father De Smet's nerve failed him. "I dared not venture to do likewise," he confessed. "To get me over, they made a kind of sack of my skin tent; then they put all my things in and set me on top of it. The three Flatheads who had jumped in to guide my frail bark by swimming, told me, laughing, not to be afraid, that I was on an excellent boat. And in fact this machine floated on the water like a majestic swan; and in less than ten minutes I found myself on the other bank, where we encamped for the night."

The next day a trail was followed out of Jackson's (Big) Hole toward Teton Pass.§ They climbed steadily through thick pine forests to an altitude of more than eight thousand feet. A heavy snow had fallen in the pass during the night, but the sky was spotlessly blue and the sun was so hot that the riders shed jackets and blankets. On the following afternoon they gazed down on the beautiful valley of Pierre's Hole, celebrated even at that time as the scene of Indian battles and annual rendezvous. It lies just west of the Tetons, and is approximately twenty-five miles in length and from five to fifteen miles in width. Named for an Iroquois trapper who discovered it, it had become a crossroads of the fur traders. In 1832, a major battle between Blackfeet on one side and trappers and Flatheads on the other had taken place there.

Father De Smet's guides had kept well the secret that in Pierre's Hole more than fifteen hundred Flatheads and Pend d'Oreilles would be awaiting him. A large lodge had been prepared for him. He could not conceal his emotion as he entered the immense camp and "men, women and children came all together to meet me and shake hands and bid me welcome. The elders wept with joy, while the young men expressed their satisfaction by leaps and shouts of happiness."

Amid the tumult and the shouting, Father De Smet was escorted into the presence of an elderly chief, Big Face, a man of "truly patriarchal aspect, [who] received me in the midst of his whole council with the liveliest cordiality."

Big Face spoke with dignity and solemnity, telling Father De Smet: "Black Robe, you are welcome in my nation. Today Kyleeyou has fulfilled our wishes.¶ Our hearts are big, for our

§ Trappers called mountain valleys of the west "holes."
¶ *Kyleeyou* means "Our Father." In another account of the same incident, Father De Smet used the word *Kaikolinzoeten*, which means "Our God," but he interpreted both words to mean "Great Spirit."

greatest desire is gratified. You are in the midst of a poor and rude people, plunged in the darkness of ignorance. I have always exhorted my children to love Kyleeyou. We know that everything belongs to him, and that our whole dependence is upon his liberal hand. Now, Father, speak, and we will comply with all you will tell us. Show us the road we have to follow, to come to the place where the Great Spirit resides. Black Robe, we will follow the words of your mouth."

Big Face indicated his willingness to step aside as the Flathead leader, but Father De Smet quickly opposed the action, replying that Big Face had mistaken the true purpose of his visit, and assuring the Indians that his only interest was their spiritual welfare. With regard to temporal affairs, they should continue as they were, respecting and obeying their chief. He understood the danger in his acceptance of any title or responsibility other than those he had as a priest. His strength and influence lay in his continued detachment from all matters political or military, and his success would come only through judicious use of that power.

During the several days he spent in the camp at Pierre's Hole, he found little time to rest. Dancing and the wild beating of drums sometimes continued far into the night. He was presented with a copper bell and told to ring it when he wished to call the people to prayer. On occasion as many as two thousand Indians would rush toward him at the first sound of the clapper. Following the prayers they would sing a solemn canticle of praise, of their own composition, "to the Author of their being."

At daylight each morning a zealous headman rode throughout the camp shouting to the Indians to arise with haste, as Black Robe would soon ring the bell. "Open your eyes," he yelled. "Address your first thoughts and words to the Great Spirit . . . the sun is about to appear, it is time you went to the river to wash yourselves. Be prompt at our Father's lodge. . . ."

If on any morning Father De Smet had thought he would take a few extra winks, he had no choice but to get up. When duty did not take him from his bed, the noise made sleep impossible. He was glad when, at the end of four days, the start for the Flathead Country was made.

The trail led up the Henry Fork of the Snake. The river, which flowed through a country of exceptional grandeur, had been named for the intrepid partner, Andrew Henry, who led a band of trappers into the valley in 1810, and built a fort there. These mountain men were the first to penetrate the remote area.

The journey northward was made in easy stages, on most days no more than nine or ten miles being traveled. "Often," Father De Smet recounted, "we passed and repassed high hills, wide and swift torrents, narrow and dangerous defiles. Often also we came upon lovely valleys, level and open, rich in pasture grounds of a beautiful verdure, dotted with flowers, and where the mountain balsam (the traveler's tea) abounds. This tea, even after it has been crushed beneath the feet of thousands of horses, still perfumes the air with its delicious scent . . . several more mountains drew our attention; some were in the form of cones, rising to a height of several thousand feet at an angle of forty-five to fifty degrees, very smooth and covered with a fair verdure; others represented domes; other were red as well-burned brick, and still bore the imprints of some great convulsion of nature; there were scoria and lava so porous that they floated on water. . . . In several places the openings of ancient craters were still to be distinguished."

Many Pend d'Oreilles had joined the Flatheads. More than two thousand men, women and children, five thousand horses, throngs of dogs, moved slowly through the immense country in long files, a wild, brilliant proccession of people whose recent ancestors had belonged to the Stone Age.

On July 22, one of the most interesting geographical points in North America was reached. Camp was established on the shore of Henry's Lake. Its waters flowed by way of the Columbia to the Pacific. Nearby was a high ridge, and just beyond it was another lake, appropriately called Mosquito Lake.* It was the ultimate source of the Missouri River, 4221 miles by watercourse from the Gulf of Mexico.

Father De Smet set out from camp alone "for a better examination of the fountains that give birth to these two great rivers." For six hours he worked his way up the side of a mountain, climbing several thousand feet. He found himself exhausted. The summit of the peak was still far above him. He was surrounded by snowdrifts, yet in the blinding sun the air was warm and sweet with the perfume of alpine meadows. He had gone far enough to gain a magnificent view. He saw the waters flowing from both lakes, "falling in cascades . . . hurling themselves with uproar from rock to rock. . . ."

He sat on a rock musing upon the works of God about him, deeply moved by the panorama. On a soft stone he cut the inscription: *Sanctus Ignatius Patronus Montium. Die Julii 23, 1840.*

Far as he was from all settlements at Henry's Lake, Father De Smet believed that not many years would pass before civilization in its impregnable advance would march beyond the Great Plains, surmount the peaks, and sweep onward to the western sea. He saw himself in the role of a conqueror, not a conqueror of land or of peoples, but a spiritual conqueror, a discoverer under the banner of God.

"Today is the accepted time to preach the gospel to these different nations," he wrote. ". . . soon the cupidity and avarice of civilized man will make the same inroads here as in the East, and the abominable influences of the vices of the frontier will interpose the same barrier to the introduction of the gospel, which all the savages seem to have a great desire to know, and which they will follow with fidelity . . ."

The destination of the Flatheads was the heart of their homeland, the Bitter Root Valley. Leisurely the long procession moved down the Beaver Head and the Jefferson Rivers. Father De Smet

* Red Rock Lake on modern maps. Nesting place of a few pairs of trumpeter swans, one of the rarest birds on earth.

held services each morning and evening, summoning the Indians with the little bell. "Their eagerness was so great that they would run to get a good place; even the sick got themselves carried thither. What a lesson for the cowardly and pusillanimous Christians of the old Catholic countries . . ." he said.

During each day he spoke and gave instructions at opportune times. As good fortune would have it, the itinerant trapper, Gabriel Prudhomme, had reappeared at Pierre's Hole. He not only spoke the Flathead language fluently, but even more important, he could write it. At Father De Smet's request he had set to work translating in writing the Lord's Prayer, the Hail Mary, the Apostles' Creed, the Ten Commandments and the Four Acts. As if he felt that was enough of a contribution at one time, he had vanished once again into the mountains. However, he left Father De Smet in a position to recite the prayers in stumbling but understandable Salishan. As an inducement to the Indians to learn them, he had announced that he would award a bright silver medal to the one who first recited them to him.

He was astonished at a camp on the Jefferson River when an aged Flathead arose during service and told him: "Father, your medal belongs to me." Thereupon, the man recited all the prayers without omitting a word. Embracing him, Father De Smet fastened the medal to his shirt, and then appointed him his catechist. Extremely proud of both the medal and his new position, the old man worked with such zeal and perseverance that in less than ten days he had a number of men and women reciting the Lord's Prayer and the Apostles' Creed as they went about their daily chores.

Game was plentiful along the trail, and Father De Smet recorded that hunters kept the little army well supplied with "the flesh of such animals as the red and black-tailed deer, elk, gazelle, bighorn or mountain sheep, grizzly and black bear, badger, rabbit and panther, killing also occasionally such feathered game as grouse, prairie hens, swans, geese, cranes and ducks. Fish abounded besides in the rivers, particularly salmon trout."

Mass was celebrated regularly on Sundays and on feast days, as well as when the Indians did not break camp in the morning at an early hour. Of these services Father De Smet wrote: ". . . the altar was made of willows; my blanket made an altar cloth, and all the lodge was adorned with images and wild flowers; the Indians knelt about in a circle of about 200 feet, surrounded by little pines and cedars, set out expressly; they took assiduous part with the greatest modesty, attention and devotion, and since various nations were among them, they chanted the praises of God in the Flathead, Nez Percé and Iroquois languages. The Canadians, my Fleming [de Velder] and I sang chants in French, English and Latin."

The Three Forks of the Missouri was reached August 21, and camp was made on the middle stream.† "In this great and beautiful plain," Father De Smet reported, "were buffalo in numberless herds. Finding themselves therefore in the midst of abundance, the Flatheads prepared to lay in their winter meat supply; they raised willowy scaffolds about their lodges for drying meat, and everyone made ready his firearm, his bow and arrows.

"Four hundred horsemen, old and young, mounted on their best horses, started early in the morning for the great hunt. I chose to accompany them in order to watch this striking spectacle from near at hand. At a given signal, they rode at full gallop among the herds; soon everything appeared confusion and flight all over the plain; the hunters pursued the fattest cows, discharged their guns and let fly their arrows, and in three hours they killed more than 500. Then the women, the old men, and the children came up, and with the aid of horses carried off the hides and the meat, and soon all the scaffolds were full and gave the camp the aspect of a vast butcher shop. The buffalo are hard to kill; they must be wounded in the vital parts. A ball that strikes a bull's forehead produces no other effect than a movement of the head and a greater exasperation; on the other hand,

† Madison River. Since joining the Flatheads he had crossed the Continental Divide at least three times.

one that strikes the forehead of a cow penetrates. Several bulls, mortally wounded in this hunt, defended themselves furiously."

During leisure daytime hours, and often far into the night, Father De Smet assiduously jotted down the information he gathered of the western Indians and their homelands. He was seemingly a tireless interrogator. The letters and journals he wrote were to give the world one of the first authentic and accurate accounts of the red peoples who inhabited the western mountains and deserts, for few, if any, men of education and literary ability had gone ahead of him into the remote areas of western Wyoming, western Montana, Idaho, and eastern Oregon and Washington.

He seemed unable to say enough in praise of the Flatheads, and throughout his notes he shows them to be people of superior intellect and character. "I was not able to discover among these people the slightest blameworthy act, unless it was their gambling, in which they often venture everything they possess," he declared. "These games were unanimously abolished, as soon as I had explained to them that they were contrary to the commandment of God, saying: 'Ye shall not covet anything that is your neighbor's.' They are scrupulously honest in their buying and selling; they have never been accused of having committed a theft; everything that is found is taken to the lodge of the chief . . . who returns them to their owner. Slander is unknown even among the women; lying is hateful to them beyond anything else . . . they abhor a 'forked tongue' . . . Quarrels and fits of rage are severely punished. No one suffers without his brothers interesting themselves in his trouble and coming to his succor. . . .

"The Flatheads may be called a grave, modest and decent people. The gross vices so common among many other nations are unknown among them. Adultery is of the rarest occurrence . . . Their charity toward the old and infirm is very great. The name of an orphan is unknown among them. Immediately after the death of their parents they are adopted by relations and friends . . . They love and esteem the whites highly and glory and take pride that they never spilt a drop of white man's blood."

Father De Smet was writing of mountain Indians who had never seen white settlers, whose only contacts with the white man had been through the few trappers that came into the country from St. Louis and Canada. In less than five years after he had first reached the Green River, the long wagon trains of the emigrants would wind through the South Pass and roll on to Oregon. The white men, whom the Indians he knew "loved and esteemed," would degrade them, infect them, destroy their means of living, and murder them, until only a few helpless and pitiable creatures remained.

This circumstance alone made the descriptions in his journals all the more valuable.

"In all the mountain tribes the costume is nearly the same," he wrote. "The men wear a long tunic of the skin of the antelope or bighorn; leggings of buckskin or dogskin; shoes of the same material, and a mantle of buffalo skin or a red, blue, green or white blanket. The seams of their garments are adorned with long fringes; they clean them by rubbing them with white earth. . . .

"The Indian loves to pile ornament upon ornament; he attaches plumes of every kind to his long hair; the eagle feather always occupies the principal place; it is the great medicine bird, the manitou or guardian spirit of the savage warrior. They attach besides all sorts of trinkets, ribbons of all colors, rings, shells and ornaments of bone. They wear on their necks collars of pearls interlaced with *apocoins* (an oblong shell that they pick up on the shore of the Pacific Ocean).‡ In the morning, all wash themselves; but for lack of a towel they make use of the end of their tunic. Then everyone returns to his lodge to make his toilet; that is, to rub his face, hair, arms and chest with bear's grease, over which they spread a thick layer of vermilion, which gives them a wild and hideous aspect. I often thought, when I met them, of

‡ Traffic in trade goods existed between the tribes of the Pacific Coast and those of the interior mountains.

those bloated visages that are called in Belgium *vagefuers gezichten* (purgatory faces).

"Boys of seven to ten years wear a sort of dalmatica of skins, embroidered with porcupine quills and open at both sides, which gives these little fellows an altogether singular appearance, without breeches or shirt. Under the age of seven they have nothing to cover them during the summer; they pass whole days playing in the water or in the mire; in winter they are lapped in scraps of leather.

"The women cover themselves with a big cape, ornamented with elk teeth and rows of pearls of various colors. This attire makes a handsome effect. . . .

"A savage takes as great pains in decorating his courser as with his own person; the animal's head, chest and flanks are covered with hangings of scarlet cloth, embroidered with pearls and adorned with long fringes, to which they attach little bells."

Father De Smet thoughtfully studied the religion of the mountain Indians, and he found that in general they "admit the existence of a Supreme Being, the Great Spirit, Creator of all things, the immortality of the soul and a future life, where man is rewarded or punished according to his desserts.

"These are the principal points of their belief. Their religious ideas are very limited. They believe that the Great Spirit directs all important events, that he is the author of all good and consequently alone worthy of adoration; that by their evil conduct they draw on themselves his indignation and wrath, and that he sends them calamities to punish them. They say further that the soul enters the other world with the same form that the body bore on earth."

In contrast to the plains tribes, wrote Father De Smet, "the savages on the west of the mountains are very peaceable and rarely make war among themselves. . . . It is only with the Blackfeet, who dwell to the east, that they often have bloody encounters. These marauders are always on the march, robbing and killing those whom they meet. . . . It is commonly said that one Flathead . . . is worth four Blackfeet; when a party of the latter meets one of the Flatheads, equal or superior in number, the Blackfoot at once manifests a desire for peace, displays a flag and presents his calumet. The Flathead chief always accepts, but he does not fail to let his enemy understand that he knows what to think of his peaceful intentions. 'Blackfoot,' he says, 'I accept your calumet, but I know very well that your heart desires war, and that your hand is defiled with murder; but I love peace. Let us smoke, since you offer me the calumet, though I am sure there will soon be fresh bloodshed.'

"The government of an Indian tribe is in the hands of the chiefs, who attain that office by merit or by exploits. Their power consists solely in the influence; it is great or little in proportion to the wisdom, benevolence and courage that they have displayed. The chief does not exercise his authority by command but by persuasion. He never levies taxes; on the contrary, he is so much in the habit of giving away his own property, as well to aid a needy individual as to further the public good, that he is ordinarily one of the poorest in the village. . . . I know of no government that allows so great personal liberty, and in which there is at the same time so little of anarchy and so much subordination and devotion."

August of 1840 would soon be gone, and Father De Smet began to be concerned about plans for the coming winter. If he remained with the Flatheads much longer, it would be impossible for him to return to St. Louis before the mountains and plains were locked in deep snow and bitter cold. He had not yet reached their homeland, but he understood that he must make a decision within the next few days.

He reviewed his accomplishments and the general situation. There remained not the slightest doubt in his mind that a mission in the Flathead Country would be successful, and unquestionably others could be profitably established among the Nez Percés, the Pend d'Oreilles, and adjacent tribes. All the great area west of the mountains on the headwaters of the Columbia appeared to be the most promising vineyard for the Church he had ever seen.

During the two months he had been among the Flatheads his progress had been both astonishing and rewarding. He had baptized nearly six hundred Indians, young and old. All the others to whom he had preached and given instruction were eager to receive the same favor. He had purposely refrained from performing more baptismal ceremonies. "I thought it prudent to put them off until the following year," he said, "to give them a high idea of the dignity of the sacrament, and to try them in regard to the indissolubility of the bonds of marriage, which is an unknown thing among the Indian nations of America; for they often part for the most frivolous causes."

Among the adults he baptized were the two head chiefs of the Pend d'Oreilles and the Flatheads, both of them octogenarians. Before bestowing the holy sacrament upon them, as he was urging them to renew repentance for their sins, the Pend d'Oreille leader, Walking Bear, suddenly spoke: "When I was young, and even as I became old, I was plunged in profound ignorance of good and evil, and in that period I must no doubt have displeased the Great Spirit. I sincerely implore pardon of him. Every time I have perceived that a thing was bad, I have at once banished it from my heart. I do not remember ever in my life to have deliberately offended the Great Spirit."

In his journal, Father De Smet asked: "Are there in our Europe many Christians who could give this testimony of themselves?

"One single man, by the influence he has justly acquired by his bravery in fight and his wisdom in the council, leads the whole tribe. He has no need of guards, nor bolts, nor iron bars, nor state prisons. . . .

"*Is it these people whom the civilized nations dare to call by the name of savages?*"

At the Three Forks of the Missouri, Father De Smet came to his decision: he would leave at once for St. Louis.

In council he explained his intentions. While he regretted that he could not go on to the Bitter Root Valley, by doing so he would make it impossible for him to return to St. Louis before the next spring. It was necessary that he go back to obtain the articles needed for the mission and the church that would be built. He also needed assistants, other Black Robes who could work among the Indians, carry the word of God to the most remote areas, and help him to build other churches.

Solemnly he gave his word that he would return as soon as he could get across the mountains after the winter snows had gone.

As he talked, many of the wild painted faces before him were stained with tears. "I performed the morning prayers among the weeping and sobs of those good savages," he wrote. "They drew from me despite myself the tears that I gladly would have stifled for the moment. . . . I urged them to continue serving the Great Spirit with fervor and to put from them every cause of scandal. . . . I gave them for their spiritual head a very intelligent Indian, whom I had taken pains to instruct myself in a most particular manner; he was to represent me in my absence. . . ."

The aged Big Face arose. "Black Robe," he said in an emotional voice, "may the Great Spirit accompany you on your long and dangerous journey. We will offer vows evening and morning that you may arrive safe among your brothers in St. Louis. We will continue to offer vows until you return to your children of the mountains. When the snows disappear from the valleys, after the winter, when the grass begins to be green again, our hearts, so sad at present, will begin to rejoice. As the grass grows higher, our joy will become greater; but when the flowers appear, we will set out to come and meet you. Farewell."

XII

The Flatheads had no intention of permitting Father De Smet and his good companion, Jean Baptiste de Velder, to set out unaccompanied on their dangerous journey to St. Louis. When they departed on the 27th of August, they had as a guard thirty skilled hunters and warriors. The number was no more than enough to assure them comparative safety in passing through the Blackfoot Country, which lay immediately eastward from the Three Forks of the Missouri. It was territory in which, since 1810, numerous disastrous fights had taken place between trappers and the implacable tribe. White men were fair game in the eyes of the Blackfeet, and there was no reason to assume they would show mercy for a Black Robe.

The trail which the company took led up the Gallatin River. After traveling for two days they traversed Bozeman Pass, the route which for centuries had been taken by tramontane Indians to the buffalo plains. Across the pass, they rode down into the valley of the Yellowstone, striking the river where it turns abruptly eastward after flowing north from its source.*

"Here," said Father De Smet, "it was needful to take the greatest precautions. . . . We had to cross plains that stretched out of sight, sterile and arid lands, cut up with deep ravines, where at every step one might come upon enemies lying in wait. Scouts were sent out in every direction to reconnoiter the country; all traces, whether of men or animals, were attentively examined.

"It is here that one cannot but admire the sagacity of the savage; he will tell you what day an Indian has passed by the spot

* At the site of the present Livingston, Montana. The river rises in Yellowstone National Park.

where he sees his tracks, he will calculate the number of men and of horses, he will make out whether it was a war or hunting party; he will even recognize, from the impression of their footgear, to what nation they belonged. Every evening we chose a favorable place to pitch our camp, and built in haste a little fort of trunks of dead trees, to shelter us from a sudden attack."

The region was heavily infested with grizzly bears. One was killed and brought into camp. "His paws," Father De Smet recorded, "were thirteen inches in length, and each claw seven. The strength of this animal is surprising; an Indian has assured me that with a single blow of his paw he has seen one of these bears tear away four ribs from a buffalo, which fell dead at his feet."

Father De Smet himself saw the power and ferocity of the grizzly demonstrated. One of the Flatheads was passing a willow thicket "when a she-bear rushed furiously upon his horse, put her formidable paw upon his croup, and rending the flesh to the bone overturned him with his rider. Luckily for my man, he gained his feet in a flash, gun in hand, and had the satisfaction of seeing his terrible adversary retreat into the willows as hastily as she had come forth."

The party followed the right bank of the Yellowstone for some distance, then left it and set out across the uplands on a course almost directly to the east. On this march they "suffered much from thirst. We found all the springs exhausted and the beds of the streams dry . . . As we went on, we perceived frequent tracks of horses. On the 5th of September we came to a place where numerous troop of horsemen had passed an hour before. Were they allies or enemies?"

He emphasized the concern of himself and his companions: "Right here I will remark that in these solitudes, though the howling of wolves, the hissing of venomous serpents and the roaring of the tiger [mountain lion] and grizzly bear are capable of freezing one with terror, this fear is nothing in comparison with that which fresh tracks of men and horses can arouse in the soul of the traveler, or the columns of smoke that he sees rising about him."

On one occasion, at the discovery of fresh tracks the escort quickly assembled to deliberate, and "everyone examined his firearm, whetted his knife and the points of his arrows and made all preparations for a resistance to the death; for to surrender in such an encounter would be to expose one's self to perish in the most frightful torments."

It was decided to follow the trail cautiously in the hope of determining the identity and the mission of the horsemen. Presently they came upon a heap of stones "piled up on a little eminence . . . these stones were covered with freshly shed blood."

After carefully examining them, the chief scout of the Flatheads told Father De Smet: "I think I can explain to you what we see before us. The Crows are not far away; we shall see them in two hours. If I am not mistaken, we are upon one of their battlefields; their nation will have met with some great loss here. This heap of stones has been raised to the memory of the warriors who had fallen. . . . Here the mothers, wives, sisters, daughters of the dead—you see their traces—have come to weep over their graves. It is their custom to tear their faces, cut their arms and legs and shed their blood upon these stones. . . ."

The scout's deductions were correct. Shortly afterward, as they crested a hill, they caught sight of a large band of Indians some three miles ahead on the bank of the Big Horn River. They rode on at a faster pace, anxious to gain the protection of the Crows, who at the time were allies of the Flatheads.

It was an enthusiastic and cordial meeting, and the Crows at once began preparations for a feast in honor of Black Robe and their mutual friends.

". . . we met groups of women," Father De Smet said, "covered with dried blood, and so disfigured that they aroused at once compassion and horror. They repeat this scene of mourning for several years, whenever they pass near the tombs of their relations, and so long as the slightest spot of blood remains on their bodies they may not wash themselves."

For the first time Father De Smet attended a council that was conducted entirely in the sign language. No one was present who could serve as an interpreter, but none was necessary, for "all the tribes in this part of America know the system and understand one another perfectly."

"The horses which the Crows have," Father De Smet noted, "are principally from the wild races of the prairies; but they had stolen some from the Sioux, the Cheyennes and other tribes . . . who in turn had got them from the Spanish in their raids into Mexican territory.† The Crows are considered the most indefatigable marauders of the plains; they cross and recross the mountains in every direction, carrying to one side what they have stolen on the other. This is how they get their name of *Absaroka,* which signifies Crow.‡ From their childhood they are practiced in this kind of larceny; they acquire an astonishing ability in it; their glory increases with the number of their captures, so that an accomplished robber is in their eyes a hero. . . . These are the best-formed savages I have met. . . ."

It was apparent to him that the morning band of Crows, with which he traveled for two days, were not curious about his religion, and he made no effort to talk on the subject. One of the reasons which had influenced him to take the Yellowstone-Missouri route to St. Louis, instead of returning over the shorter route by which he had gone out, was that he would have an opportunity to visit the trading posts in the upper Missouri area. Also, the more tribes he saw, the better and more comprehensive would be the report he would make to his superiors. This was, perhaps, a somewhat transparent excuse for visiting people and countries he had never seen.

Reaching the Yellowstone again at the mouth of the Big Horn, the company proceeded down its right bank to the Rosebud,

† Which began south of the Arkansas River in what is now Colorado.
‡ Actually sparrow-hawk.

then crossed to the American Fur Company's post, Fort Alexander. More than a thousand Crows were camped there, and Father De Smet visited them. Here a Crow elder expressed a wish to hear something of Black Robe's beliefs. An interpreter being available, he gladly complied, and had no more than "explained the main articles of the Christian faith—depicting in lively colors the torments of hell—when one of the chiefs uttered an exclamation I would not think of translating. . . ."

"I think there are only two in all the Crow nation," declared the chief, "who will not go to that hell you speak of; those are the Otter and the Weasel; they are the only ones I know who have never killed, nor stolen. . . . Still, I may be mistaken about them, and in that case we will all go to hell together."

The chief may have intended his remarks to be humorous. He displayed a liking for Father De Smet, put a bell on his horse and invited him to take a tour of the camp.

Being informed that for the next two hundred miles he must pass through a country that was frequently overrun by war parties of Blackfeet, Assiniboines, Gros Ventres and Sioux—all nations with hostile dispositions toward the Flatheads—Father De Smet insisted that his escort turn back. He also gave De Velder an opportunity to remain, but the trapper refused.

The two men set out on the dangerous trip. There was no trail. Father De Smet's account said: "For a long time we followed the course of the Yellowstone [left bank], except in some places where chains of rocks intercepted our march and obliged us to make long circuits, crossing rough hills four or five hundred feet high. At every step we were aware . . . they might contain lurking enemies . . . one is constantly looking death in the face. . . . There one feels in a very special manner that he is wholly in God's hands. It is then easy to offer him the sacrifice of a life which belongs less to you than to the first savage who may see fit to take it; and to form the most generous resolutions a man is capable of. That was, in fact, the best 'retreat' that I have ever made in my life. My only consolation was the object for which I had undertaken the journey. . . ."

If these were the words of a man of God, they were as well the words of a man of unbounded courage.

"On the second day of the journey," he wrote, "I espied, upon waking very early in the morning, the smoke of a great fire a quarter of a mile away; only a rocky point separating us from a . . . war party. Without losing time, we saddled our horses and started at full gallop; at last we gained the hill, and crossing the ravines and the dry bed of a torrent, we reached the top without being perceived.

"That day we made forty to fifty miles . . . and did not camp until two hours after sunset, for fear of the savages coming upon our trail and following us. The same fear prevented our lighting a fire, and so we had to do without supper. I rolled myself in my blanket and stretched on the sod, commending myself to the good God. My grenadier, braver than I, was soon snoring like a steam engine in full swing; running through all the notes of the chromatic scale, he closed each movement of his prelude with a deep sigh, by way of modulation. As for me, I turned and rolled, but spent a sleepless night; what they call *nuit blanche*.

"At dawn next morning we were already underway. . . . Towards noon, a fresh cause for alarm; a buffalo had been killed, not more than two hours before . . . his tongue, marrowbones and some other delicate morsels had been taken. We trembled at this sight, thinking the enemy not far away; but we ought rather to have thanked the Lord, who had thus prepared food for our evening meal. We turned in the opposite direction to the tracks of the savages, and that night we camped among rocks that are the resort of bears and tigers. There I had a good sleep. This time the music of my companion's snoring did not trouble me.

"We always took the road early in the morning, but it was to confront fresh dangers each time. . . . Towards ten o'clock we came to an abandoned camp of forty lodges; the fires were not yet out; but luckily we saw no one.

"Finally, we crossed the Missouri at the same place where, only an hour before, a hundred lodges of ill-minded Assiniboines had passed, and we arrived safe and unmolested at Fort Union, situated a few miles above the mouth of the Yellowstone."§

When Father De Smet related to a chief he met at the fort their narrow escapes, the Indian remarked: "The Great Spirit has his manitous [guardian spirits]; he sent them out to you on your way to stupefy and put to flight the enemies who might have harmed you."

Pleased by the explanation, Father De Smet thought that he had "never seen a plainer instance of the special Providence that protects the poor missionary."

He had not been so frightened on the journey from Fort Alexander to Fort Union, however, that he neglected to note that the Yellowstone country abounded in game, expressing the view that he did not believe "there is in all America a region better adapted to the chase. I was for seven days among innumerable herds of buffalo. Every moment I perceived bands of majestic elk . . . while clouds of antelope took flight before us with the swiftness of arrows. The ashata or bighorn alone seemed not to be disturbed by our presence; these animals rested in flocks or frolicked upon the . . . crags, out of gunshot. Deer are abundant, especially the black-tailed. . . . It is a noble and beautiful animal, covered with a dark brown *pelisse*. . . . All the rivers and streams that we crossed in our course gave evident signs that the industrious beaver, the otter and the muskrat were still in . . . possession of their solitary waters. There was no lack of ducks, geese and swans. This country abounds in coal and iron mines. The Yellowstone is not navigable, unless [except] in the middle of summer, when the water from the melting snows rushes down in torrents from the mountains."

Fort Union was built chiefly for trade with the Blackfeet and Assiniboines and other tribes which ranged along the far upper

§ Probably about the 20th of September.

Missouri, above the Mandans, and with an eye to capturing trade from the British establishments along the Canadian border. It was the headquarters post of the American Fur Company for all the upper river territory.

The American Fur Company's commander, or partner, at Fort Union when Father De Smet first visited it was James Kipp, a distinguished mountain man and trader, whom he described as "a gentleman well worthy of his station . . . I was treated with . . . the greatest politeness and kindness, and all my wants were liberally supplied."

Kipp's private house stood on the opposite side of the open square from the entrance. It was solidly built, two stories in height, with glass windows, stone fireplaces, and a rare convenience, an inside commode. Besides Father De Smet, this touch of luxury and modernity was greatly appreciated by such distinguished guests as the artist George Catlin, John James Aububon, and Maximilian, Prince of Wied.

Two or three days of rest in the affluent environment of James Kipp's house restored Father De Smet's strength and gave a new lift to his spirits. He had not been troubled by fever for several weeks, and he felt that, at last, it had been driven from his body. He would have enjoyed spending more time at Fort Union, but the morning airs contained the nip of frost, the buffalo herds for the last moon had been pushing southward, at night one heard the geese honking as they drove in their great wedges through the brilliant fall sky, and the coats of the ponies were beginning to thicken with new fur—winter was moving down from the Arctic upon the great plains. He had no time to linger. Ahead of him remained a journey of eighteen hundred miles.

On September 23rd the start was made for the Mandan villages, two hundred and fifty-five miles down the Missouri. With Father De Smet and De Velder were three trappers who were going to the Arikaras to sell horses. The five men, keeping a sharp lookout for renegades and wandering war parties, maintained a steady pace along the right bank of the great river. Father De

Smet noted that the soil of the upper Missouri Valley was "much more fertile than that of the Yellowstone; but it is still the same vast prairie . . . The river beds are dry through a part of the year . . . On the hillsides and in the bottoms, on the banks of the rivers, handsome groves are found here and there . . . The soil is strongly impregnated with sulphur, copperas, alum and Glauber's salts; the strata of earth give a strong color to the rivers. . . .

"There are some sandy places . . . full of natural curiosities; I noticed great trunks of trees petrified, and the skeletons of various species of animals. . . ." When he came upon a large buffalo skull that had been "changed to stone as red as porphyry," he could not resist taking it with him. Its weight, however, proved to be too great, and he reluctantly abandoned it.

One day they came to the camp of a war party of fifteen Assiniboines. It was learned that these Indians were returning "from a fruitless expedition against the Gros Ventres . . . ," and they were in a bad mood, and it was "chiefly on such occasions that it is dangerous to meet the savages. To come home without horses, prisoners, scalps, is for them the climax of dishonor and shame; accordingly they showed us much displeasure, and their looks were nothing if not sinister.

"These Indians are, however, cowards, and this particular band was poorly armed . . . and though we were only five, each of us laid his hand upon his weapon, assuming an air of determination, and we had a little talk with them and continued our route without being molested."

The day following this meeting, the party passed through a forest on the bank of the Missouri which had been a winter camping ground in 1835 of many Gros Ventres, Arikaras and Mandans. They saw a tragic sight, and Father De Smet wrote: ". . . it was there that these unfortunate nations had been attacked by that epidemic, which, in the course of a year, made such ravages among the Indian tribes; several thousand . . . died of smallpox. We observed in passing that the corpses, wrapped in buffalo hides, had remained bound to the branches of the largest trees. . . ."

Two days later the five men reached the village of the Mandans, where some of "the miserable remnants of these three unfortunate tribes" dwelt together. He estimated that only three thousand persons of the three nations were alive.

Black Robe was known by reputation, for the Indians had heard of his "house" near the Council Bluffs and of his peace mission to the Sioux on behalf of the Potawatomies the previous year. He was made welcome, and they "forced us to pass the afternoon and night in their camp. The kettles were soon filled in all the lodges, and the roasting pieces were set to the fire. . . . Here again, as among the Crows, it was a succession of invitations to feasts that we had to undergo until midnight." The ordeal was not quite as strenuous, however, as it had been in the Crow camps, in one of which, Father De Smet recalled with distaste, he had been obliged to attend twenty-two feasts in a single afternoon. The people of the Mandan villages saw many more travelers than the Crows, and the novelty of entertaining them had worn off.

The little party was ferried across the Missouri on the next day in bull boats paddled by squaws, who were very expert at the task. Some of their horses, which crossed by swimming, became mired in the bank, and several hours were required to extricate them.

That same evening an Arikara village was reached. Father De Smet thought the houses "very commodious and roomy; they are made with four great crotched tree trunks set on end, supporting the beams and a roof of stout poles interwoven with osiers; the whole structure is covered with earth . . . Inside the lodge is surrounded with alcoves, resembling the bunks on a ship and concealed by skins instead of curtains. At the extremity of each lodge, or else upon the summit, you will see a kind of hunting or war trophy, consisting of two or more buffalo heads painted in an odd manner, and surmounted with shields, bows, quivers and other weapons."

The Arikaras usually wore no garment but a loincloth. However, "on feast days, they put on a handsome tunic, leggings and moccasins of gazelle skin embroidered with porcupine quills of lively colors; then they envelope themselves in a buffalo robe loaded with ornaments . . . throw their quiver filled with arrows over the left shoulder, and cover their head with a bonnet of eagle feathers," he recorded. "He who kills a grizzly bear wears the claws of that animal in the form of a collar, and it is the most glorious trophy of an Indian hunter. The warrior who returns from the enemy with one or several scalps paints a red hand across his mouth to show that he has drunk enemies' blood."¶

Father De Smet also noted that the warriors of the Arikaras and the Gros Ventres, "before starting on the warpath, keep a strict fast . . . they abstain totally from eating or drinking for four days. In this interval their imagination is exalted to the point of delirium; whether it is the enfeebling of their organs or the natural effect of the warlike plans they are nursing, they claim to have strange visions. The elders and wise men of the tribe, being called in to interpret these dreams, draw from them auguries more or less favorable to the success of the enterprise; their explanations are received as oracles by which the expedition is to be regulated. While the preparatory fast continues, the warriors make incisions in their bodies, thrust pieces of wood into their flesh beneath the shoulder blade, tie leather straps to them and let themselves be hung from a post fastened horizontally upon the edge of a chasm . . . often they even cut off one or two

¶ Here again Father De Smet was influenced, probably unconsciously, by the writings of Washington Irving. Irving, however, got his descriptions second, or even third, hand. That is, he composed them from documents and reports in the possession of John Jacob Astor, to which he alone was given access. Irving never saw most of the Indians about whom he wrote, while Father De Smet seldom wrote about Indians he had not visited. His accounts, therefore, must be credited with greater authenticity than Irving's, for he gathered the information himself.

fingers, which they offer as a sacrifice to the Great Spirit, that he may grant them scalps in the warfare they are about to undertake. . . ."

Father De Smet had been a witness to gruesome and terrible sights, horrifying orgies, mutilations and scalpings (and he was to see many more), but he restrained his pen in most instances in referring to them, as was expected of an educated and cultured man of his time. However, in two letters he included a description of a victory celebration, commonplace among the tribes of the upper Missouri, in which he omitted few details. The letters went to his friend, Father de la Croix of Ghent, and to the Father-General of the Jesuits. They are not for persons with weak stomachs.

"In one of their last skirmishes with the Sioux," he said, "the Arikaras killed twenty of the enemy and placed their bodies in a heap . . . Then began their grand war dance; many women and children took part. After having celebrated . . . the exploits of their braves, they rushed like wild beasts on the inanimate bodies, hacked them to pieces and stuck the scraps on the ends of long poles, with which they danced several times around the village.

"One can form no idea of the cruelty of a great number of these savage tribes in the continual warfare that they wage with their neighbors. When they know that the warriors of a rival tribe have gone for a hunt, they come unexpectedly upon their village, massacre the children, women and old men, and carry away prisoners all men they can lead. Sometimes they put themselves in ambush and let part of the band pass quietly, then all at once they give a hideous yell and shower upon the enemy a hail of bullets and arrows. A deadly combat begins instantly, they rush upon one another, war club and ax in hand, and make a horrible butchery, boasting of their valor and spewing a torrent of insults upon the . . . vanquished; death shows itself in a thousand hideous forms, the sight of which, though it would freeze with horror any civilized man, only inflames the rage of

these barbarians. They insult and trample under foot the mutilated corpses; they tear off the scalps, roll in the blood like
ferocious beasts, and often even devour the quivering members
of those who still breathe.

"The conquerors return to their village dragging with them the
prisoners destined to torment. The women come to meet them,
uttering frightful howls on the supposition they will have to weep
the death of their husbands or brothers. A herald calls out the
circumstantial details of the expedition; the roll of the warriors
is called, and their silence indicates they have succumbed. Then
the piercing cries of the women are renewed and their despair
presents a scene of rage and grief that passes imagination. The
last ceremony is the announcement of the victory; forgetting at
once their own troubles, they [the women] hasten to celebrate
the triumph of their nation; by an inexplicable transition, they
pass in an instant from frantic sorrow to the most extravagant joy.

"I could not find words to describe to you the torments that
they inflict upon the poor prisoner devoted to death; one tears
out his nails by the roots, another chews the flesh off his fingers,
sticks the torn finger into his pipe and smokes its blood; they
crush their toes between two stones, apply red-hot irons to all
parts of their bodies, skin them alive and feed upon their quivering flesh. These cruelties continue for several hours, sometimes
for a whole day, until the victim succumbs . . . The women, like
veritable furies, often outdo the men . . ."

At Fort Clark, a short distance below the mouth of the Big
Knife River, Father De Smet was hospitably received by the
American Fur Company traders stationed there. Located near a
large Arikara village, it had been an important trading site since
1822.* Father De Smet was surprised to see "fair fields of maize,
cultivated with the greatest care," and he was interested to learn
that the Indians there "continue to make the same earthen vessels (and every lodge has several of them) that are found in the

---

* The fort was on the right bank of the Missouri, about fifty miles north of
the present Bismarck, North Dakota.

ancient tombs scattered throughout the United States, and which the antiquarians of the country assume to have belonged to an earlier race than the savages of today."

He was fascinated by the magicians he saw at this Arikara village, and he remarked that they "enjoy a high reputation among the Indians, by reason of the astonishing tricks they perform to give themselves greater importance; they pretend to have communication with the spirit of darkness.

"They plunge their arms to the elbows in boiling water . . . they eat fire and shoot arrows at one another without injury."

Father De Smet, De Velder and a Canadian trapper who chanced to be going downriver to Fort Pierre, left Fort Clark on the 6th of October. They had before them a journey of ten days through the Sioux Country, and they were duly warned before their departure to keep themselves concealed as much as possible. They followed the advice, maintaining the steadiest pace they could without exhausting their horses. At noon on the fifth day they were in an area ranged by the Blackfoot Sioux.† They took refuge in a ravine to eat a cold meal, congratulating themselves on their progress and believing they were undetected.

Suddenly they found a score of Indians gazing down upon them. Of that tense moment, Father De Smet said: "They were armed with guns, bows and arrows, almost naked, and painted in the most outlandish manner. I rose at once and presented my hand to him whom I believed to be the chief of the band."

The Canadian, who spoke some Sioux, found his tongue, and he interpreted for Father De Smet the chief's blunt question: "Why are you hiding in this ravine?"

Father De Smet answered that they had halted to eat and rest. With obvious suspicion and wonder the chief stared at him, saying at last: "I have never seen such a man in my life. Who is he?"

"My long black robe and the missionary's cross that I bore upon my breast especially excited his curiosity," Father De Smet

† No relationship to the Blackfeet of the mountains.

remembered. "The Canadian answered him—and under the circumstances he was prodigal with his titles—'It is the man who talks to the Great Spirit. It is a chief, a Black-gown of the Frenchmen.' His fierce look at once changed; he ordered his warriors to put away their weapons and they all shook hands with me. I made them a present of a big twist of tobacco, and everybody sat down in a circle and smoked the pipe of peace and friendship. He then besought me to accompany him and to pass the night in his village, which was at no great distance. I [we] followed him, and on coming in sight of the camp, which comprised some hundred lodges, or about 1000 souls, I stopped a quarter of a mile away in a fair meadow on the bank of a fair river, and there pitched my camp. I had the head chief, Goes Barefoot, invited to sup with me. When I said the Benedicite, he asked the Canadian what I was doing. The Canadian answered that I was speaking to the Great Spirit to thank him for having procured us whereof to eat. The chief uttered an exclamation of approval."

An exciting evening followed the meal. Thirteen warriors in full costume presented themselves at Father De Smet's tent, and spread a large and fine buffalo robe before him. He was directed to be seated on it, and presumed he was to smoke with the group.

"Judge my surprise," he wrote, "when I beheld the twelve warriors seize this kind of carpet by the ends, lift me from the ground and, preceded by their chief, carry me in triumph to the village, where everybody was instantly afoot to see the Black Robe. The most honorable place in the chief's lodge was assigned to me, and he, surrounded by forty of his principal warriors, harangued me in these terms: 'Today for the first time we see among us a man who comes so near to the Great Spirit. Here are the principal braves of my tribe. I have bidden them to the feast that I have prepared for you, that they may never lose the memory of so happy a day.'

"Then he requested that I would speak again to the Great Spirit before commencing the feast; I made the sign of the cross and said the prayer. All the time it [the prayer] lasted, all the savage company, following their chief's example, held hands raised toward heaven. . . . I asked the chief for an explanation of this ceremony. 'We raise our hands,' he replied, 'because we are wholly dependent on the Great Spirit; it is his liberal hand that supplies all our wants. We strike the ground afterward, because we are miserable beings, worms crawling before his face.' Then he took from my dish a piece of *pomme blanche‡* and put it in my mouth with a little piece of buffalo meat."

Father De Smet had hoped to speak to the Blackfoot Sioux on the main points of Christianity, but found to his disappointment that the Canadian was not sufficiently skilled in their language to interpret religious words. He returned to his lodge, and went to sleep with a feeling of security among Indians reputed to be the most dangerous and untrustworthy of all the Sioux nations.

On his trip from Fort Clark to Fort Pierre, he and his companions met several other Sioux bands, but on no occasion were they threatened, always being welcomed and treated with respect. It was on this journey through the heart of the Sioux Country that he laid the foundation for the great influence he was to have among almost all of the Sioux, the strongest influence, as many historians of the West have written, ever wielded by a white man.

Fort Pierre was reached on October 16. Next to Fort Union, it was the most important American Fur Company post on the Missouri. It was named for Pierre Chouteau, scion of the distinguished St. Louis family, a dynasty in the fur trade. Father De Smet was a close friend of the Chouteaus and received favors from them and from the American Fur Company.

There were many Sioux in the vicinity of Fort Pierre, and Father De Smet sat in council with several chiefs. He thought their lodges "worthy of attention; each tribe has a different form which it is easy to recognize. The Sioux lodges have a gay exterior; they are painted in wavy red, yellow and white lines, or

‡ A kind of root widely used for food by the Sioux.

decorated with figures of horses, deer and buffalo, moons, suns and stars."

The Sioux were not only the largest, but, in his opinion, the most warlike of all people. He made an effort to secure information as to their number, and from the facts obtained, estimated that the Sioux nations along the Missouri contained about 23,000 persons. Eight to ten thousand others dwelt in numerous bands in the triangle bordered by the upper Mississippi, the Des Moines River and the Red River of the North.

From the standpoint of intelligence, the Sioux ranked high on the aborigine scale. They also were a people of large stature and great vigor. Ever since he had begun to study American Indians, with the hope of becoming a missionary among them, Father De Smet had had a desire to establish a church and mission among the Sioux. At Fort Pierre he reiterated his belief "that a mission among them would have the most consoling results."

It was October 17 when Father De Smet, De Velder and two Canadians en route to a camp on the *Rivière à Jacques,* rode out of Fort Pierre. Although there was no snow, cold winds frequently swept across the plains, and ice formed on the stream banks at night. Often they could find neither wood nor buffalo dung along their trail for fuel and were obliged to cook their meals with dry grass, which made a very unsatisfactory fire. They encountered only a few wandering Indians, no large parties, and they were not delayed by the necessity of sitting in council and attending feasts.

For nineteen days they rode steadily toward the southeast along the rim of the Missouri River Valley, through an immense sea of grass all but devoid of either wild game or human beings. Fort Vermilion, which Father De Smet had visited on his first peace mission to the Sioux, was a welcome sight, but the situation he found there was deeply distressing to him.

A Santee war party had just returned from an attack on his beloved Potawatomies, and displayed a scalp to him. Dejectedly he wrote that "the murderers had blackened themselves from head to foot with the exception of their lips, which were rubbed with vermilion. Proud of their victory, they performed their dance near his camp, carrying the scalp on the end of a pole."

"I appeared all at once in their presence . . ." he related. "I reproached them vigorously with their unfaithfulness to the solemn promise they had made me the year before, to live in peace with their neighbors, the Potawatomies. I made them feel the injustice they were guilty of in attacking a peaceable nation that wished them nothing but good, and who had even prevented their hereditary foes, the Otoes, Pawnees, Sauks, Foxes and Iowas from coming to invade them. Finally I advised them to employ all means to effect a prompt reconciliation and avoid the terrible reprisal which would not fail to come upon them; being well assured that the Potawatomies and their allies would come soon to take vengeance for their perjury, and perhaps to wipe out the whole tribe."

Father De Smet's account of this incident was colored by mildness and modesty. The traders and half-breeds of Fort Vermilion who heard his scathing denunciation of the raiders were struck with amazement. Never before had they known of a white man marching with seeming fearlessness into the midst of a wild victory dance, halt it, and deliver a stinging rebuke to men with blood on their bodies. His eyes blazed and his voice thundered as he stood straight and defiant before the celebrants. He made it clear, and he demanded that his words be repeated to all the Sioux nations, that he did not propose to be the victim of broken promises, that he would not stand idly aside while men he had believed flaunted their unfaithfulness and untrustworthiness in his face. His own integrity, his own honor, were at stake, and he would not suffer them to be sullied.

But Father De Smet concluded his remarks on the dramatic scene with the simple statement: "Abashed at their fault and dreading its consequences, they conjured me to serve once more as their mediator, and to assure the Potawatomies of their sincere resolution to bury the hatchet forever."

Winter was closing in, and Father De Smet left Fort Vermilion as soon as he could. He was still some two hundred miles by river from St. Joseph's Mission at the Council Bluffs, the next haven where he might be assured of assistance and security, and St. Louis was nearly seven hundred miles beyond that point.

On November 14, in the hope of speeding the journey, he engaged the services of a half-breed Iroquois as a paddler and pilot, and with this competent man at the helm, he and De Velder embarked in a canoe.

For several days fine, clear, fall weather prevailed, then winter suddenly descended, and the "snow and cold that followed filled the stream with ice cakes, which, striking upon the snags of which the river is full, rendered navigation doubly dangerous. We were . . . in a region where all the prairie grasses and plants . . . had been burned by the Indians to the very banks of the river, and from which in consequence all the animals had withdrawn. We did, however . . . kill a fine deer, which . . . stood motionless upon the bank of the river as if to receive the mortal blow. Five times we were on the point of perishing by being overturned . . . despite all our efforts.

"We passed ten days in this disquieting and dangerous navigation, sleeping on sand bars at night and taking only two meals, evening and morning; besides, we had nothing in the way of food but frozen potatoes and a little fresh meat."

On the night they arrived at St. Joseph's the Missouri was closed by ice.

The conditions he found at the mission brought pain to his heart. It would soon have to be abandoned. Sadly he wrote of "the grief of observing the ravages which unprincipled men, liquor sellers, had caused . . . ; drunkenness, with the invasions of the Sioux on the other hand, had finally dispersed my poor savages [the Potawatomies]. While waiting a more favorable turn of events, the good Fathers Felix Verreydt and Christian Hoeken busy themselves with their cares of the holy ministry among some fifty families that have had the courage to resist these two enemies."

The continued failure of the federal government to suppress the illegal sale of intoxicants to the Indians of the Council Bluffs area was, however, merely one cause of their downfall. The government was also criminally negligent in failing to uphold treaties it had signed, and under which the Indians would have been able to retain their homes. The government stood knowingly aside and let swindlers take the Indian lands. It did nothing to prevent settlers from swarming over Indian property. It let the Indians, helpless, penniless and starving, be driven out or wantonly murdered.

Once again Father De Smet and his faithful Fleming companion, De Velder, set out on horses, and after eight days of travel, and seven nights of sleeping in vermin-infested Indian camps and cabins, they reached the little house in Westport in which Father Nicholas Point resided.

Still driven by his urgent desire to reach St. Louis, make a report, and begin preparations for building a mission among the Flatheads, Father De Smet rejected an invitation to spend Christmas in the crude but warm quarters of Father Point. He and De Velder enjoyed hot baths, rid themselves of the Indian lice, donned fresh clothes generously supplied by their host, and had a good sleep.

The next day, December 22, they boarded a stage in Independence for the final leg of their long journey. It was New Year's Eve when they knocked on the door of the Father Superior at St. Louis University.

In slightly more than nine months—exactly two hundred and forty-nine days—Father De Smet had traveled by horseback, except for comparatively short distances by canoe and stage, through the western wilderness, most of the time in country never before visited by a man of the cloth, for 4814 miles.

XIII

A few days after he had returned to St. Louis, Father De Smet had good reason for saying a special prayer. He had been regretfully informed by his superiors that the exchequer was so badly depleted that financing the plans he had proposed for a Flathead mission was quite impossible. The funds available for missionary work would not amount to half of the minimum sum he would need.

His prayer was not so much a plea for divine assistance in securing the money as it was a fervent request for aid in his struggle to remain calm. Moreover, the great strength of his body, hardened by months in the saddle and the endurance tests he had been obliged to meet in the western wilderness, was menaced by his despondency. He was bitter, and he was thoroughly angered, but even to a larger extent was he grieved by the thought that he would fail to keep his pledge to the Indians of the Bitter Root Valley. They had trusted him, and they were looking forward to his return with the eagerness of children awaiting St. Nicholas. He did not propose to disappoint them. No effort, no sacrifice, would be too great for him to make so that he might fulfill his promise. He would take matters into his own hands, even though he might have to violate protocol.

His first move was to get off urgent letters, fully stating the case, to the editor of the *Catholic Herald*; to the coadjutor of Philadelphia, whom he had been informed was an enthusiastic supporter of a program for western missions; and to other prominent persons he thought might be interested in participating in a campaign to raise the necessary funds. That accomplished, he boarded a steamboat for New Orleans.

The results of his one-man crusade were recorded in letters he wrote in the spring of 1841 to the *Herald,* which had published his appeal, and to his brothers, Charles and Francis, in Belgium. The Bishop of Philadelphia gave his sanction to a simultaneous collection throughout his diocese, and the people of Philadelphia "liberally responded to the call of their pastors." Of his trip to New Orleans, he wrote: "The Bishop received me with great kindness; gave his approbation to a collection, and placed his name first on the list. His clergy followed his example. As I had only a few days at my disposal, I thought it was best to solicit subscriptions through several generous ladies who offered themselves for this purpose. In the space of three or four days, they collected nearly $1000.

"You have no idea with what spirit the pious portion of the people entered into the affair. Almost every moment of my stay persons came to offer me something for the Indian mission. Several ladies gave me various trinkets, such as earrings, bracelets, and ornaments of every description; others brought implements and articles which will be of great use in the Indian Country. . . . I left New Orleans with $1100 in cash and six boxes full of various and most useful articles."

Contributions came to him from other places, and he mentioned receiving from "the Reverend Mr. Durkin of Kentucky . . . $300, and the Reverend Jno. Reilly remitted $140, the amount collected in St. Paul's Church, Pittsburgh. St. Louis supplied the balance of what was necessary for the outfit, the expense of the journey and the commencement of the establishment. . . ."

If Father De Smet's superiors in St. Louis had been apprehensive about exhausting their mission treasury, the attitudes of the Bishops of Philadelphia and New Orleans prompted them to take a broader view of the matter. Not only did they willingly turn over to him all money that had not been earmarked for other causes, but they assigned to him a most satisfactory contingent of assistants.

When he sailed April 24, 1841, for Westport on the steamboat

Oceana, he was accompanied by a staff of two Fathers and three lay Brothers.

Father Nicholas Point was a zealous missionary with experience among the Indians. Father Gregory Mengarini had recently arrived from Rome and had been selected for the mission because of his "great facility with languages and his knowledge of medicine and music." Brother William Claessens, a Belgian, was a blacksmith. Brother Charles Huet, also a Belgian, was a carpenter. Brother Joseph Specht, a German, was a tinner and "a sort of factotum."

Father De Smet knew profound gratification as the steamboat thrashed its way against the surging yellow spring flood of the mighty Missouri, but at Westport his joy was dampened by the severe disruption of the plans he had formed. It had been his intention to attach his group to either one of two caravans known to be departing for the mountains, but both were indefinitely postponed. He found himself stranded, for it would have been the height of foolhardiness to have led his little contingent out on the trail without protection. As he said in a progress report sent back to the Father-Provincial, they had need of "firearms, implements of every kind, wagons, guides, a good hunter, and experienced captain—in a word, whatever becomes necessary when one has to traverse a desert of 800 leagues, and expects nothing but formidable obstacles to surmount, and thieving, and sometimes murder, enemies to combat—and swamps, ravines and rivers to cross, and mountains to climb . . ."

In Westport, dismayed and apprehensive, the six men took refuge in an abandoned little cabin, where an Indian woman had died the day before, and there they existed in extreme discomfort for ten days.

Father De Smet at last was able to make arrangements to travel with a caravan leaving on May 10th for Oregon. It was a heterogeneous company of sixty-four, composed of emigrants from Missouri, three families from Arkansas, an invalid from Illinois, two or three men who professed to be scientists, an

English adventurer, several sportsmen and others traveling for pleasure. Most of the group were destined for what Father De Smet termed "the too highly boasted land of California."

A Missourian, John Bartelson, who claimed to be a minister without a flock, demanded that he be named captain of the train. When some of the emigrants protested that he was inexperienced and had never been west of his own state, he threatened to leave and take with him eight men, all well-armed, of whom he was the leader. Not wishing to have the ranks of the able-bodied decreased by such an extent, the objectors acquiesced in his appointment. Fortunately, Bartelson's unsuitability as a leader was offset when the members were able to engage one of the most competent guides in the West, a veteran mountain man, Thomas Fitzpatrick.

The route taken from Westport was generally that which Father De Smet had traveled the previous year. He did, however, enjoy a new experience. On Big Soldier Creek,* the caravan camped near a large village of Kansas Indians, a tribe with which he had never held council. But if he did not know them, they knew him by reputation, and he was warmly welcomed by a chief who displayed with great pride one of the meaningless scrolls which the Indian Department distributed in a puerile attempt to cater to what it thought was the savage intellect.

Father De Smet accepted an invitation to visit the village, and took with him the Englishman, Captain Romaine, and Father Point. The three men were impressed by the "strongly characterized physiognomy" of these Indians, as well as "their vivacity of expression, singular costume, diversity of amusement and fantastic attitudes and gestures."

The warriors in the council lodge appeared to be unabashed or uninhibited by the presence of the distinguished Black Robe, continuing to occupy themselves as they might have done had no guest been there. The meeting was hardly more than informal,

* Eastern Kansas.

for Father De Smet observed that "some were preparing to eat—their great occupation when they are not asleep . . . others were smoking, discharging the fumes of the tobacco by their mouths and nostrils, reminding one of the funnels of a steamboat; they talked, they plucked out their beard and the hair of their eyebrows, they made their *toilette,* the head receiving particular attention.

"Contrary to the custom of the other tribes, who let the hair on their heads grow—one Crow has hair eleven feet long—the Kansas shave theirs, with the exception of a well-curled tuft on the crown. . . . While we were smoking I could not help watching the motions of a young savage, a sort of dandy, who ceased not to arrange, over and over again, his bunch of feathers before a looking glass, apparently unable to give it the graceful finish he intended.

"Father Point, having suffered his beard to grow, soon became an object of curiosity and laughter—a beardless chin, a shaved head and well-picked brows and eyelashes being, among them, indispensable to beauty."

If they were beau brummels, the Kansas lacked nothing of the qualities of ferocity, fighting skill and courage. Only a short time before Father De Smet's visit they had virtually wiped out a Pawnee village, carrying off the scalps of ninety victims. In their belief, revenge was not a vice but the greatest of virtues, and Father De Smet thought, "It would be time lost to attempt to persuade them that there can be neither merit nor glory in the murder of a disarmed and helpless foe."

In the accounts of his westbound trip across the plains in 1840, Father De Smet had made no mention of meeting the Pawnees, yet he had passed through a portion of their country along the Platte River. This was not a strange circumstance. Indians were frequently drawn from a territory by war, by the hunt, and by ceremonies, leaving it virtually deserted for long periods.

When his train reached the Platte in the early summer of 1841, however, several large bands of Pawnees were encountered. He spent some time among them, and narrowly missed seeing a human sacrifice . . . that of a young captive Sioux maiden. While he was thankful that he had been spared the ordeal, his unquenchable interest in the customs and religious practices of Indians would not permit him to refrain from an investigation. He questioned several Pawnees and half-breeds who had witnessed the terrible spectacle, making voluminous detailed notes with the intention of preparing a long account as time permitted.

"The Pawnees are one of the few aboriginal tribes," he wrote, "firmly persuaded that human sacrifices are most agreeable to the Great Spirit. Hence, when the Pawnee takes a prisoner and wishes to render himself acceptable to heaven, he devotes it to the morning star. . . . I was in the neighborhood when one of these bloody sacrifices took place.†

His narrative of the sacrifice is one of his most famous papers, and the best account of this type ever written. It is not pleasant reading.

At South Pass the route he had taken in 1840 turned northwestward toward the valley of the upper Green River. From this point on the country would be entirely new to him. They were now on the western slope of the continent, and five miles beyond South Pass the caravan reached springs whose waters flowed into the Pacific. The main Oregon Trail, which they were following, bore toward the southwest. The country, sweeping away on every side in great uplifts, was dry and barren, and the heat and dust at times was almost overpowering. Through the last half of July and the first half of August, animals and humans suffered thirst in the dry reaches, then struggled for hours to get the wagons across a stream. The water and grass and shade along the banks

† In one letter, Father De Smet mentions that the sacrifice took place in 1837. This is an error, either on his part, that of the translator, or the printer, for he was not in the Pawnee Country until 1839, and in several other papers he sets the date as 1841. Mistakes of this kind often occurred in his writings.

were blessings, but the work of crossing the torrents was looked upon as representative of the tortures of hell.

Green River was reached on the 24th of July. For several days smoke and other Indian signs had been seen, and the terrified members of the train were overjoyed to meet a company led by the noted trader and fur hunter, Henry Fraeb, on its way from California to St. Louis. Several men and women with the west-bound expedition decided they had seen enough of the West, and went back with Fraeb.

Father De Smet was both startled and delighted to see suddenly standing before him Francis Xavier, a son of the Flathead chief, Old Ignace. It had been Old Ignace who, with his two young sons, had made a futile journey to St. Louis in 1835 seeking to have a Black Robe sent to his country. The boys had been baptized by Bishop Rosati. On a similar mission in 1837, Old Ignace had been killed by the Sioux.

Francis Xavier told Father De Smet that when the summer of 1841 had begun his people had discussed plans for meeting him, as they had done the previous year. Some disbelievers had argued that he would not return, that he was like other white men, who once gone never came back, that the promises of all white men were worthless and the product of forked tongues. Most of the Flathead leaders, especially the chiefs Big Face and Insula, had remained firm in the conviction that unless death had intervened, Black Robe would keep his word, and it was decided to send a delegation over the mountains to watch for him.

The delegation had reached Green River, where some of the fur hunters were gathering, on July 1. When Father De Smet had not arrived by the 16th, they were forced to leave because of a lack of provisions. All the traders had departed. However, three young warriors were left behind with orders to continue the watch as long as possible. Francis Xavier had not given up hope, and he had shrewdly deduced that Father De Smet must have chosen to travel by the main Oregon Trail.

With premeditated deception, Francis Xavier permitted Father

De Smet to think that his companions had gone home unaware that he had been found. The truth was that all three of the scouts had known that Father De Smet and the other Black Robes were in the caravan, and two of them had left at once with the news.

After two days rest, the expedition set about making the perilous crossing of Green River. Father De Smet recalled that "We put our confidence in God; the teamsters lashed their mules, the mules did their duty, and presently the river was crossed, and the line of wagons spread out as best it could, twisting and straying in almost every direction, amid a labyrinth of mountains and valleys, obliged to open a road, now in the bottom of a ravine, now on the slope of a cliff, often through the brush; in one place the mules would have to be unhitched, in another teams must be doubled, and again all hands would be called upon to support the wagons on the inclined edge of an abyss or hold them back in some too rapid descent, to prevent what after all was not always prevented . . . how many overturnings did we behold?

"Our good Brothers especially . . . had become teamsters from necessity much more than from choice . . . how often were they not astonished at finding themselves, one upon the croup, another on the neck, another among the hoofs, of their mules, without any clear idea of how they had come there, but thanking the God of the traveler that they had gotten off so easily. The same protection covered the horsemen; in the course of the journey, Father Mengarini had six tumbles and Father Point quite as many; once while riding at full gallop my horse fell and I flew over his head, and not one of us in these various occurrences received the least scratch."

The trail crossed the Black Fork.‡

‡ Two years later, the famous mountain man, James Bridger, wrote to Pierre Chouteau in St. Louis: "I have established a small fort, with a blacksmith shop and a supply of iron, on the road of the emigrants on Black's Fork of Green River, which promises fairly. They, in coming out, are generally well supplied with money, but by the time they get there are in want of all kinds of supplies. Horses, provisions, smith-work, etc., bring ready cash from them,

The next important stream was the Big Muddy, and the trail ascended it for more than thirty miles to the crest of a high divide. Sixteen miles further on it reached Bear River, a stream with an unusual course, rather like a gigantic horseshoe. Rising in the Uinta Mountains, it flowed northward through almost two degrees of latitude, turned completely around and flowed south for more than a hundred miles to empty into the Great Salt Lake.

For eight more days the caravan crept down the beautiful Bear River Valley. The arduousness of the trip was relieved for Father De Smet by meetings with Indians and the sight of geological phenomena, both of which delighted him.

He wrote of meeting "several families of Shoshone, or Snake, Indians, and the Sohocos, or Root Diggers. They speak the same language and are both friends of the whites. The only difference we could observe between them was that the latter were by far the poorer. They formed a grotesque group, such as is not to be seen in any other part of the Indian Territory.

"Represent to yourself a band of wretched horses, disproportionate in all their outlines, loaded with bags and boxes to a height equal to their own, and these surmounted by rational beings young and old, male and female, in a variety of figures and costumes, to which the pencil of a Hogarth or a Brueghel could scarcely do justice, and you will have an idea of the scene we witnessed. One of these animals, scarcely four feet high, had for its load four large sacks of dried meat—above which were tied several other objects—and on the summit . . . were seated cross-legged on a bearskin a very old person smoking his calumet . . . on another Rozinante was mounted an old one-eyed Goody, probably his wife, seated in the same manner on the top of sacks

and should I receive the goods hereby ordered will do a considerable business in that way with them."

The event was important in history, for not only was Fort Bridger the first private enterprise launched for the accommodation of emigrants in the western mountains, but it signaled the end of the great days of the fur trade and the beginning of the era of mass emigration.

and bags. . . . Sometimes we have seen a whole family on the same animal, each according to his age, the children in front, the women next, and the men behind. On two occasions I saw thus mounted five persons, of whom two at least had the appearance of being able to carry the poor horse as the horse was to support the weight of these two Sohoco gentlemen."

He was particularly attracted to a "square plain of a few acres" which presented "an even surface of fuller's earth of pure whiteness, like that of marble, and resembling a field covered with dazzling snow. Situated near this plain are a great many springs, differing in size and temperature. Several of them have a slight taste of soda, and the temperature of them is cold. The others are of milk-warm temperature." He expressed the thought that the springs might be wholesome, like the celebrated waters of Spa, but added quickly that he was not advising either sick or well to test them.

From Soda Springs, at the great northern bend of Bear River, the trail mounted another divide and then descended to the Portneuf River. A tributary of the Columbia system, it, too, was a stream of unusual formation. Its flow was repeatedly interrupted by natural low rock dams which converted it into a series of quiet rock pools separated by cascades of exquisite beauty.

By the 14th of August, both travelers and beasts were near exhaustion. Camp was made that evening on the Portneuf. According to Francis Xavier, they were "virtually in sight of Fort Hall," and he proposed that he and Father De Smet push on ahead of the train. He did not reveal why he was anxious to have Father De Smet reach the fort.

Francis declared he knew the trail, and he and Father De Smet rode away into the night. The result was, Father De Smet recalled, that they were "soon involved in a labyrinth of mountains . . . My poor guide, being able to see nothing by the weak light of the moon but frightful precipices . . . confessed himself lost. This was not a place, nor was it a time, to wander at random; I therefore took what I considered the only alternative, that of waiting for the morning sun to extricate us . . . Wrapped up in my blanket and with my saddle for a pillow, I stretched myself upon a rock, and immediately fell into a sound sleep."

Early the next morning they were able to make their way out of the hills and onto a plain bordering the Portneuf. During the day they rode some fifty miles through a burning, tortured country made grotesque by ancient volcanic eruptions. Late in the evening they could see some distance ahead the faint light of campfires at Fort Hall, and being unable to find a trail in the darkness, they camped beside a small brook amid a cloud of mosquitoes.

As he rode into Fort Hall on the morning of August 16th, Father De Smet found awaiting him a cheering, dancing delegation of Flatheads. They had ridden hard for several hundred miles so they might meet him there.

The leader of the embassy was Wistilpo, a rising chief who declared he had not once despaired of Black Robe returning. With Wistilpo was Simon, believed to be the oldest man of the tribe. Father De Smet said of him that he "was so burdened with the weight of years that even when seated he needed a stick for his support. Yet, he had no sooner ascertained that we were on our route . . . than mounting his horse and mingling with the young warriors who were prepared to go forth to meet us, he said: 'My children, I shall accompany you; if I die on the way, our Fathers, at least, will know the cause of my death.' . . . he led his youthful followers at the rate of fifty miles a day."

Other old friends greeted Father De Smet in the compound of Fort Hall: Francis, a boy of seven years and a grandson of old Simon, who had served at the altar in the Flathead camps the previous year, and Pilchimo, brother of one of the Flatheads of the 1837 delegation to St. Louis who had been killed by the Sioux. Although still young, Pilchimo had won renown as a warrior. On one occasion his presence of mind and courage had saved seventy Flatheads from being trapped and slain by a force of nineteen hundred Blackfeet.

There, too, to meet him was the interpreter, Gabriel Prud-homme, who had done such valuable work in translating prayers into phonetic Flathead.

One of the delegation ceremoniously handed Father De Smet a small rabbitskin packet. When he opened it he found a letter, addressed in French, to "Reverends Priests, Catholic Missionaries, The Flatheads."

"With what joy and contentment have I learned of your arrival among the Flatheads," the letter said. "I thought at first that you had been sent to our assistance to share the immense task which we have on our hands. For from the upper waters of the Columbia to the wild tribes scattered far down the Pacific Ocean is what we have to cover and visit, without mentioning the two Canadian establishments . . . one on the Willamette River and the other on the Cowlitz. . . . You have no doubt heard that we were sent thither in 1838 by way of the canoes of the Honorable Hudson's Bay Company, which gave us our passage *gratis* . . . I am at no great distance from you [now] . . . I have heard today from an Indian that you are to come to Colville. In that case I should have the satisfaction of seeing you . . ."

The letter was dated "Camp of the Pend d'Oreilles, August 6, 1840." It was signed by Father Modeste Demers.

Prudhomme told Father De Smet its history. Late in August 1840, when Father De Smet left the Flatheads at the Three Forks and started back to St. Louis, the Indians had moved slowly toward their home valley. On the trail they met several Pend d'Oreilles bearing the letter. For nearly a month it had been carried by these messengers while they indulged in a leisurely journey through the mountains, stopping each day to enjoy the rich bounties of the late summer.

Big Face had taken the letter and had wrapped it carefully in a rabbitskin to preserve it until Father De Smet's return. So Father De Smet learned at last that Canadian Black Robes were on the lower Columbia and had established missions there.

The reunion at Fort Hall was made all the more pleasant by

the extraordinary hospitality of Frank Ermatinger, an Englishman who was the Hudson's Bay Company factor at the post. Ermatinger had been long a mountain trader. He was related by marriage to the famous Dr. John McLoughlin, Hudson's Bay Company governor for all the Northwest. Father De Smet was unstinting in his praise for the factor, who "although a Protestant by birth . . . gave us a most friendly reception. Not only did he repeatedly invite us to his table, and sell us, at first cost, or at one third of its value, in a country so remote, whatever we required, but he also added, as pure gifts, many articles which he believed would be particularly acceptable." What especially endeared Ermatinger to Father De Smet was that he urged him to establish a mission among the Snakes, and offered to aid the project.

The journey to Fort Hall had taken a hundred and fifteen days. Of the total distance of 1678 miles, 390 had been traversed by steamboat, and 1288 in a saddle. Although he was still some six hundred miles from his destination—a hard journey through an immense land of great peaks, deep canyons and dense forests that could be made only by following game trails—Father De Smet had the gratifying feeling of being close to the goal he had thought of achieving for so long.

He was unaware that the world believed he was dead. Several men and women, who had separated from the caravan with which he had come West, had been slain by Indians. A report had gone back along the trail that he and the missionaries with him had been killed. Heavy was the sorrow in both the United States and Europe . . . until later caravans brought to St. Louis letters written by the "dead men."

XIV

The journey from Fort Hall to the Bitter Root Valley began under ominous circumstances. Brother Huet drove his team over a bank into the Snake River. Three fine mules were drowned, and Huet was saved only by the heroic action of an Indian who plunged into the water and pulled him to shore. Father De Smet returned to the fort for replacements of the equipment and supplies lost in the accident, and once more Ermatinger demonstrated his friendship by selling the articles without profit to his company.

The route went up the Snake River as far as Henry's Fork, then turned toward the northwest. It was a barren, inhospitable land, with little water or grass, and the suffering of both men and animals was acute. Far eastward the magnificent spires of the Tetons were etched against the sky, and to the west were the Three Buttes, the sight of which was always welcome to weary travelers seeking landmarks on the desolate Snake River plain.

The guides were taking the most direct trail possible for the carts. From the desert it twisted into the high country of the Continental Divide. A great chasm in which the verdure was rich, and through which a clear mountain stream teeming with trout and grayling passed, was given the name of *Father's Defile* and the river was christened *St. Francis Xavier*. The valley of the Beaver Head River was reached on August 30th. Ahead was a fine land of grass hills, lush valleys and forested mountains.

Waiting for Father De Smet in the Beaver Head Valley was virtually the entire tribe of Flatheads. Big Face, wearing a bright red scarf, "after the fashion of the marshals of France," rode out

146

to meet him. He gripped his hand, and said with fervor, "Welcome home, Black Robe." Father De Smet thought Big Face "the handsomest warrior of my acquaintance."

"The tribe had the appearance of a flock crowding with eagerness around their shepherd," he said. "The mothers offered us their little children . . . This evening was certainly one of the happiest of our lives. We could truly say that we had reached the peaceful goal. All previous dangers, toils and trials were at an end and forgotten."

A triumphal procession miles in length crept slowly out of the Beaver Head Valley, following a game trail to the high country, and once more the Continental Divide was crossed. The descent brought them to "a remarkable spring—called the Deer Lodge— and into a land well watered, for it abounds with small lakes and rivulets. . . . In no part of the world is the water more limpid or pure, for whatever may be the depths of the rivers, the bottom is seen as if there were nothing to intercept the view."

To the stream beside which the great spring stood, Father De Smet gave the name *St. Ignatius,*° and he noted with great interest that the waters at the base of the spring were "of different temperatures—hot, lukewarm and cold—though but a few steps distance from each other. Some indeed are so hot that meat may be boiled in them. We actually tried the experiment.†

Suddenly the peaceful journey was disrupted by a report that a large band of Blackfeet was only a short distance away. Several warriors, led by Pilchimo, raced out to reconnoiter, while the main camp prepared for a defense.

The alarm was false. The invaders were not Blackfeet but Bannocks who were very frightened and wanted nothing so much as to put the area behind them. Although not a large tribe, the Bannocks were warlike, were notorious bandits and accomplished horse thieves. They ranged an enormous country between the

---

° Later named Deer Lodge Creek.
† The State of Montana gave the unimaginative name of Warm Springs to the phenomenon, and built an asylum for the insane on the site.

Great Salt Lake and the Snake River, menacing travelers on both the Oregon and California Trails.

Under a sign of peace, Father De Smet rode out to meet them. He conferred with a Bannock chief whom he thought "showed the most favorable disposition." The situation was tense, however, for there were men present on both sides who had lost fathers, brothers and sons in the countless fights between the two nations. The Flatheads refused to smoke with the Bannocks, by whom they had been betrayed so many times in the past, but the meeting concluded without violence, and the Bannocks at once began a swift retreat toward their own country.

The Flatheads continued down Deer Lodge Creek and the Clark Fork to its confluence with the Bitter Root.‡ Big Face informed Father De Smet that during his absence a study had been conducted for possible sites for the mission, and he led the way up the valley of the Bitter Root to point them out. The place which Father De Smet thought most suitable was some thirty miles above the mouth of the Bitter Root.§ In addition to its beauty there was an abundance of timber just beyond the meadowlands that bordered the river.

The date of the establishment of the mission was September 24, 1841, and, as Father De Smet noted, it was the day of the feast of Our Lady of Mercy.

"On the first Sunday of October, the feast of the Rosary," he wrote, "we took possession of the promised land by planting a cross on the spot . . . Today too we celebrate the Divine Maternity, and what may we not expect from the Virgin Mother . . . ? So many favors have induced us unanimously to proclaim Mary the protectress of our mission, and give her name to it."

The responsibility of making a report to his superiors weighed upon him. In the hope that he would find a means of getting letters to Fort Hall, where they might be picked up by some eastbound caravan and taken to St. Louis, he assiduously applied

‡ Site of Missoula, Montana.
§ Near the present town of Stephensville, Montana.

his pen to paper. With the mountains and plains already in the grip of winter, there would be no possibility of the messages going east from Fort Hall until the coming spring. He prepared them, nevertheless, for he might have an opportunity to get them out toward the west. Trappers and messengers of the Hudson's Bay Company did travel on occasion down the Columbia during the winter months. From the mouth of the Columbia they might be picked up by a ship, taken to the Sandwich Islands, thence to Panama, across the Isthmus by land, by ship to New York, and to St. Louis in the regular United States mails.

As he sat at a desk made of supply crates, he could see the buildings of the mission taking shape, and he could "hear the joyful voices of the carpenters, re-echoing to the blows of the smith's anvil, and see them engaged in raising the house of prayer."

Father Point, an artist of considerable talent who made innumerable sketches on the Oregon Trail and among the Indians, had drawn the plans for the mission. It was to be a compound of some thirty or forty paces on each side, surrounded by a strong stockade. Bastions would stand at two corners, and they would serve as residences as well as observation posts. The church would rise against the rear wall, opposite the main gate, and it would have a steeple and cross rising above the other structures. Beside the church would be other dwelling quarters and storehouses. Buildings also had been planned to serve as stables, granaries and tool houses on the farm that would be cultivated nearby.

As October drew to a close, Father De Smet concluded that, although the season was far advanced, pressing needs required that he make a trip to Fort Colville, the Hudson's Bay Company post on the Columbia River, three hundred and twenty miles northwest of the mission. In addition to increasing the staples in their larder, he had several other reasons for going. He could send word of his presence to the Fathers at St. Paul's on the Willamette and to Dr. John McLoughlin, the chief Hudson's Bay

Company factor, or governor, for the Oregon Territory and Western Canada, at Fort Vancouver. He could secure seeds to be planted in the spring, and perhaps purchase a few head of cattle from the herd he had been informed was maintained at Fort Colville. Also, he had promised the Pend d'Oreilles that he would visit their territory, and he could carry out this mission en route.

The Flatheads promptly responded to his request for an escort by providing ten men, each of whom had been tested in battle and had suffered one or more wounds. Of them Father De Smet said: "With pleasure I bear testimony to their devotedness, their childlike simplicity and docility, politeness, complaisance and rare hilarity; but, above all, to their exemplary piety. These good Flatheads endeavored in every manner to divine and anticipate all my wants."

The party left St. Mary's on October 28th, passing down the Bitter Root and crossing the Clark Fork. The next day snow fell but it was not heavy enough to delay them. Father De Smet noted humorously that mountain men had given to a beautiful canyon the name of Hell Gate, "for what reason, however, I know not," and added, as a possible explanation, "These gentlemen have frequently on their lips the words devil and hell . . . Be not alarmed when I tell you that I examined the Devil's Pass, went through the Devil's gate, rowed on Satan's stream, and jumped from the Devil's horns."

His guides informed him that the Indians he wished to visit had been located near Flathead Lake. The journey required several days of traveling over mountain trails. He was struck by the richness and beauty of the country, especially remarking about the dark forests, which gave to the mountains a "very somber appearance, particularly in the autumn, in which season the snow begins to fall. They abound in . . . sheep, whose wool is as white as snow and as fine as silk; also . . . in carcajoux, an animal with short paws, some four feet long and remarkably powerful; when he has killed his prey, deer, antelope or bighorn, he tears off a piece of skin big enough to stick his head through after the fashion of a hood, and drags it off whole to his den.¶ There are also found tiger cats, wildcats and whistlers, a species of mountain rat. The moose is found here . . . Amongst the most remarkable birds we distinguished the Nun's Eagle, so called on account of the color of its head, which is white, whilst the other parts of the body are black. . . ."

Most of the Indians he had expected to meet at Flathead Lake had left the area and were scattered throughout the valleys, and he could do no more than attempt to visit available groups as he continued on his way. He thought the plain from which he looked over the great lake "one of the most fertile in the mountainous regions. The Flathead River runs through it . . . It is wide and deep, abounding with fish and lined with wood . . . There are beautiful sites for villages, but the vicinity of the Blackfeet must delay for a long while the good work, as they are only at two days' march from the great district occupied by these brigands . . . A second obstacle would be the great distance from any post of the Hudson's Bay Company; consequently the difficulty of securing what is strictly necessary. The lake is highly romantic . . ."

As he went on it became obvious that word of his approach had preceded him. Frequently he found groups of Indians looking for him or awaiting his arrival. His account of the journey gave to it the tenor of a religious procession on which blessings were generously bestowed and ceremonies frequently performed.

". . . we proceeded to cross a smiling little plain, called the Camas Prairies,* where the Flatheads come every spring to dig up that nourishing root. . . .

"The first of November—All Saints' Day—we met two encampments of the Kalispel tribe. . . . Men, women and children ran to meet us, and pressed our hands with every demonstration of sheer joy . . . The chief was called Chalax . . . I baptized

¶ This was the wolverine, or Canadian lynx.
* Camas, herb of the lily family.

twenty-four children in his little village, and one young woman, a Kootenai, who was dying . . ."

The old man with the good memory who had won a medal the previous year for reciting his prayers without an error was recalled to Father De Smet's mind. In a small Kalispel village a young man presented himself with an air of great pride, and flawlessly recited both the Apostles' Creed and the Lord's Prayer. He had learned them during the past winter from the Flatheads, and he had taught others in his village to recite them in part and to make the sign of the cross before and after each meal. "It was, as you can easily imagine," said Father De Smet, "a great consolation for me . . . in a wilderness, where a Catholic priest had never been before. They [the Kalispels] were overjoyed when they heard that I hoped before long to be able to leave a missionary among them . . . The next day . . . I baptized twenty-seven children . . ."

In the vicinity known as Horse Prairie large, ferocious wolves were exceptionally numerous and constantly terrorized the horses. Beyond the plains their course took them through a steep and rough pass. Father De Smet recalled that on previous occasions he had seen "landscapes of awful grandeur, but this one certainly surpassed all others in horror. My courage failed at the first sight . . . my mule Lizette was sufficiently docile and kind to allow me to grasp her tail, to which I held on firmly. . . ."

On the 4th of November the riders entered a forest which required four days to traverse, and which Father De Smet thought was "certainly a wonder of its kind; there is probably nothing similar to it in America . . . so dense that in its whole length we could scarcely see beyond the distance of twenty yards. Our beasts . . . suffered a great deal in it for want of grass . . . It was a real labyrinth; from morning till night we did nothing but wind about to avoid thousands of trees fallen from either fire, storms or age . . . The savages speak of it as the finest forest in Oregon, and really every tree which it contains is enormous in its kind . . . Cedars of four and five fathoms lying on the ground measured more than 200 feet in length. The delicate branches of these noble trees entwine themselves above the birch and beech; their fine, dense and evergreen foliage forming an arch through which the sun's rays never penetrate; and this lofty vault, supported by thousands of columns, brought to the mind's eye the idea of an immense temple, reared by the hand of nature . . ."

Beyond the great forest they looked down on "the whole surface of the lake called Pend d'Oreille, studded with small islands, covered with woods. Sunday, November 7, was spent in devotional practices on the shore of the lake. Two Hudson's Bay Company boats, rowed by eight half-breeds, and low in the water with heavy cargoes of merchandise, stopped at the camp. One of the men with the boats was Charles, a Flathead interpreter Father De Smet had engaged the previous year. Charles had been at Fort Vancouver when word reached there from Fort Hall that Father De Smet had returned to the Flathead Country to build a mission. Dr. McLoughlin at once had sent Charles to serve the new mission as long as he was needed.

After traversing high country for three days and passing a divide, Father De Smet came upon what he thought to be a "fine location for a mission. There is a large and fertile prairie, wood will never fail, the river abounds in fish. At the bottom of the prairie is a little lake or marsh about six miles in circumference, which is a rendezvous for all sorts of aquatic birds. A large number of Indian tribes would there be close at hand: the Coeur d'Alenes, the Spokans, the Kettles, the Simpoils, the Kootenais, the Gens-du-lac, the Nez Percés, and several others are scarce more than two or three days' travel away. Besides, Fort Colville is within a long day's ride, which would make it very easy to procure victuals, tools and clothing." On November 14th the party crossed a high snow-covered ridge. The next day they descended Mill Creek to Fort Colville on the Columbia.

"Wherever one finds the gentlemen of the Hudson's Bay Company," said Father De Smet, "one is sure of a good reception.

They do not stop with demonstrations of politeness and affability, they anticipate your wishes in order to be of service to you."

The accolade came as a result of the attention he received from Archibald Macdonald, the factor at Fort Colville, who had been for twenty years in the service of the company and had been entrusted with numerous important assignments.

Three days were spent at the fort securing supplies and repairing saddles. Father De Smet celebrated Mass for the French-Canadians stationed there, and enjoyed a long talk with a chief of the Kettle Indians. They started on the return trip on November 18. At their camp on the first night out, Father De Smet discovered that Macdonald had gone "so far as to have his lady prepare and put among our provisions, without my knowledge, all sorts of little extras, such as sugar, coffee, tea, chocolate, butter, crackers, flour, poultry, ham and candles."

On the outbound journey they had left five bags of dried meat in a village of the Pend d'Oreilles. When they called to pick them up, they found only two. Father De Smet indignantly demanded to know from the chief what had happened to the three bags that were missing.

"I am ashamed, Black Robe," the chief told him. "I am afraid to speak to you. You know that I was absent when you left your bags in my lodge. My wife opened them to see whether the meat had molded; the *dépouilles* [the fat] looked so fair and so good that she tasted. When I came in, she offered me some, and to our children as well; the news was spread through the village; the neighbors came, and we all ate together."

The Kalispels had assembled at Horse Prairie to meet Father De Smet on his return trip, and he spent three days with them. During the night of December 2, a fierce storm roared through the mountains. He feared that "hell had been unchained against us. A terrible gust of wind carried my tent away and cast it into the branches of a great pine." He took refuge under a buffalo robe while hail, snow and finally rain beat upon him. Morning brought a bright sun and warm, cleanly washed airs. That day he baptized forty-seven Kalispel children and thirteen adults.

Following the same route they had taken out, they reached St. Mary's on the 8th of December, "amid shooting and shouting from our good Indians running to meet us."

Father De Smet was astonished by the building which had been accomplished during the forty-two days he had been away. Assisting "with their whole heart and strength," the Flathead workers had cut three thousand strong and straight stakes. The palisade had been completed, and most of the structures within it were ready for occupancy. Services already had been held in the church. The lay Brothers had constructed, "with no other tools than the ax, saw and auger . . . a chapel with pediment, colonnade and gallery, balustrade, choir, seats, etc., by St. Martin's Day; when they assembled in the little chapel all the catechumens, and continued the instructions which were to end on the 3d of December, the day fixed for their baptism. . . . The compound and buildings could shelter from 400 to 500 souls."

XV

During the short days and long nights of the winter, Father De Smet spent many hours in his study writing in his journal, reflecting upon the accomplishments of the past year, and striving to anticipate the problems of the future so that he might face them in an adequate and beneficial manner.

Much more was involved in establishing and managing a mission than the dispensing of religious instruction and the celebrating of holy ceremonies. Religion was not a thing apart from the daily life of the Indians, not a thing to which they gave their attention only at certain hours or on certain days. It was irremovably woven into their every act and thought. All creation, the sun, the moon, the stars, the forces of the atmosphere, the darkness and the light, were inextricable components of a creed born of immeasurable time, incomprehensible space, and the mysterious, inexplicable and incredible functioning of the human brain.

If the Indian was idolatrous, if he worshiped many minor gods, his greatest obeisance was paid to a Great Spirit, a Supreme Deity who ruled over all, who possessed incomparable power. Not without qualification could the Indian be called an unbeliever.

Enlightenment and direction were the weapons with which idolatry, immorality, cruelty and injustice could be diminished and destroyed. Environment, isolation, a way of life governed largely by the realities of an animalistic existence, had molded the Indian in body and mind. If he appeared childlike, he was not without the capacity to learn, to comprehend, to lift himself. All races were the same in that there were in each of them the wicked and the good, the intelligent and the dumb, the moral and the immoral, the competent and the helpless.

Father De Smet was too knowledgeable, too sophisticated, and most of all too practical, to permit himself to believe that his swift success with the Flatheads meant that he could march on to similar easy victories among other tribes. He might achieve equal accomplishments as easily among the Nez Percés, the Kalispels and the Pend d'Oreilles, but that would not indicate that the road ahead for Catholic missionaries would be free of dark pitfalls, extreme discouragements and tragic defeats.

Economic and social factors would create barriers that might very well prove to be insurmountable. The Flatheads occupied superior intellectual and physical levels, equal to those of the Blackfeet, the Crows and the Sioux among northern nations. They dwelt in a land with a comparatively mild climate, a land incredibly rich with the bounties of nature. Seldom did they know real want, and seldom did they suffer, as did the nations of the plains and desert wastes, from prolonged drought, pestilence and adverse elements. Moreover—and perhaps the most significant factor of all—they had not yet been subjected to large invasions of their homeland by unscrupulous and filthy white men; not yet had they been corrupted, cheated, defiled and diseased by the riff-raff pushing westward across the Missouri River. Oh God, if only the men of government had the strength to obey and uphold the noble principles upon which the American nation had been founded!

Father De Smet had no proven formulas, no precedents, to guide him. St. Mary's was the first mission in the western mountains.* In the hope of obtaining beneficial advice, he studied the narratives of the Jesuits who had founded the highly successful missions among the natives of South America, but conditions were not comparable. The first South American missions had been

* It was also the first permanent white settlement in what was to become the state of Montana. Fur trading posts were not permanent establishments. They frequently were abandoned or moved for business reasons.

established in 1610, and they were maintained for a hundred and fifty years. However, during this time the missionaries had an almost clear field in which to work because of laws which made it difficult for intruders to introduce the vices of Europe. Between 1757 and 1766 the Jesuits had been expelled from Spanish South America, and all their accomplishments had been negated.

There were laws of the United States which would have helped the missionaries, but they were not enforced, and Father De Smet held forth no belief that this condition would change.

The dispute between England and America over their respective claims in the Oregon country was once again becoming acute. A substantial migration of American farmers to the Willamette Valley was fanning the flames, creating a new facet to the old controversy. For many years the conflict had been solely over the territory between 42° and 54°40′, or more precisely between the Columbia River and the forty-ninth parallel. Now it was also between the fur trader and the settler. Still, no matter how the boundary question was settled, the continued influx of emigrants would inflict growing hardships and adversity upon the Indians.

When the Jesuits had launched their mission program west of the Mississippi River, it had been deemed advisable for missionaries to accompany the Indians on the customary long hunting expeditions. The reasoning behind this policy was that the hunting bands, which often consisted of several hundred persons, would not be for a number of weeks without religious instruction, and priests who went on the hunts would be available to minister, both medically and spiritually, to the injured and dying. Another thought also entered into the matter: it was that the presence of Black Robes in the hunting camps might restrain the Indians from indulging in disorders and excesses that successful hunts usually inspired them to commit.

Father De Smet had begun to doubt the wisdom of the policy. Accompanying a hunting band placed the missionary in a delicate position. The buffalo plains were not only the hunting grounds of tribes bitterly hostile to each other, but were for the most part common battlefields. The presence of a Black Robe with any one tribe under such circumstances was, Father De Smet thought, "greatly to the detriment of his influence and efficiency." Indians who saw him in the camp of an enemy might very well consider him an adversary. If a battle took place, and prisoners were captured, the Father would be obliged to advocate mercy for them. This would be resented, even by Indians who might in every other respect value and adhere to advice from a Black Robe. Furthermore, Indians on a hunt usually were filled with the wildest excitement, and there was little time or opportunity to give them religious instruction.

Despite his reservations, Father De Smet permitted Father Point to go on a winter buffalo hunt with two hundred lodges of Flatheads and Pend d'Oreilles.†

Father Point and the hunters were gone nearly two months. The way was long and difficult, and for several weeks their quarry eluded them.

The first Christmas of St. Mary's Mission was a brilliant success and a joyous day. At an early hour the compound was crowded. The decorations of the chapel were things of beauty. Some days previously the Brothers had requested that all who wished to contribute to the festivity of the occasion make mats of rushes. Many women and girls responded, and they had woven enough mats to cover the entire floor, the ceiling and the walls.

As Father De Smet described the scene, the mats, "ornamented with festoons of green, made a pretty drapery around the altar. On a canopy was inscribed the holy name of Jesus. Among the

† An insoluble discrepancy occurs here in Father De Smet's papers. In one place he sets the date for the start of the hunt as December 23rd. In another place he mentions that immediately after Christmas, Father Point was to visit the camps of several tribes, and that Father Point prepared for the journey by a retreat of eight days. In still another passage, he says that Father Point left on the hunt December 29th. Whatever, the correct date, Father Point did go on a hunt. This fact is made indisputable by his own journal, and by succeeding incidents.

ornaments they placed a picture of the Blessed Virgin over the tabernacle; on the door of the tabernacle a representation of the heart of Jesus. The pictures of the way of the cross, in red frames; the lights, the silence of the night, the approach of the important day . . . all these circumstances united had, with the grace of God, so well disposed the hearts and minds of our Indians, that it would have been scarcely possible to find on earth an assembly of savages more resembling a company of saints."

Upon his return from Fort Colville, Father De Smet had begun to give daily instruction to a large group of men and women. With pleasure he could write: "They profited so well that 115 Flatheads, with three chiefs at their head, thirty Nez Percés with their chief, and the Blackfoot chief and his family, presented themselves at the baptismal font on Christmas day.‡ I began my Masses at seven o'clock in the morning; at five o'clock P.M. I still found myself in the chapel. The heart can conceive, but the tongue cannot express the emotions which such a consoling spectacle may well awaken.

"The following day I celebrated a solemn Mass of thanksgiving . . . From six to seven hundred new Christians, with bands of little children . . . assembled in a poor little chapel . . . in the midst of a desert, where but lately the name of God was scarcely known."

Of all the difficult social problems to be faced, probably the most vexing and complicated was that of the Flatheads' attitude toward marriage. Father De Smet bemoaned the fact that former missionaries with experience among the Indians in both the United States and Canada had "left nothing in writing on the conduct we should observe" with regard to the delicate and aggravating matter. He feared that he might be making serious

‡ This Blackfoot had some time before deserted his own tribe and taken up residence among the Flatheads. He was obviously an exception among his people, for he demonstrated his trustworthiness several times, sought to effect peaceful relations between the Flatheads and his own tribe, and became an extremely pious member of the mission church.

mistakes, and he took steps to protect himself by setting down his policies and his thoughts, "in order that our conduct might be rectified if it has not been judicious."

He and his colleagues held the principle that, "generally speaking, there are no valid marriages among the savages of these countries." They had not found a single Flathead or Pend d'Oreille who had married according to Indian customs, "who did not believe himself justified in sending away his first wife, whenever he thought fit, and taking another. Many even had several wives in the same lodge."

The Indians who had qualified for marriage in the church were greatly perplexed by the matter of godfathers. They seemed unable to comprehend the meaning of the term, which was not to be found in their language. It was learned in time that in an effort to make the word *godfather* understandable to them the interpreter had translated it as *second father*. This had left them all the more confused. A person could not have two fathers, and he certainly didn't need them. Moreover, if he was given two fathers he was forced to make a choice between them. One father was all anyone properly should have.

When Father De Smet at last was able to make them understand that a godfather in no way suggested physical conception, that a godfather was a sort of spiritual sponsor, and that the title carried with it special honors, they resigned themselves to accepting it. In fact, after that there was considerable squabbling among elders as they vied with each other to acquire the special honors. To further simplify matters, Father De Smet decreed that godfathers would be given only to men and godmothers only to women.

In a great many of his letters and papers the prevailing voice was that of Father De Smet the scholar, rather than that of Father De Smet the missionary seeking contributions and assistance.

The characters, customs and personal lives of the Indians never failed to attract him as subjects worthy of thorough study and of long and detailed reports. It seems doubtful that his sole purpose was to leave to posterity scientific treatises. Despite his many interests, he was first a man of God. Perhaps he believed that the more his superiors and friends knew of the Indians, the more they would be inclined to support the missions program.

"When I speak of the Indian character, I do not mean to include the Indians that live in the neighborhood of civilized man . . . [who] not only demoralize them by the sale of spiritous liquors, but communicate to them their own vices, of which some are shocking and revolting to nature. The Indian left to himself is circumspect and discreet in his words and actions. He seldom gives way to passion; except against the hereditary enemies of his nation. . . . With respect to others, the Indian is cool and dispassionate, checking the least violent emotion of his heart . . . To give signs of disappointment or impatience is looked upon by the Indians as a mark of cowardice. . . ."

Father De Smet believed that the Indian was "endowed with extraordinary sagacity," and that he easily learned to perform tasks, even those requiring technical skill, when instructed under proper circumstances. "Experience and observation," he added, "render him conversant with things that are unknown to the civilized man. Thus, he will traverse a plain or forest 100 or 200 miles in extent, and will arrive at a particular place with as much precision as the mariner with the aid of a compass . . . he will point out the exact place of the sun when it is hidden by mists or clouds . . . he follows with the greatest accuracy the traces of men or animals, though these should have passed over the leaves or the grass, and nothing be perceptible to the eye of the white man. He acquires this knowledge from a constant application of the intellectual faculties, and much time and experience are required to perfect this perceptive quality. Generally speaking, he has an excellent memory."

Father De Smet disagreed with writers who had asserted that Indians were guided by instinct, "and have even ventured to assert that their children would find their way through the forests as well as those farther advanced in age.

"I have consulted some of the most intelligent Indians on this subject, and they have uniformly told me that they acquire this practical knowledge by long and close attention to the growth of plants and trees, and to the sun and the stars . . . Parents teach their children to remark such things . . . They measure distances by the day's journey. When an Indian travels alone, his day's journey will be about fifty . . . English miles, but only fifteen or twenty when he moves with the camp. They divide their journeys, as we do the hours, into halves and quarters; and when in their councils they decide on war or on distant excursions, they lay off these journeys with astonishing accuracy on a kind of map which they trace on bark or skins . . . nothing but the degrees of longitude and latitude are wanting in some to make them exact."

Father De Smet had received both material assistance and moral support from Scotsmen and Englishmen employed by the Hudson's Bay Company, whom one would hardly have expected to be enthusiastic about helping Catholic missionaries, especially since there were Protestant ministers in the Oregon country. Perhaps their generosity and kindly attitudes were no more altruistic than they were realistic. The Hudson's Bay officers had been trained in Canada, where priests had been active and influential for three centuries, and they were fully aware of the Indians' preference for the Black Robes.

The great difference between the British and American traders lay in the policies which motivated their respective conduct. The Americans thought not at all about a long-range program. They thought only of the day at hand, as if their motto might have been, "Get it all now, and to hell with tomorrow." The British for the most part sought to build their trade with the Indians on a sound foundation, looking to the future, and to prevent irreparable injury to either the supply or the suppliers.

In Dr. John McLoughlin were combined the qualities of integrity, justness, business acumen and great dignity. He had been born in Canada in 1784, and had been educated in Europe. In 1818 he had married a Scotch-Indian half-breed, the widow of Alexander McKay, who had been killed in the disaster of Astor's trading vessel *Tonquin*. Assigned to command on the Columbia in 1824, he had selected the site for Fort Vancouver and transferred company quarters there in 1825.

As a shrewd trader McLoughlin was without a peer, yet his innate kindness and sense of justice never permitted him to deal unscrupulously with American competitors. On numerous occasions he had assisted rivals whose furs had been stolen by Indians or who were in need of aid as a result of other adversities. When emigrants from the States began to arrive in Oregon, his generosity to them brought severe criticism from his superiors.

McLoughlin had been reared in the Anglican Church. Always devout, he came to prefer the creed and rituals of the Catholic faith, and after the Black Robes had reached the lower Columbia, he was converted to Catholicism. This in no way prejudiced him against other faiths. His personal code did not permit him to be either antipathetical or antagonistic toward persons whose religious beliefs differed from his own.

"I am extremely happy," McLoughlin wrote Father De Smet at St. Mary's, "to find that you and your worthy associates are to be residents in this part of the world and intend to devote yourselves to the laudable object of teaching the doctrine of the Christian religion . . . we will be happy to furnish you with anything our stores contain and to assist you as much as we can to transport it to the interior . . . the cost and expense of which you will have to pay by bill on London, and if there is anything else in which I can be of use to you, please command me . . ."§

Father De Smet was eager to acquire cattle for the Flatheads, and McLoughlin informed him some cows were available in the

§ In acquiring his college degrees, Dr. McLoughlin seemed not to have discovered the period, and though he was aware of the existence of the comma, he appeared to find little use for it. His letters were virtually one long, uninterrupted sentence.

Snake Country. Sending him an order to buy the animals in the name of the Hudson's Bay Company, McLoughlin wrote: "If you take the cattle, I will, to replace them, purchase the like number on your account from the settlers here."¶

During the early spring of 1842, Father De Smet busied himself with finishing a detailed report to St. Louis, remarking in it with understandable pride:

"The whole Flathead nation converted—400 Kalispels baptized —eighty Nez Percés, seven Coeurs d'Alene, many Kootenais, Blackfeet [?], Snakes and Bannocks—the Simpoils, the Chaudières, who open their arms to us, and eagerly ask for Fathers to instruct them; the earnest demands from Fort Vancouver on the part of the Governor—and of the Reverend Mr. Blanchet, assuring us of good desires and dispositions of a great number of nations, ready to receive the gospel—in a word, a vast country, which only awaits the arrival of true ministers of God, to rally round the standard of the cross—Our number is very far from sufficient for the pressing and real wants of this people. The Protestants are on the *qui vive*. Send us then some Fathers and Brothers to assist us . . ."

It was a fine and consoling record of accomplishments, but Father De Smet had no thought of resting on his laurels. He saw more to be done than ever before, and he considered the main task of the moment to be the securing of their achievements, giving them strength and permanency, making them impregnable.

With this conviction in mind, he packed his saddlebags. He would journey to the lower Columbia to confer with the Reverends Blanchet and Demers and with the estimable Dr. McLoughlin in regard to the program for the coming year.

¶ Punctuation inserted.

XVI

Early in April 1842, Father De Smet was riding down the Bitter Root Valley with a small escort of Flatheads and the interpreter, Charles, en route to Fort Vancouver. His trip had been undertaken chiefly for the purpose of conducting church business, but he soon found that the Indians had some plans of their own for him.

He found himself very soon helplessly involved in an evangelistic procession through the wilderness that gave indications of assuming alarming proportions. Word of his journey had preceded him, and he was besieged with requests to hold meetings, give instruction, celebrate Masses, attend feasts, minister to the sick, conduct mass baptismals, go on hunts and perform rites that would drive the evil spirits from the land.

He followed the trail he had taken in 1841 to Flathead Lake, planning to go on from there as he had the previous year to Fort Colville, but he was met by emissaries from the Coeur d'Alenes whose pleas to visit their tribe were so fervent that he was unable to refuse them. In the company of a delighted and excited group of Coeur d'Alenes he set out on a lengthy detour by way of Coeur d'Alene Lake, where the nation had gathered to await his coming.

He found the area suitable for one of the branch missions he was eager to establish, and during the three days he spent with the Coeur d'Alenes he looked over the country for a specific site. It was his intention to send Father Point to reside with the Coeur d'Alenes during the coming fall and winter.*

* The mission was built on the St. Joseph River, but spring floods forced its removal to the bank of the Coeur d'Alene River, where it was maintained for several years.

Taking the most direct route from the Coeur d'Alenes to Fort Colville, Father De Smet passed through the country of the Spokan Indians, another tribe he had not previously visited. The reception he received was wildly enthusiastic, and the tribe trailed along with him as he continued on his way.

In contrast to the land of the Coeur d'Alenes, the homeland of the Spokans was bleak and forbidding, "sandy, gravelly and badly calculated for agriculture. The section over which I traveled consisted of immense plains of light, dry and sandy soil, and thin forests of gum pines. We saw nothing in this noiseless solitude but a buck . . . From time to time the melancholy and piercing cry of the wood snipe increased the gloomy thoughts which this sad spot occasioned."

Father De Smet reached Fort Colville early in May to find to his great disappointment that because of the early melting of snows many rivers could not be crossed, "the mountain torrents had overflowed, and the small rivers that usually move quietly along in the month of April had suddenly left their beds and assumed the appearance of large rivers and lakes, completely flooding all the lowlands. This rendered my journey to Vancouver by land impossible . . ."

He was informed that a wait of some three weeks would be necessary before Hudson's Bay Company barges could be sent downstream. Nothing made Father De Smet unhappier than enforced idleness, and he at once planned ways to keep himself busy until his departure was possible. The first task he undertook was to translate several prayers into the tongue of the Skoyelpi Indians who resided near the fort. The language of the Skoyelpi, Flatheads and Kalispels stemmed from the same linguistic family. Although he had resided among the Flatheads less than a year, he had become so proficient in their tongue that he was able to complete the translations in a single day.

On May 13th, he set out on a hundred-mile journey by horseback to the main village of the Okinagan Indians, which was located north and west of Fort Colville. He was the first Black

Robe to visit this tribe. During the several days he spent among the Okinagans he baptized a hundred and six children and a number of elderly men and women. As he moved through the rough country he was accompanied by two hundred horsemen and accorded every honor the Indians were capable of bestowing.

The start down the Columbia from Fort Colville was made on May 30th. Two large barges had been constructed for the journey, and they put out heavily loaded with furs taken during the past winter. On the bales rode trappers and other employees happy to be off on a furlough to headquarters, where they would meet men from sailing vessels and enjoy for a brief time the amenities of Fort Vancouver and the settlements near the mouth of the great river. One of the men making the trip was the noted explorer and fur trader, Peter Skene Ogden, whom Father De Smet found to be a thorough gentleman, an excellent conversationalist and possessed of an inexhaustible fund of entertaining anecdotes and *bon mots*.

Father De Smet was deeply impressed by his first sight of the cascades and rapids which, he noted, were "called by the Canadian *voyageurs* the Great Dalles. A *dalle* is a place where the current is confined to a channel between two steep rocks, forming a prolonged narrow torrent, but of extraordinary force and swiftness . . . Some of these channels are navigable at certain seasons of the year, although with very great risk, even to the most experienced pilot . . . In this state the river flows with imposing grandeur and majesty . . ."

It was at one of the Dalles that Father De Smet's death was prevented by what he felt could have been no other force than that of the "Divine Hand of Providence." For some unknown reason he had asked to be put ashore just before his barge entered the rapids, intending to walk around them and rejoin his boat on the lower side.

He wrote of the tragic accident that he ". . . was walking along the bank, scarcely thinking what might happen; for my breviary,

papers, bed, in a word, my little all, had been left in the barge.
I had proceeded about a quarter of a mile, when seeing the
bargemen push off from the bank and glide down the stream
with an easy, careless air, I began to repent having preferred a
path along the river's side, so strewn with fragments of rocks
. . . all at once the barge is so abruptly stopped that the rowers
can hardly keep their seats . . . they ply the oars with redoubled
vigor, but without any effect on the barge.

"They are already within the power of the angry vortex; the
waters are crested with foam . . . I distinguish the voice of the
pilot encouraging his men to hold to their oars. . . . The danger
increases every minute, and . . . all hope of safety has vanished.

"The barge, the sport of the vortex, spins like a top upon the
whirling waters—the oars are useless—the bow rises—the stern
descends, and the next instant all have disappeared.

"A deathlike chill shot through my frame—a dimness came
over my sight . . . Overwhelmed with grief and utterly unable
to afford them the slightest assistance, I stood a motionless
spectator . . . All were gone, and yet upon the river's breast there
was not the faintest trace . . . Soon after the whirlpool threw up,
in various directions, the oars, poles, capsized barge, and every
lighter article it had contained. Here and there I beheld the
bargemen vainly struggling in the midst of the vortex. Five of
them sank never to rise again. My interpreter was thrown upon
the bank. An Iroquois saved himself by means of my bed; and
a third was so fortunate as to save himself by seizing the handle
of an empty trunk, which helped him to sustain himself until he
reached land."

The party stopped at Fort Okinagan, a post established at the
mouth of the Okinagan River in 1811 by David Stuart for Astor's
Pacific Fur Company, and later taken over by the British. The
next station visited was Fort Walla Walla. At each of these posts
Father De Smet found that his name was well known. He celebrated Masses, and baptized a number of Indians and half-breed
children.

Fort Vancouver was reached on the 9th of June. He was astonished by its comforts and size. The compound measured five hundred by seven hundred and fifty feet. Within the palisade were some forty buildings, and he was delighted to find that one was a small Catholic chapel. Nearby was a village of some sixty dwellings, and beyond them was a farm nine square miles in extent, with more than 1500 acres in cultivation.

Fathers Blanchet and Demers were on hand to receive him, and all three were assigned guest rooms in the spacious and well-furnished house of Dr. McLoughlin, a host whose generosity and kindness appeared to be without limit.

After he had made a journey to the Willamette with the two Canadian priests, visiting the mission they had built there in 1838, Father De Smet wrote enthusiastically to St. Louis of the plans he and the other Fathers had formulated. He expressed the conviction that the Catholic Church would know greater success than any rivals in the Oregon Territory, and he repeated the advice Dr. McLoughlin had given him, to the effect that if "Catholicity was rapidly planted in these tracts where civilization begins to dawn"—that is, the growing settlements of the emigrants along the lower Columbia—"it would be more quickly introduced thence into the interior."

Father De Smet prayed in his letters that ways would be found to "send us numerous fellow laborers; for in so extensive a field we are but five, and beset with so many dangers that at dawn of the day we have often reason to doubt whether we will live to see the sun go down."

He set out for St. Mary's as a passenger in a big Hudson's Bay Company trading canoe on the 30th of June. Father Demers accompanied him, intending to visit several tribes along the river. Both the weather and the wind were favorable, so that much of the time sails were raised to aid the rowers.

Fort Walla Walla was reached June 11, and on the next day Father De Smet left with the interpreter, Charles, to continue the return journey on horseback. Their course took them across both the so-called Nez Percé and Spokan Deserts in a northwestward direction. Few Indians were encountered before they reached Lake Coeur d'Alene, where they spent two days in a large village. They then rode up the valley of the St. Joseph River, at last turning away from the stream and entering what Father De Smet described as "terrific mountains . . . and impenetrable forests. I could scarcely believe that any human being had ever preceded us over such a road."

It was the 27th of July when they ascended the Bitter Root Valley and saw the cross of St. Mary's chapel ahead.

They found the mission deserted, except for Father Mengarini and a few Flatheads serving as guards. The lay Brothers were in the field, and Father Point had left ten days before with the Flatheads on a summer buffalo hunt in the Three Forks country.

While Father De Smet had been at Fort Vancouver, Dr. McLoughlin and both Fathers Demers and Blanchet had urged him to return to the eastern United States and to Europe to secure funds and recruits for the Oregon missions. They were united in the opinion that through his personal efforts progress could be speeded and delays that might work to the detriment of the expansion program they wished to see executed might be averted.

He had given serious consideration to their advice as he rode back from Fort Vancouver, and after more reflection on it he decided he would heed it. He directed Father Mengarini to leave as soon as possible to build a residence and chapel among the Coeur d'Alenes. Then he repacked his saddlebags once again.

The last day of July found him riding up the Bitter Root Valley with an escort of six Flathead warriors, once more setting out on the long and hazardous journey to St. Louis.

XVII

The hunting camp of the Flatheads, whom Father Point had accompanied, was found on the Madison River. After resting several days there with his good friends, Father De Smet prepared to continue eastward. Ten Flatheads volunteered to ride with him to the Crow Country, and the party started out on the 16th of August.

They had been on the trail only two days when they reached an immense Crow village, which Father De Smet estimated contained no less than three thousand men, women and children.

Cries of "The Black Robe! The Black Robe!" rose when he was seen approaching. Young and old raced out to meet him, and what he termed "a comical scene" took place.

He was surrounded by a yelling, dancing horde in which there were many who had seen him two years before, and he recounted, "I was literally assailed by them. Holding me by the gown, they drew me in every direction, whilst a robust savage of gigantic stature seemed resolved to carry me off by main force. All spoke at the same time, and seemed to be quarreling, whilst I, the sole object of this contention, could not conceive what they were about. I remained passive, not knowing whether I should laugh or be serious. The interpreter soon came to my relief, and said that all this uproar was but an excess of politeness and kindness toward me, as everyone wished to have the honor of lodging and entertaining the Black-gown."

He was soon rescued and lodged in the house of the chief, whom he had met on his previous trip through the Crow Country, as befitted a visitor of his distinction. During preparations for a feast in his honor, he was suddenly confronted by his wizened, battle-scarred host, who proclaimed in solemn tones: "It is you, Black Robe, that I owe all the glory I have gained in the victories over my enemies."

Completely surprised, Father De Smet asked for an explanation. He got it, and he wrote of the incident:

"In 1840, I first met the Crows in the Valley of the Big Horn . . . I had with me a stock of lucifer matches, which I used from time to time to light my pipe . . . The effect of these matches surprised them greatly; they had never seen any. They conversed about them in all the lodges, and called them the mysterious fire which the Black Robe carried. I was at once considered the greatest medicine man that had ever visited their tribe . . . Before my departure the chiefs . . . of the council requested me to leave them a portion of my matches . . . I readily distributed them, reserving only what was necessary for my journey."

Father De Smet had forgotten the occurrence, until the old chief "took from his neck his Wah-kon, or medicine bag, wrapped in a bit of kid. He unrolled it and displayed to my wondering view the remnant of the matches I had given him in 1840! 'I use them,' said he, 'every time I go into battle. If the mysterious fire appears at the first rubbing, I dart upon my enemies, sure of obtaining victory.' As you see, it requires little to acquire a reputation among the Indians: with a few lucifer matches, you may be a great man among the Crows, and receive great honors."

If the Crows held Father De Smet to be a medicine man, in addition to being a man with the power to speak with the Great Spirit, they were not so certain he was not speaking with an unreliable tongue when he answered their question as to how many whites lived in the world.

"Count the blades of grass upon your immense plains, and you will know pretty nearly the number of the whites," he told them.

Head shaking, dubious smiles and laughter followed this reply. Their incredulity became even more evident when he told them "of the vast extent of the villages inhabited by the white men, of New York, London, Paris, of the grand lodges [houses] built as near each other as the fingers of my hand, and four or five piled up, one above the other—meaning the different stories of our dwellings . . ."

Father De Smet appeared to be cheered by the news that the Crows were making stringent efforts to prevent traders from bringing large quantities of liquor into their country.

"For what is this fire-water good?" a Crow headman asked. "It burns the throat and the stomach; it makes a man like a bear who has lost his senses. He bites, he growls, he scratches and he howls, he falls down as if he were dead . . . fire-water does nothing but harm . . . we do not want it . . . we are fools enough without it."

Quite possibly this attack against liquor was made simply to please Father De Smet, for it was not altogether true. Traders had been bringing liquor into the Crow Country for years, and especially during the regime of the dynamic and colorful Kenneth McKenzie, general manager of the American Fur Company's Upper Missouri Outfit. McKenzie was ousted after he had boldly defied federal officers and set up a still at Fort Union. Moreover, Father De Smet understood that neither the government nor the Crows themselves could keep liquor out of the Crow Country, but he did not reveal that he realized he was being deceived.

He left the Crow post, Fort Alexander, for Fort Union on the 25th of August. With him were an Iroquois, Ignatius, a Cree half-breed named Gabriel, two American trappers, and a French-Canadian interpreter who had spent eleven years among the Crows.

At the end of six days' ride they found themselves "upon the very spot where a combat had recently taken place. The bloody remains of ten Assiniboines who had been slain were scattered here and there—almost all the flesh eaten off by the wolves and carnivorous birds. At the sight of these mangled limbs—of the vultures that soared above our heads—I own that the little courage I thought I possessed seemed to fail me entirely, and give place to a secret terror, which I sought in vain to stifle or conceal from my companions."

After narrowly avoiding war parties whose trails were seen, the little band reached Fort Union on September 10th. Even three days of rest in the most comfortable of quarters failed to give Father De Smet the strength, both physical and spiritual, he would have liked to possess in facing the long journey down the Missouri River to St. Louis. Yet, he had no alternative but to remain at Fort Union through the bitter winter that would soon descend upon the northern plains.

At the time, however, warm Indian Summer weather prevailed, and experienced men approved the proposal that he attempt to travel down the river by canoe. All signs indicated that the clement days and nights would continue. With good luck and hard paddling they could progress much faster than by horseback.

On September 14th, he set out in a skiff with Ignatius and Gabriel, and for three days they moved swiftly downstream, their courage and their hopes rising with the passage of each mile.

Suddenly they caught sight of smoke against the clear fall sky, beyond a distant bend of the river. Not long afterward they heard the unmistakable puffing of a steamboat.

That night Father De Smet wrote: "It was a real Godsend to us . . . We soon beheld her majestically ascending the stream. It was the first boat that had ever attempted to ascend the river in that season of the year, laden with merchandise for the [American] Fur Company.

"Four gentlemen from New York, proprietors of the boat, invited me to enter and remain on board. I accepted with unfeigned gratitude . . . I was an object of great curiosity—my black gown, my missionary cross, my long hair, attracted attention. I had thousands of questions to answer . . ."

Father De Smet, Ignatius and Gabriel returned on the steamboat to Fort Union. The cargo was unloaded with all possible speed, for the water was falling, and the captain understood that any day he might find himself trapped and forced to spend the next six or seven months fighting to save his boat from being crushed by ice floes.

The downstream trip, which was harrowing in the extreme, consumed forty-six days. "The waters were low," Father De Smet said, "the sand banks and snags everywhere numerous . . . We were frequently in great danger of perishing. The boat's keel was pierced by pointed rocks, her sides rent by the snags. Twenty times the wheels had been broken. . . ."

A tornado struck, and the pilot's house was "carried away . . . the whole cabin would have followed if it had not been made fast by a large cable. Our boat appeared to be little more than a mere wreck. . . ."

One day early in November 1842, Father De Smet knelt before the altar of the St. Louis Cathedral and gave his thanks to God for the protection he had received. During the year, he had traveled in the wilderness between the Mississippi River and the Pacific Coast nearly five thousand miles without serious illness or injury.

XVIII

For almost three years, Father De Smet had kept a secret which frequently had disturbed him, both in his waking hours and through long sleepless nights. In the winter of 1842–43, again finding the financial cupboard in St. Louis bare, and faced once again with the necessity of raising funds to carry on his work in the Far West, the secret became especially aggravating to him.

In the mountains he had discovered gold, not a few isolated grains, not a nugget or two, but gold in immense quantities.

On his first journey to the Flatheads in 1840, he had traveled along an unnamed mountain stream not a great distance from the Three Forks of the Missouri River. In places the stream's bed appeared to be composed entirely of gold sand. The precious metal was so abundant that he had had difficulty believing his eyes. He had mentioned the discovery to no one.[*]

In 1840 and in the following year he had come across unmistakable indications in other places of the presence of gold, silver and copper in enormous quantities. In all of these locations white trappers had for two decades taken beaver while walking over inconceivable fortunes in precious metals. Father De Smet took not a pinch of gold dust, not even a tiny nugget, for fear that his find would be revealed.

How greatly the history of the West would have been changed had he disclosed his discoveries! He had not for a moment considered such a thing. On the contrary, he had sworn to himself that he would never do it, that he would keep his secret as long as possible.

[*] Father De Smet had found the famous Alder Gulch in Montana. Twenty years later it would become one of the richest placer mines in the world.

He had no illusions about his success in such an effort. At any moment someone else might find the precious deposits. Yet, any time gained in keeping them from becoming known would benefit the Indians. Once the world knew of them, the western mountains would become overnight a wild, mad country, perhaps another Mexico, another Peru. The helpless Indians would be driven from their homes, their hunting grounds, their own lands, tortured and murdered.

If only he might devise some scheme by which the great earthly bounties could be put to work for his beloved red people. He felt certain that the Almighty Father of Creation could have had no other purpose in putting such riches in ground that belonged to the Indians.

He could devise no feasible scheme. Certainly, after seeing with his own eyes what had happened on the Missouri River, how there the government had failed to enforce its own liquor laws, how it had permitted the Indians to be debauched, cheated, robbed and killed by unscrupulous settlers, how it had tolerated corruption in its own ranks, how it had violated treaties it had sworn to uphold, he dared not turn even to the highest officials in Washington. He could not have faith that any pledges they made to him or to the Indians would be kept.

Knowing the location of fabulous fortunes, Father De Smet set out in the spring of 1843 to beg the little money he must have to carry on. In lieu of financial support, which they could not give, his superiors were prodigal with good wishes and words of encouragement, promised to pray for his success, and gave him *carte blanche* in selecting his own itinerary. He viewed the road ahead with something less than ecstasy.

Having no definite plan of campaign in mind, he went down the Mississippi by steamboat to New Orleans, then traveled through parts of the South by river and stage, gradually working his way to Philadelphia, New York and finally to Boston. Catholic communities in the United States being generally small and poor, reactions to his requests were marked more by good spirit than by pecuniary and material contributions.

He did not complain. If he found himself inclined to grumble, he had only to glance back through memory to the remote valley of the Bitter Root in order to remind himself how valuable was a hoe, an ax, a bolt of cloth, a bushel of wheat in the far lands beyond the mountains. Gratefully he dropped the small coins given to him into his money sack and shipped the equipment, tools, and varied commodities donated off to St. Louis.

He did not look on his journey as a failure, but he knew that it might well have been less successful if he had not resorted to some showmanship. He had taken with him a trunk containing an exhibit of Indian artifacts, and he had entertained the groups before which he had appeared by donning deerskin clothing and feathered headgear, waving a tomahawk, smoking a calumet and beating on a painted drum.

At times he winced at his histrionics, and asked himself if, after all, he had absorbed some of the proclivities of the medicine men he had so often condemned. He had not yet taken to brewing potions from entrails and tree bark, dancing to unholy chants, or proffering ointments made of toadskins and snake oil, but he wondered if he would be forced to descend to such a level. If so, he determinedly continued his shows, feeling that the end justified the means.

Before he reached Boston it was apparent that securing volunteers was hardly less difficult than obtaining satisfactory amounts of hard cash. There were few men willing to make the tremendous sacrifice—even men whose piety was unquestionable—of going off into the wilderness to spend years, if not the remainder of their lives, among savages. Under the circumstances he considered himself fortunate to have enlisted six, all of whom he was convinced would successfully meet the challenges and hardships of long isolation.

Three of them were in a position to start at once, and he decided to escort them to the frontier. There was still time to catch a westbound caravan with which they could travel to Fort Hall, or even on to the Columbia, where the Hudson's Bay Company factors would assist them to reach the Flatheads.

The other three volunteers—Fathers Joseph Joset and Peter Zerbinati, and Brother Vincent Magri—would not be available because of previous commitments until summer, too late to start for the mountains. They would remain in St. Louis, where they would be quite useful, until the following spring.

Father De Smet traveled westward with Fathers Peter De Vos and Adrien Hoeken, and Brother J. B. McGean. Father De Vos, a native of Ghent, had been in the United States since 1836. A somewhat frail man who had been afflicted with internal hemorrhages, he hoped that the western climate might benefit his health. Father Hoeken was a younger brother of Father Christian Hoeken, who for several years had been a missionary among the Missouri River tribes. Brother McGean was a skilled mechanic and miller, and Father De Smet had no more than interrogated him as a prospective recruit than he had visions of a fine gristmill rising beside the Bitter Root.

The four men paused only long enough in St. Louis to assemble the tools and equipment which Father De Smet had sent there from his southern and eastern trip. Loading them on a steamboat, they set out for Westport.

On the edge of Westport one morning a few days later, Father De Smet watched a long caravan wind its way into the western hills. He seemed to be able to see best among all the varied colors of the long train the black robes of three riders, and he watched them, tears filling his eyes, until they had vanished into the sky. Turning away, he asked God to protect them.

Two weeks later he stood on the deck of a ship watching the entrance to New York Harbor grow fainter over the stern.

Father De Smet's European trip, during the summer and fall of 1843, was both financially profitable and personally rewarding. His letters and articles which had appeared in newspapers and religious publications in numerous countries had won him distinction as both an explorer and a missionary. He was continually astonished by the receptions he received, the cordiality displayed toward him, and the hospitality of his hosts. American correspondents and European journalists sought interviews with him. Church dignitaries welcomed him with enthusiasm, and the doors of civil officials and prominent citizens stood open to him. His invitations numbered many more than it was possible for him to accept.

His arrival in Europe was marked by a somewhat comical incident. When his ship became becalmed in the English Channel, he had gone ashore in a fisherman's boat, landing at Court McSherry, Ireland. There he was promptly accosted by a British Army officer who suspected him of being a French spy. British Intelligence, it was subsequently learned, had been advised that French military men would attempt to infiltrate Ireland disguised as priests. The London *Times* carried a dispatch relating how the American missionary had convinced the suspicious officer that he was, indeed, both an American and a bonafide man of the cloth.

In Dublin he again aroused the suspicions of the British by calling upon the famed Irish patriot, Daniel O'Connell, and later attended an O'Connell rally. Upon reaching Liverpool he expressed his unlimited admiration for the rebellious Irish leader. "What a man!" he said to newspaper reporters. Such sentiments did nothing toward endearing him to the troubled British authorities.

Father De Smet's travels on the continent took him from London to Antwerp. He went to Termonde and met boyhood friends, visited the graves of his father and mother and other members of his family, and spent some time with his brothers, Charles and Francis, both of whom were prominent businessmen.

From Belgium he went to Paris, where he was invited to speak at the Sorbonne. He appeared in full Indian regalia, with tomahawk, bow and arrows, and calumet among his props, and regaled his distinguished audience with frightening tales of missionary life among the American aborigines.

Upon reaching Rome, he found that an audience had been arranged for him with the Pope. He was overwhelmed when, as he was ushered into the throne room, His Holiness Gregory XVI arose and embraced him.

The Pope had read some of Father De Smet's letters and articles, and he asked him a number of questions about his experiences. For an hour he held the Pope's rapt attention with anecdotes. He told him, for one thing, how on beautiful summer evenings he often would sit in a flowery meadow of the lovely Bitter Root Valley with a hundred or more Flatheads and entertain them with Biblical and historical stories. He would tell the Indians of George Washington and the founding of the American nation, of Napoleon and Waterloo, of how for eighteen hundred years evil forces had tried to destroy the Church.

One evening, visibly moved by the fear that the Pontiff might be injured by the Church's enemies, Chief Victor of the Flatheads arose and told Father De Smet: "If the Great Chief of the Black Robes be in danger, you speak on paper to him in our name and invite him to our mountains. We will raise his lodge in our midst; we will hunt for him and keep his house provided, and we will guard him."

Pope Gregory was highly amused but greatly appreciative of Victor's invitation when Father De Smet delivered it to him. He smiled and then grew serious. "Truly the time is at hand when we shall be forced to quit Rome," he said with solemnity. "Wither shall we go? God alone knows. Give those good savages my apostolic benediction."

If there had been any doubt that Father De Smet's only ambition in life was to remain a humble missionary among the Indians, it was dispelled once and for all time during his stay in Rome. He was informed to his dismay, if not horror, that he was to be made a bishop. In great alarm he appealed to the Father-General of the Jesuits to secure his release from such a burden, and he accompanied his plea with the argument that Father Blanchet was in every way more qualified for the episcopal dignity, besides being his senior both in years and as a missionary. The appeal was successful, and Father Blanchet, far away on the Columbia and unable to speak his own thoughts on the matter, became a bishop.

Father De Smet hurried out of Rome before any other schemes to honor or promote him could be hatched. On the 12th of December, at the mouth of the Schelde River, he boarded the *Infatigable* with four other priests, six Sisters from the Congregation of Notre Dame de Namur, and a lone lay Brother. The vessel had been chartered by the Society of Jesus to take them, several tons of supplies and a large quantity of tools and other equipment to the mouth of the Columbia, by way of Cape Horn. In what he referred to as his "medicine bag," Father De Smet carried a substantial amount of good British pounds, an asset that brought him no little comfort and satisfaction.

One of the Fathers, Louis Vercruysse, and the lay Brother, Francis Huybrechts, were Belgians. Fathers John Nobili, Michael Acolti and Anthony Ravalli were of Italian descent and had served in several European countries.

For twenty-eight maddening days they waited at anchor for an east wind which would let them put into the North Sea. When at last it came it blew in a veritable gale. For the next ten days the little brig was driven through raging seas, on two occasions narrowly averting bars on the English and French coasts. All the passengers were prostrated by seasickness. The month of January, 1844, had nearly gone before the winds abated, and a bright sun spread its beneficent warmth over the rolling Atlantic.

Cape Horn was passed during the last days of March. As they entered the Pacific a terrible storm struck, sails were torn from the masts, and in an almost helpless condition the vessel was driven southward for days until the sixty-sixth degree of south latitude had been reached. They were among great icebergs. But the *Infatigable* lived up to its name, and by mid-April they were sailing along the Chilean coast.

On the trip northward they visited Valparaiso, Santiago, Callao and Lima. When, on the 28th of July 1844, they sighted the dark misty coast of Oregon, they had circumnavigated a large part of the world, they had survived fierce tempests and wild seas, bitter cold and terrible heat, all the terrors of seven months at sea, yet they could not permit themselves the pleasure of thinking their long voyage was nearing a successful end. They had only a little distance to travel, but of all the perils known to voyagers of the oceans one of the greatest still awaited them . . . the crossing of the bar at the mouth of the Columbia River.

The captain, who had never taken a ship into the river, had no chart of the mouth. Ahead they could see only forested capes shrouded in ever changing gray mists. The roar of breakers came to them.

On the afternoon of the 30th, a small boat in charge of the second officer was sent out to sound for a passage. It was gone until the next afternoon. A channel thought to contain no less than five fathoms of water had been found.

Father De Smet's journal graphically portrayed the scene and the emotions of the passengers:

"Under a light breeze, we advanced slowly . . . It was a most beautiful day—a cloudless sky—a blazing sun—everything seemed to combine for a day of joy and gladness.

"As we drew near the redoubtable bar . . . the sounders had several times reported seven fathoms—soon six fathoms were heard—after that five—then four and one-half—presently four, and so it went, always growing less.

"Each cry was a shock that oppressed our hearts, and at the repeated cry of 'three fathoms' all countenances were visibly discomposed, for that was the vessel's minimum draft—several of us thought that it was all over, that the ship was about to strike . . .

"Soon the cry of 'four fathoms' caused something of a revival of joy. But of the five miles of the bar we had as yet made only three. Suddenly a cry of 'three fathoms' plunged us again into consternation—at the cry of 'two and a half fathoms' I felt, as it were, annihilated. I expected to see the anchor let go, and then a mad scramble for the boats.

"But our imperturbable captain cried, 'She is *passepartout,* this *Infatigable!* Go ahead!'

"Heaven was for us—the next cast of the lead showed four fathoms, and the depth increased at every plunge until we heard the cry of 'no bottom.' We were out of danger in the south channel."

Shortly afterward a large canoe paddled by a dozen Clatsop Indians and commanded by an American trader came out to the ship. It was then they learned that they had been even closer to disaster than they had realized. "We thought you dead men," the trader told them. "No ship ever came in that way before."

He then explained that the Columbia divided near its mouth into two channels, one on the north skirting Cape Disappointment, which is the deepest and should have been used, and one on the south which mariners shunned because of its narrowness and heavy seas.

The American was James Birnie, manager of the Hudson's Bay Company post, Fort George, the former Astoria. Indians had informed him two days previously that a ship was attempting to enter the river by the south passage. He at once had gone out to Cape Disappointment and had lighted large fires, fired a small cannon and waved signal flags in an effort to draw the *Infatigable* toward him.

"We had indeed observed all these signals, but seafaring makes people suspicious," Father De Smet said. "It was feared that it was some ambush of the Indians, desirous of capturing the vessel."

The priests and nuns got their first close look at American Indians when a score of Chinooks visited the ship. Father De Smet noted: "My companions . . . wondered extremely at the poverty of their raiment, their uncleanliness, their long hair and their tranquil manners. I warned them that it was necessary to be very reserved with savages if they did not want them to become too familiar. It is natural for all Indians to be lazy, but it is worse with these because of the great ease with which they can secure fish and game. They live from day to day, and spend the greater part of the daytime motionless in the sun. . . ."

On August 1 the missionaries and nuns visited Birnie's station, receiving "a most cordial welcome from Mrs. Birnie and her ten children . . . the Sisters seem to have won from the first the entire friendship of the seven young ladies who belong to this honorable family. We were shown a tree that is spoken of by Blabi in his geography, which is forty-two feet in circumference . . . it would be impossible to imagine grandeur or more beautiful forests than those which cover both banks of the Columbia. Mr. Birnie took me to the tomb of the famous chief Tecumle,† who was buried in the forest behind the fort. When he used to come to Vancouver in the days of his glory, 300 slaves would precede him, and he used to carpet the ground that he had to traverse . . . with beaver and otter skins."

After the long sea voyage, a few days on steady ground in the pleasant environment of Astoria would have been most welcome, but Father De Smet, tired as he was, could not be content in idleness. On August 2, he was back on the water in a canoe manned by nine Chinook Indians, on the way up the Columbia to Fort Vancouver. On the evening of the second day he was sitting at the governor's sumptuous table at the fort. Present, in addition to the kindly Dr. McLoughlin and his charming lady, were Father Demers; the prominent Hudson's Bay Company officer, James Douglas; and the company surgeon, Dr. Forbes Barclay, who, in his younger days had been an Arctic explorer in the expedition commanded by Sir John Ross. It had been Douglas who had negotiated the arrangements by which Fathers Blanchet and Demers were granted the site on the Willamette for their mission, the first Catholic establishment in Oregon.

Father De Smet had arrived just in time to save Father

† Probably Comcomly.

Demers from a transcontinental journey to Montreal. He had been planning to leave the next day in the hope of obtaining Canadian nuns for St. Paul's Mission.

Father Demers had good news as well for Father De Smet. It was that Father De Vos and his two companions, Father Adrien Hoeken and Brother McGean, had arrived safely at St. Mary's on the Bitter Root. During the past year almost the entire tribe of the Coeur d'Alenes had been converted, a church had been built for them, and, in addition, 436 savages had been baptized among the nations of New Caledonia.‡

Favorable winds permitted the *Infatigable* to reach Fort Vancouver on August 5. The captain and several members of the crew were stricken with a strange intestinal malady. A few days later, Father Blanchet arrived from St. Paul's, accompanied by several score Indians, and preparations were made for the trip up the Willamette to the mission.

The time had come for what Father De Smet spoke of as "an affecting adieu," saying farewell to the unwell captain and crew, indeed, to the staunch little brig itself, on which, "for eight months we had shared the same dangers, and so often stood together, gazing in the very face of death: could we then restrain the parting tear . . . ?"

The start was made on August 14th, 1844.

‡ New Caledonia was the name given to a department established by the North-West Company, predecessor of the Hudson's Bay Company in the western mountain trade. It embraced an enormous area extending generally from the upper Columbia to the upper Frazer and Peace Rivers in the present Province of British Columbia. The name came to be somewhat loosely applied, and Father De Smet was speaking of Indians who lived in the area of the present international border in what is now northern Washington and Idaho.

XIX

The flotilla which pushed off from Fort Vancouver consisted of four immense Indian cargo canoes and a small sailing sloop. The canoes were low in the water with the weight of the supplies from the *Infatigable* and the twenty paddlers assigned to each craft. On the sloop, with the Fathers, were the first Sisters to arrive in the far western United States.

The trip to St. Paul's required two days, and as the first night approached the boats were moored in a small bay of the Willamette, and a camp set up on shore. "There, grouped around the fire," said Father De Smet, "we partook of our evening meal. The night was calm and serene—all nature was hushed in profound silence—all invited us to repose; but the swarms of mosquitoes with which these woods abound prevented our slumber. The nuns, to whom we had yielded the tent, suffered equally with those who had nothing but the star-spangled canopy of heaven above them . . . the night appeared somewhat long . . . the morning's dawn found us on foot. It was the festival of the glorious Assumption of the Mother of God . . . Aided by the nuns, I erected a small altar . . ."

When he was in Rome, Father De Smet had been charged by the Father-General of the Jesuits with establishing a convent, which would be supervised by a Mother Superior, adjacent to the mission in the Willamette Valley. He made this duty the first order of business. Immediately after reaching St. Paul's he began a series of excursions into the surrounding countryside in search of a suitable location.

He had been informed that he could purchase the buildings and grounds of the abandoned Methodist Mission, not far from

St. Paul's, and he went to look at it. The Methodist Mission had been established in the fall of 1834 by the Reverends Jason and Daniel Lee. It had been closed in the spring of 1844, and the property had been sold to residents of the area several months before Father De Smet arrived.

Who offered him the property was not stated by Father De Smet. His inference that the proposal was made by the Methodists was not correct, for they did not own it at the time.

Father De Smet had no intention of buying the property, finding it "entirely destitute of wood and arable land." Several other locations which would have been suitable were either already occupied by emigrants or owned by persons who refused to sell to the Catholics. He and Father Blanchet at last concluded it would be wisest to locate the convent on land already owned by St. Paul's, and they selected a site within two miles of the mission buildings.

As Father De Smet described it, it looked out upon an "immense plain extending southward as far as the eye can reach . . . the snowy crests of the gigantic [Mounts] Hood, Jefferson and St. Helens . . . towering majestically upward, and losing themselves in the clouds; on the east a long range of distant hills, their blue-tinged summits melting . . . into the deep azure of the sky; on the west the limpid waters of two small lakes . . . We have also a fine view of the Willamette River, which in this place makes a sudden bend, continuing its course amongst dense forests . . . In no part of this region have I met with a more luxuriant growth . . . The intervening country is beautifully diversified with shadowy groves and smiling plains, whose rich soil yields abundant harvests, sufficient for the maintenance of a large establishment . . . There are a number of springs on one side of the hill . . ."

The work of building the convent was soon underway, but was suddenly brought to a halt by an epidemic of the virulent form of dysentery which had afflicted persons on the *Infatigable*. Word was received that a number of people, including the ship captain, had died of it at Fort Vancouver. The disease had appeared to sweep up the Willamette, and large parties of its victims were seen camped along the river. Indians who were too weak "to proceed were abandoned by their friends; and it was truly painful to see these poor creatures stretched out and expiring on the sand."

Few at St. Paul's escaped the pestilence. Three of the Sisters and Father Acolti lay for several days at the door of death, and almost all Indian and white craftsmen were unable to work. Father De Smet was confined to his bed for fifteen days, during which his strength almost completely failed him and he could keep little food on his stomach. Full recovery of all the sufferers was not achieved until mid-September.

Meanwhile, Father Mengarini had arrived from the mountains, and Father De Smet was eager to start back with him. The passes would soon contain snow.

Although the convent buildings were still without doors and sashes, the Sisters insisted on opening their school. They held classes in the open air for their first pupils, who ranged in age from six to sixty, most of them no less eager to receive an education than their teachers were to give it.

It was discovered that one Indian woman, desirous of becoming a teacher among her own people, had attended classes for two days without anything to eat. Dogs had got away with the small supply of provisions she had brought with her. She was too ashamed of her own carelessness to ask for food, and she did not want to interrupt her studies by taking the time to go home for more. Father De Smet thought it "passed belief how these Indian women cherish and respect the Sisters and what thankfulness they show them; some bring melons, others potatoes, butter, eggs, etc."

When they were not busy with their students, the Sisters attempted to help the carpenters, wielding planes, saws and hammers, glazing windows and painting. In addition to the Indian pupils, some thirty children of French-Canadian families were soon enrolled at the school. Both Indians and whites appeared to assume that orphans properly belonged under the convent roof, and the Sisters soon had a number of homeless waifs on their hands. Room was made for them, but Father De Smet shook his head in dismay at the problem of securing funds with which to keep them in clothing. The small profits derived would not be more than sufficient to pay for their board.

The profits were to a large extent not cash but excess food. While contributions of money were always sought and gratefully received, the tuition charged was expected to bring in, per quarter: 100 pounds of flour, 25 pounds of pork or 36 pounds of beef, 1 sack of potatoes, 4 pounds of hog lard, 3 gallons of peas, 3 dozen eggs, 1 gallon of salt, 4 pounds of candles, 1 pound of tea and 4 pounds of rice—far less than enough to sustain boarding pupils and the faculty. Survival depended in large part on the bounties provided, not only by the Lord, but by the mission farm.

All believed that spirit and determination would succeed despite inevitable failures and disappointments. Actually, both the Fathers and Sisters thought the prospects so good that they were soon contemplating the establishment of a second mission school near the settlement of Oregon City. Of course, more Sisters would be required. Father Blanchet was leaving for Montreal to become a bishop, and he agreed to go on from there to Europe, after his consecration, for the purpose of obtaining both men and women recruits.

Although he had not yet regained his full strength, Father De Smet felt that he could not wait longer to leave for the interior, and he and Father Mengarini set out on horseback on October 3. They followed a course which took them along the base of Mount Hood, across the Deschutes and John Day Rivers to Fort Walla Walla, which they reached October 20th. Father De Smet arranged with the factor, Archibald McKinlay, to purchase twenty horses and saddles and several head of young cattle. An Iroquois and a French-Canadian were engaged as guides and helpers.

The four men, driving the livestock, left Fort Walla Walla

October 28. From the Snake River they traveled as directly as possible across the sagebrush plains and endless arid reaches in a northeastward direction toward the Spokan River. The weather remained favorable, and they found sufficient forage for the animals without trouble.

After several days of travel they fell in with a seventeen-horse packtrain of the Hudson's Bay Company. The two parties continued on together for two days, crossing a high ridge of mountains. On the second night they camped beside a lake that was "literally covered with wild swans, geese and ducks. One of the hunters fired off his gun . . . and the innumerable multitude of birds rose in a mass, the beating of their wings resembling the deep sound which ordinarily accompanies an earthquake."

They were overjoyed when they met Father Hoeken and a number of Kalispel Indians. Father Mengarini and two guides pushed on at once with the horses for St. Mary's. The cattle were left with the others, who continued on the trail to the Sacred Heart Mission.

Father Point and Brother Huet had opened the mission in the fall of the previous year on the site selected by Father De Smet. It was on the St. Joseph River, a short distance from Lake Coeur d'Alene, and was established expressly for the Coeur d'Alene tribe. Anxious to keep his promise to erect a similar mission for the Pend d'Oreilles, Father De Smet hurried on to Lake Pend d'Oreille and chose a site about thirty miles above the mouth of Clark's Fork. He gave it the name of St. Ignatius and placed Father Hoeken in charge.

Still determined to reach St. Mary's in the Bitter Root, he set out from the Sacred Heart Mission on the 19th of November. The Indians were strongly opposed to his attempting the journey, for snow and rain had been falling steadily for several days, but he would not listen to their pleas to wait until spring. Thereupon, four hunters volunteered to go with him.

Eight days later they had got no farther than the foot of the mountains. They pushed on through November 27, the snow growing heavier as they ascended the divide. On November 28, they met two Nez Percés traveling westward who gave them "a most terrifying description" of the state of the trail ahead.

Father De Smet concluded "that the passage was at present impracticable and impossible; moreover, the waters were now coming down from the mountains so fast and in such volume that we thought of nothing but returning in haste." All streams had burst from their beds and were flooding the valleys. Father De Smet came close to losing his life in crossing a river that was "carrying down great masses of tree trunks . . . I found myself under water and under my mule; but I held fast to my beast, which dragged me to the farther shore."

Father De Smet made his way to the Indian camp at Lake Pend d'Oreille, hoping for better weather. There a messenger arrived with a letter from Father Mengarini, who reported that he had reached St. Mary's safely but only after great difficulties and the loss of twelve horses.

Despite this bad news and his own experience, Father De Smet refused to admit defeat, and early in December he started again for the Bitter Root, accompanied this time by four Pend d'Oreilles. He had decided that he might have better luck going by way of Clark's Fork, and they set out across Lake Pend d'Oreille in two small canoes. For four days they made good progress, then ran into thin sheet ice. "We were constantly having to land to regum the thin bark of which our canoes were composed. Thus I found myself stopped for the second time . . . my pilots declared that to advance was to expose ourselves to imminent danger."

One of the Indians offered to carry a message to St. Mary's on snowshoes, and Father De Smet wrote Father Mengarini: "I have done what I could . . . to come to you . . . now finally the ice stops me on Clark's Fork. I find myself frustrated in my most earnest desire, that of seeing the mother mission once more."

Shortly before Christmas, Father De Smet was settled in an Indian camp near Lake Pend d'Oreille, resigned to spending the balance of the winter in a small log lodge which had been built for him. He wrote in his journal that the place "was well chosen, picturesque, agreeable and convenient . . . A dense and interminable forest protected us from the north winds, and a countless number of dead trees standing on all sides furnished us with abundant fuel . . . We were encircled by ranges of lofty mountains, whose snow-clad summits reflected in the sun their brightness on all the surrounding country . . . thousands of deer . . ."

He thought the festival of that Christmas would never be effaced from his memory. At midnight there was a general firing of guns, "and 300 voices rose . . . from the midst of the forest, and intoned in the language of the Pend d'Oreilles the beautiful canticle: *Du Dieu puissant tout annonce la gloire* . . . Here, indeed, the Indian missionary enjoys his greatest consolations: here he obtains his strength, his courage, his zeal to labor . . . The trifling things of the world he abandons are nothing to be compared with the blessings he finds in the wilderness."

During the winter plans were drawn for the St. Ignatius Mission. There would be fourteen log houses, a large barn, a church, three hundred acres planted in grain and surrounded by a high pole fence. The squaws had already learned how to milk the cows and to churn butter. Eventually a gristmill would be constructed, and Father De Smet would arrange to bring in hogs and fowl and beef cattle during the next year.

He was given the honor of felling the first tree for the church. When the warm days of early spring arrived he started again for the Bitter Root. The snow was still too deep in the mountains to travel by horse, and he left the Pend d'Oreille camp with a single guide in a small canoe.

XX

Father De Smet spent the Easter season of 1845 at St. Mary's with his beloved Flatheads. Soon afterward he was once more in a canoe with two hunters moving swiftly down the spring flood of Clark's Fork. His destination was Fort Vancouver.

The task of managing and directing the business affairs of the Jesuits in Oregon Territory was no longer a simple one which might be easily handled by one administrator. There were now five missions widely scattered throughout the immense mountainous region, two more would be built as soon as the other recruits he had obtained in Europe arrived on the Columbia, and on the Willamette were two establishments in addition to the convent. All of the stations in the upper country needed more equipment, supplies, tools, domestic animals, medicines and household articles. His role was swiftly becoming that of a combined business manager, procurator, fiscal agent and spiritual adviser. He found himself in need of being in several places at the same time.

From Indians they met on their way down Clark's Fork they learned that four unidentified white men, "travelers from the United States," had been recently swept to their deaths by the raging stream. The site of the tragedy was pointed out to Father De Smet by a Pend d'Oreille.

Father De Smet's guides, however, knew the river so well and were so skillful in applying their paddles, fore and aft, that they slipped down the great canyons and through the rapids without mishap, traveling sometimes at a speed which dizzied him. It had taken him sixteen days to reach St. Mary's from the Pend d'Oreille camp. The same journey downstream was made in four.

He continued on at once to Fort Colville by horseback. Five days after embarking from there in a Hudson's Bay Company canoe he reached Fort Vancouver. With Father Nobili he ascended the Willamette to St. Paul's.

Although anxious to start back to the mountains with tools badly needed there, he took time to prepare a long report which he knew would cheer his superiors as it did himself. Nowhere, he told them, did "religion make greater progress, or present brighter prospects for the future, than in Oregon Territory."

In the late spring of 1845, Father De Smet was on his way to Lake Pend d'Oreille with eleven horses packing plows, spades, pickaxes, scythes and carpenters' tools. With him was Brother McGean, the expert mechanic, and two half-breed helpers. His journal shows that they "encountered many obstacles and difficulties among the Cascade Mountains owing to the water which at this season descends on every side in torrents and with irresistible fury . . .

"In the narrow valleys between these mountains, the rhododendron displays all its strength and beauty; it rises to the height of fifteen or twenty feet. Entire groves are formed by thousands of these shrubs . . .

"Our path was strewn with the whitened bones of horses and oxen, melancholy testimonies of the miseries endured by other travelers . . . We passed the foot of Mt. Hood . . . We were twenty days going from the Willamette to Walla Walla . . . Game is scarce . . . however, we found large partridges and pheasants . . ."

It was the second week of July when they reached Lake Pend d'Oreille. Hearing that some nine hundred Indians had gathered at the Kettle Falls, on the Columbia near Fort Colville, to fish for salmon, Father De Smet rode on to hold services for them.

He celebrated one Mass beside the falls, which was attended by several hundred members from the Skoyelpi, Simpoils, Zingomenes, Kalispels, Okinagans and other tribes who lived in the upper Columbia Valley. He felt it to be a "most imposing spectacle . . . The noble and gigantic rock, the distant roar of the cataracts breaking in on the religious silence of that solitude, situated on an eminence overlooking the powerful Oregon river, and on the spot where the impetuous waters, freeing themselves from their limits, rush in fury . . . casting upwards a thousand *jets d'eau,* whose transparent columns reflect in varied colors the rays of the dazzling sun."

As Father De Smet made short excursions to various villages in the triangle between Fort Colville and Lakes Pend d'Oreille and Coeur d'Alene during the summer of 1845, he picked up fragments of distressing news. The Blackfeet had been for the past eighteen months engaged in a series of bloody raids. The mission on the Bitter Root had been threatened, a number of Flatheads and other Indians had been killed, and there were indications that this reign of terror was to become more intense in the coming months.

The menacing situation gave rise in his mind to thoughts of attempting to negotiate a peace treaty between the Blackfeet and the mountain tribes. He had no authority to undertake such a mission, no official portfolio, yet it was inconceivable to him that any objections to whatever efforts he made in such a cause might come from either the British or American Governments. It was his reasoning that if he failed to secure a formal treaty, he might succeed in inducing the Blackfeet to accept an interim agreement under which their incursions would be temporarily halted. Such a truce might open the way for further talks in the coming year.

It was both a commendable and a daring plan, one that would involve great risk to himself, but in deciding to undertake it he was not motivated solely by the desire to bring a cessation of the destructive warfare. He permitted other factors to influence both his purpose and his course.

The shortest and easiest way to reach the heart of the Blackfoot Country was to travel over the mountains to the Missouri River. Yet, he laid out a route which would take him in a great arc northward into Canada and then southward, eventually bringing him to the area of the Great Falls of the Missouri, where he would be certain to meet bands of the Blackfoot nation.

The Indians he consulted about the journey shook their heads in wonder, unable to understand why he proposed to travel such a circuitous route, four or five times as long as the most direct one to his destination. They pointed out that the summer season was far advanced, and even though he used the most feasible trails across the mountains to the Three Forks, the snow would be deep before he could complete the mission and return.

Father De Smet was a man with a great and an absorbing dream. He was also an incurable explorer.

His dream was to build an immense spiritual empire that recognized no geographical, national or territorial boundaries, no governments, but only the authority of God. He saw as the only way to achieve fulfillment of his dream the appointment of himself as a spiritual ambassador, and in such a high office he would, indeed, be armed with a powerful portfolio, that bearing the holy endorsement of the Lord. Northward were tribes he had never seen, who had never been visited by a Black Robe, and even a brief appearance among them would bring them within the spiritual realm he had pledged himself to create on earth.

His blood raced at the thought of carrying the missionary's cross among these unblessed, unanointed people. It raced, too, at the thought of seeing new countries, countries into which no man of the cloth—and few white men of any persuasion—had gone. There had been Fathers east of the mountains in Canada, but he had heard of none being among the Indians within the mountains.

He organized a small expedition. It was comprised of six Indians and a dozen horses. However, he set out by canoe, ascending the Pend d'Oreille River, and sending the horses ahead to wait for him near Lake Pend d'Oreille.

Camped at the rendezvous on the lake, he was astonished to see several horsemen "in tattered garments" ride out of the forest.

One of them saluted him "by name, with all the familiarity of an old acquaintance." He did not recognize the speaker. "A small river separated us, and with a smile he said, 'Wait till I reach [you] . . . and you will recognize me.'"

He was delighted to meet again the famed British mountain man and Hudson's Bay Company official, Peter Skene Ogden. Ogden was accompanied by two white men whom Father De Smet identified as British Army officers, Captains Ward and Vavasseur. All three had left England the previous April, and while Father De Smet thought it a great pleasure to receive "recent" news from Europe, he felt "the Oregon question appeared . . . somewhat alarming."

It was his belief that neither curiosity nor pleasure "had induced these two officers to cross so many desolate regions, and hasten their course to the mouth of the Columbia. They were invested with orders from their government to take possession of Cape Disappointment, to hoist the English standard, and erect a fortress for the purpose of securing the entrance of the river in case of war.

"In the Oregon question, John Bull, without much talk, attains his end, and secures the most important part of the country; whereas Uncle Sam loses himself in words, inveighs and storms! Many years have been passed in debates and useless contention, without one single practical effort to secure his real or pretended rights. The poor Indians of Oregon, who alone have a right to the country, are not consulted. Their future destiny will be, undoubtedly, like that of so many other unfortunate tribes who . . . will finally disappear, victims of vice and malady, under the rapacious influence of modern civilization."*

* As to the mission of Ward and Vavasseur, historical records do not entirely bear out Father De Smet's statements. There was no doubt that they were instructed to study and report on the situation on the Columbia, perhaps, as they were reputed to be engineers, even to consider sites for defense installations. Chittenden said their "orders in this regard were somewhat elastic." Bancroft said they were sent out by the Hudson's Bay Company to look into the "state of the country generally," with the additional assignment "to examine into McLoughlin's policy and proceedings."

As he set out northward from Lake Pend d'Oreille on a rough trail that ran through the dense forests and over the high ridges of the Selkirk Mountains, Father De Smet knew once more the stimulating feeling of entering country he had never seen. He reached the Kootenai River in the vicinity of the present Bonner's Ferry, Idaho. This was an area inhabited by Arcs-à-plats, of whom he did not have a very high opinion. They lived in a land abounding in fish and game, the soil of which was extremely fertile, yet they were "strangely improvident" and passing "from the greatest abundance to extreme scarcity. They feast well one day, and the following is passed in total abstinence. The two extremes are equally pernicious. Their cadaverous figures sufficiently demonstrate [this]."

Going on, he ascended the Kootenai River through the northwestern corner of the present state of Montana, "enchanted by the beautiful and diversified scenery."

Dense, dark and damp forests always seemed to depress Father De Smet, and now he spoke of the "gloomy and harrowing thoughts which imagination conjures up in these dismal regions. The most fearful apprehensions dismay the bravest heart and cause an involuntary shudder . . ."

He asked himself: "What would this now solitary and desolate land become under the fostering hand of civilization?" He saw outcroppings of coal, and "great quantities of lead . . . and some mixture of silver.

"Poor unfortunate Indians! They trample on treasures, unconscious of their worth, and content themselves with the fishery and the chase. When these resources fail, they subsist upon roots and herbs; whilst they eye with tranquil surprise the white man examining the shining pebbles of their territory."

At Prairie du Tabac he was pleasantly surprised to find several lodges of Kootenais whom he had met more than three years before at Flathead Lake. With them was a Hudson's Bay Company trader named Berland. The Indians hailed Father De Smet with a "long and boisterous discharge of musketry." Then they showed him the "journal" they had kept in his memory. It was a squared stick on which they had computed with notches the passage of forty-one months since their previous meeting.

It was while he was with the Kootenais that he wrote significantly in his notebook that he had taken "spiritual possession of this land, which was now for the first time trodden by a minister of the Most High."

With him when he started were two young Kootenais who claimed they knew how to find the Blackfeet, and a half-breed who was an expert hunter and interpreter. Early in September they were passing through a country he described as "highly picturesque and agreeably diversified by beautiful prairies, from which poured forth spicy odors of flower and shrub and fresh spirit-elating breezes, smiling valleys and lakes, surrounded by hoary and solemn pines . . ." East and west were gigantic chains of mountains.† They crossed, "magnificent dark Alpine forests, where the sound of the ax had never resounded," and made their way with difficulty on a faint game trail over an immense ridge, leaving the valley of the Kootenai behind them. The small stream they saw below was one of the headwaters of the Columbia River.

Going down the unidentified stream they reached two charming mountain lakes covered with "coots, ducks, cormorants, bustards, cranes and swans; whilst beneath the tranquil water lay shoals of salmon in a state of exhaustion . . . cut and mutilated after their long watery pilgrimage . . . These two lakes form an immense tomb, for they there die in such numbers as frequently to infect the whole surrounding atmosphere."

As he was at all times, Father De Smet was fascinated by wild animals, and he made careful notes on them as he advanced through the Canadian wilderness, remarking that in "the absence of man, the grizzly, black and brown bear, the wolf, the eagle and the vulture assemble in crowds this season of the year. They fish their prey on the banks of the river and at the entrance of

† South of Banff National Park.

the lakes—claws, teeth and bills serving them instead of hooks and darts. From thence, when the snow begins to fall, the bears, plump and fat, resume the road back to their dens . . . there to pass the winter months in complete indolence . . . all hunters and Indians remark that it is a very uncommon incident for a female bear to be killed when with young . . ."

In a passage which illustrated his astuteness as an observer and a prophet, he stated unequivocally that when "emigration, accompanied by industry, the arts and sciences, shall have penetrated into the numberless valleys of the Rocky Mountains, the source of the Columbia will prove a very important point . . . the laborious hand that would till these valleys would be repaid a hundredfold. Innumerable herds could graze through the year in these meadows, where the sources and streams nurture a perpetual freshness and abundance . . . The advantages nature seems to have bestowed on the source of the Columbia will render its geographical position very important . . . The magic hand of civilized man would transform it into a terrestrial paradise."

It was in a mountain valley near the lakes of the Columbia that he was astounded to find a white family named Morigeau dwelling in complete isolation, hundreds of miles from the nearest civilized community.

"The Canadian!" he told his journal. "Into what part of the desert has he not penetrated? The monarch who rules at the source of the Columbia is an honest emigrant from St. Martin, in the district of Montreal, who has resided for twenty-six years in this desert.‡

"Here no one disputes his right, and Polk and Peel,§ who are now contending for the possessions of his dominions, are as unknown to our carbineer as the two greatest powers of the moon. His scepter is a beaver trap—his law a carbine—the one on his

‡ Many explorers of Father De Smet's generation used the word *desert* when they meant *wilderness,* and not necessarily an arid territory.
§ President James K. Polk and Sir Robert Peel.

back, the other on his arm . . . He embarks on horseback with his wife and seven children and lands wherever he pleases . . . he reviews his numerous furry subjects, the beaver, otter, marten, fox, bear, wolf, the sheep and white goat, the stag . . . He exacts and receives from them the tribute of flesh and skins. Enriched by so much grandeur, undisturbed proprietor of all the skyward palaces, the strongholds, the very last refuge which nature has reared to preserve alive liberty in the earth—solitary lord of these majestic mountains—Morigeau does not forget his duty as a Christian. Each day, morning and evening, he may be seen devoutly reciting his prayers midst his little family.

"Many years had Morigeau desired to see a priest; and when he learned that I was about to visit [his home] he [prepared] to procure for his wife and children the signal grace of baptism. The feast of the Nativity of the Blessed Virgin, this favor was conferred on them, and also on the children of three Indian families who accompany him in his migrations . . . In memory of so many benefits a large cross was erected in the plain . . ."

Father De Smet felt it incumbent upon him to make "honorable mention of the royal *cuisine à la sauvage*. The first dish he [Morigeau] presented me contained two paws of a bear. In Africa this ragout might have given some alarm . . . it bears a striking resemblance to the feet of a certain race. A roast porcupine next made its appearance, accompanied by a moose's muzzle, which had been boiling all night. The latter I found delicious. Finally the great kettle, containing a sort of hotchpotch or salmagundi, was placed in the midst of the guests . . . there was the choice back fat of the buffalo cow, venison, cutlets, beavers' tails, quail, rabbits, dumplings and substantial broth."

Leaving the Morigeau family on the Columbia, the four men ascended a narrow valley "along the bank of a great torrent, between the lofty chains of mountains. This valley and the mountain stream bear the name of 'the place where the man lied.' I learned from my guides that the Indians speak of the place with horror to their children, as of an accursed land, and inspire them with an aversion for lying. They assured me that when the savages traverse Liar's Valley, they observe profound silence."

After a lengthy and difficult climb they found themselves once again going down into the valley of the Kootenai. "We crossed the river in order to attempt the passage of another defile . . . where the waters of the Vermillion [River] have forced an opening . . . Projecting mountains rise like holy towers where man might commune with the sky . . . terrible precipices hang in fragments overhead . . ."

They ascended the Vermillion almost to its source, crossed the Continental Divide and, passing close to an exquisite lake,¶ rode down into the valley of the Bow River, a tributary of the South Saskatchewan.

Here Father De Smet was treated to what he called a "ravishing scene." It was a magnificent display of the aurora borealis. One of his Indians declared it was the "dance of the manitous or spirits, and the glorious entrance of departed champions into the country of souls."

On the Bow they came upon the recent campsite of an Indian party composed of at least nine lodges, an estimated fifty to sixty persons. After a careful examination the guides reported that the Indians were Blackfeet traveling toward the northeast. While Father De Smet was glad that he had reached Blackfoot territory, his companions displayed no little fright, and advised taking a trail in an opposite direction. One claimed that he had sighted two smokes far ahead during the day which he took to be a warning signal. Another declared that he had dreamed that a bear had devoured him, a particularly evil omen. The third swore he had seen ravens and vultures hovering over Black Robe.

Father De Smet ignored the superstitions, and ordered the march to continue. Ahead spread the great rough plains that wash against the feet of the Canadian Rockies. It was estimated that the Indians were five days ahead of them. He set as

¶ Lake Louise.

his next destination—unless the Indians were overtaken first—Rocky Mountain House at the junction of the Clearwater and North Saskatchewan rivers.

The month of September was drawing to a close, and the nights were brilliant and cold. Father De Smet sent a scout ahead, but instead of finding the Blackfeet the scout came upon a small camp of Assiniboines. He returned to report that a disease had afflicted them, two men had recently died, and they were desirous of seeing the Black Robe.

He reached the Assiniboines the next day, and found that the sickness was on the wane. These were Indians of the forest and were seldom seen on the vast plains. He was pleased by the opportunity to talk with them and add a bit of material to the studies he never ceased to conduct.

The Assiniboines of the forest lived in small bands, owned few horses, and "performed most of their journeys on foot. They had a long file of famished dogs, loaded with their little provisions, etc. Every family has a band of six to twelve of these animals, and each dog carries from thirty to fifty pounds weight . . . Every evening we find it necessary to hang all our property upon the trees, beyond the reach of these voracious dogs. We are even compelled to barricade ourselves within our tents; for whatever is of leather, or whatever has pertained to a living being, these crafty rogues bear away and devour . . . One evening having neglected the ordinary precaution of blocking up the entrance of my tent, I next morning found myself without shoes, and minus one leg to my *culottes de peau!*

"One of the chiefs of this little camp recounted to me that last winter one of his nation, having been reduced to extreme famine —and such cases are not rare—had eaten successively his wife and four children. The monster then fled, and has never been heard of since.

"The Assiniboines [of the forest] are filthy beyond conception; they surpass all their neighbors in this unenvied qualification. They are devoured by vermin, which they, in turn, consume.

Through complacency, I one day overcame natural disgust and assisted at their porcupine feast . . . they had disrobed themselves for the purpose of providing a tablecloth! . . . they carved their meat on their leathern shirts, highly polished with grease, filthy and swarming with vermin. They dried their hands in their hair . . . and as the porcupine has naturally a strong and offensive odor, one can hardly endure the fragrance of those who feast upon its flesh and besmear themselves with its oil.

"If a bit of dried meat or any other provision is in need of being cleansed, the dainty cook fills her mouth with water and spurts it . . . upon the object.

"A certain dish . . . is prepared in a most singular manner, and they are entitled to a patent for the happy faculty of invention. They [the women cooks] commence by rubbing their hands with grease, and collecting in them the blood of the animal, which they boil with water. Finally they fill the kettle with fat and hashed meat. But—hashed with the teeth! Often half a dozen old women are occupied in this mincing operation for hours; mouthful after mouthful is masticated, and thus passes from the mouth into the cauldron, to compose the choice ragout of the Rocky Mountains.

"Add to this, by way of an exquisite dessert . . . pulverized ants, grasshoppers and locusts that had been dried in the sun, and you may be able to form some idea of Assiniboine luxury."*

Father De Smet and his three companions parted from the Assiniboines of the forest on the 27th of September, taking a trail that led into a thick cypress forest. His guides told him it was the last forest through which they would pass, and he murmured *"Deo Gratias."* It was a difficult ride because of the

---

* Father De Smet, and following him Father Point, were the first priests to do missionary work among the Assiniboines of the forest. The Assiniboines of the plains were a much larger nation, owned a great many horses, were of a commanding stature, expert in thieving, great drinkers of liquor, and perpetually at war with their historic enemies, the Crows, Blackfeet, Arikaras and Sioux. They roamed for immense distances between the Saskatchewan, the Red River of the North, the Missouri and the Yellowstone.

low branches and heavy underbrush. At one place, although bending over the neck of his horse, he was caught by a branch on the collar of his surtout, "the horse still continuing his pace. Behold me suspended in the air, struggling like a fish at the end of a hook." His coat and hat were torn, his eye was blackened, and he received two deep scratches on a cheek.

At sundown on the 4th of October they reached Rocky Mountain House. He was deeply regretful that they had failed to find the Blackfoot band, but his disappointment was alleviated when J. E. Harriote, the post factor, expressed the belief that Blackfeet would come in to trade before the month had ended.

Harriote, whom Father De Smet characterized as being one of "the most amiable gentlemen I have ever had the pleasure of meeting," offered to use his influence to persuade the Blackfeet to negotiate a treaty of peace with the mountain tribes of the United States. He frankly admitted that it would not be an easy thing to accomplish, and he warned Father De Smet of the dangers involved in an attempt to achieve the feat by himself.

At the fort a band of some twenty Crees called on Father De Smet and extended a cordial welcome to their country. They had been visited by a Black Robe some time previously—Father Thibault—and several of them wore medals and crosses. Once more Father De Smet was delighted to sit in council with a tribe he had never known. He spoke of them as "a very powerful nation, numbering more than 600 lodges, and one of the most formidable enemies of the Blackfeet, from whom in the previous year they carried off more than 600 horses. The present limit of the country they traverse extends from the bases of the Rocky Mountains, between the two forks of the Saskatchewan, some distance beyond the Red River. Their turbulent and warlike spirit and rapacity for plunder, especially for horses, are among the great obstacles which retard the conversion of the larger portion of this tribe.

"The Crees have a singular custom . . . one contrary to the practices of other nations. They stain the faces of the warriors who fall in combat, clothe them in their richest ornaments, and thus expose them in places conspicuous to their enemies. They place near them their guns, bows and arrows . . . and this they do purposely that they may be cut to pieces—an opportunity which an enemy never suffers to escape, and which a Cree warrior regards as the height of his wishes. Other nations, on the contrary, carry off and conceal their dead, to save them from the insults . . . of their enemies, and to be cut into pieces, even after death, is considered a great dishonor . . ."

Some of the Crees camped near Rocky Mountain House were willing to have their children baptized and to attend religious services, but Father De Smet found himself thwarted to a large extent by a veteran medicine man who injected racial bias into his attacks on the Catholic Church. The shaman declared that he had once died and had made a trip to the heaven of the white man, where Jesus Christ dwelt, and had been refused admission because of his red skin. Thereupon, he had gone to the country in which the souls of his ancestors lived. Once again he was cast out because he had permitted a priest to baptize him. Angered by such treatment he had returned to earth, renounced the promise he had made at his baptism and "resumed his medicine bag," hoping to expiate his errors and "render himself once more worthy of the beautiful and spacious plains and delightful abode" of the Crees, where numberless flocks and herds afforded an abundant and everlasting existence.

As Harriote had anticipated, a party of Blackfeet arrived at Rocky Mountain House. There were only thirteen of them, hunters with skins to trade, but Father De Smet held the hope they would guide him to larger bands with which he might hold peace talks. He was not long in broaching the subject, and was greatly encouraged when they saluted him "with a politeness truly *à la sauvage,* rough and cordial at the same time. The old chief embraced me quite tenderly when he learned the object of my journey. He was . . . decorated from head to foot with eagles' plumes . . . He cordially invited me to his country, offering to be my guide and to introduce me to his people."

Never one to neglect his scientific observations, Father De Smet noted that the "difference of physiognomy existing between the Indians inhabiting the plains east of the mountains and those near the upper waters of the Columbia is as great as the stupendous rocks that separate them. The latter are remarkable for their mildness, serenity and affability, while cruelty, craft—the word blood, in fine—may be read in every feature of the Blackfeet . . ."

He learned that the year of 1845 had been a sad and disastrous one for the Blackfeet. In two skirmishes with the Flatheads and Kalispels they had lost twenty-one warriors. The Crees had taken twenty-seven Blackfoot scalps. The Crows had struck them a severe blow, massacring fifty families, the entire band of Little Robe. A hundred and sixty Blackfoot women and children had been taken into captivity by enemies.†

Preparing to leave with the Blackfeet, Father De Smet had difficulty finding an interpreter, for "the only one now at the fort is a suspicious and dangerous man; all his employers speak ill of him . . . he makes fine promises. In the alternative of either renouncing my project or being some utility . . . I accepted his services. May he be faithful to his engagement!"

The start from Rocky Mountain House was made on the 31st of October. Snow had fallen and the weather was menacing. Father De Smet's staff consisted of the reputedly unreliable interpreter and a young Cree half-breed whom he had engaged to handle his horses.

It was a foolhardy mission, undertaken against the advice of the factor and clerks at the post. Blizzards might at any time sweep across the plains, and he might expect to be trapped in a

† Father De Smet's reference to Little Robe was of great importance to historians. It explained the mysterious disappearance of the Little Robe band of Blackfeet, which until 1844 had been known to exist on the plains of southern Alberta and northern Montana.

Blackfoot tepee through the long months of the winter . . . if he survived. He rejected all pleas to wait until spring.

The party soon made a camp beside two lakes, which the Blackfeet called the "Lake of the Men and the Lake of the Women." According to their traditions, from one issued a band of young men, handsome and vigorous, but poor and naked. From the other came "an equal number of ingenious and industrious young women, who constructed and made themselves clothing. They lived a long time separate and unknown to each other, until the great manitou . . . conducted the men to the dwelling of the young women, who received their guests with dances and cries of joy . . . Each young woman selected her guest, and presented him with a dish of seeds . . . Both parties began to think they were necessary to each other . . . it was agreed that the men should become the protectors of the women, and provide all the necessities for their support: whilst all the other family cares should devolve upon the women.

"The Blackfoot squaws often bitterly complain of the astonishing folly of their mothers in accepting such a proposition . . ."

The interpreter soon showed his true colors, and Father De Smet philosophized that the "wolf cannot remain concealed beneath the sheep's clothing."

The interpreter "became sullen and peevish, always choosing to halt in those places where the poor beasts of burden could find nothing to eat after their long day's journey. The farther we penetrated . . . the more and more sulky he became. It was impossible to draw from him a single pleasant word, and his incoherent mutterings and allusions became subjects of serious apprehensions."

For ten days they pushed almost directly southward, coming gradually closer to the mountains. A wandering French-Canadian trapper was encountered, and Father De Smet induced him to accompany them for a few days. On the twelfth day out from Rocky Mountain House the interpreter vanished and was not again seen.

The trapper informed Father De Smet that an able and reliable interpreter named Monroe lived only two or three days' ride toward the southeast, and he set out at once on a quest for him, planning to rejoin the Blackfeet farther to the south. For another eight days he wandered with only the company of the young half-breed Cree through an endless succession of valleys. The Cree found signs that his own people were marauding in the country, and the tracks of large bands were seen but no living soul was found.

". . . we began wandering as chance might lead, to the point of discouragement . . ."

For four days snow fell. The trail of the Blackfeet with whom they had left Rocky Mountain House was obliterated. Indeed, they could find no mark of any kind to guide them. Their supplies were dangerously low.

In the third week of November, Father De Smet resigned himself to defeat. Had it been possible, he would have crossed the mountains to the Kootenai or the Columbia, but he knew that snow had closed all passes. The Cree informed him that the snow eastward on the plains would not yet be as deep as it was close to the mountains, and with a sad heart he turned in that direction.

He was probably within seventy or eighty miles of the International Border when he abandoned his quest. When they came to a small creek that was a tributary of the Bow River, the Cree turned northward on a trail with which he was familiar.

It was mid-December when they arrived at Fort Edmonton on the North Saskatchewan,‡ and Father De Smet "begged hospitality for the winter." It was graciously extended to him by the Hudson's Bay Company factor, John Rowan, his kindly wife, and their two daughters.

Fort Edmonton was the headquarters factory for an enormous district bordering the Saskatchewan and Athabaska Rivers, and

‡ Near the present large city of Edmonton, capital of the province of Alberta.

including Forts Jasper, Assiniboine, Little Slave Lake, Pitt, Carrolton, Cumberland and Rocky Mountain House. The number of employees and their families "is about eighty. Besides a large garden . . . the lakes, forests and plains of the neighborhood furnish provisions in abundance . . . the icehouse contained 30,000 white fish, each weighing four pounds, and [the meat of] 500 buffaloes, the ordinary amount of the winter provisions. Such is the quantity of aquatic birds in the season, that hunters often send to the fort carts full of fowls. Eggs are picked up by the thousands . . . in the marshes.

"The greater number of those employed being Catholics, I found sufficient occupation."

The Rowans showed Father De Smet "every attention. Never shall I have it in my power to cancel the debt of gratitude I owe them."

He remained at Fort Edmonton until March 1846, with the exception of the single excursion he made to the mission on Lake St. Anne, about forty miles to the west, to visit Fathers Thibault and Bourassa who resided there.

Father De Smet was very well liked by the people of Fort Edmonton. Most of them attended church each day, and he was seldom without an invitation to dinner or to some social affair. Many expressed the wish that he would remain with them, and they offered to contribute to the building of a church. He learned in time that their attitude toward Father Thibault was quite different, and when he sought from Rowan the reason for the antagonism he received the vague reply, "Your ways and those of Father Thibault are so very different. They cannot have the same regard for him. He only comes to Edmonton when he is sent for." Father De Smet deemed it a situation in which he could be of no help, and kept his silence.

As the days lengthened and the first signs of the coming spring were seen, he knew a consuming restlessness, and he felt that it would be to his advantage, even though winter would not relinquish its grip for weeks to come, to move closer to the mountains. He would cross them to the Columbia as soon as possible.

By the 12th of March he could contain himself no longer, and he set out for Fort Assiniboine on the Athabaska River, some hundred miles to the northwest. Had he been content to wait a few more weeks, he might have gone by horseback in a much more direct route to the mountains, that is, straight westward from Fort Edmonton. But that would have prevented him from seeing more of the country, more places and faces new to him.

XXI

On a bright but extremely cold day in March 1846, Father De Smet left Fort Edmonton with three dog sledges driven by half-breed Crees. Provisions, beds and baggage were carried on two of the sledges, and on the third, which was drawn by four powerful Malemutes, he rode well wrapped in fur robes.

He found "the mode of traveling quite a novelty; and on the glittering ice of the rivers and lakes, it was particularly convenient and agreeable." The weather continued favorable, although at night the mercury fell well below zero. However, he found himself quite comfortable in his furs and blankets in lean-tos facing roaring campfires. They reached Fort Assiniboine after five days of easy travel.

Two days later they drove their dog teams onto the thick ice of the Athabaska River and started for Jasper House, some two hundred and fifty miles upstream and in the shadows of the Canadian Rockies. They advanced at a steady pace that put the miles behind them with smooth rapidity, and nine days later, on the 28th of March, pulled up before the log structures of Jasper House. A hearty welcome was given Father De Smet by the factor, Colin Fraser, and his wife. He was the only white man "from the outside" who had visited them during the winter.

En route, on the shore of Lake Jasper, Father De Smet had met an old Iroquois named Louis Kwaragkwante, or Walking Sun, accompanied by his family clan, thirty-six in number. He had been forty years absent from his own country, during which time he had rarely seen a priest.

The old man was overwhelmed with joy. "Today I behold a priest, as I did in my own country . . . my heart rejoices . . .

wherever you go I shall follow you with my children . . . all will hear the word of prayer . . . all will have the happiness to receive baptism."

The old Iroquois kept his promise. He and his big family had pursued Father De Smet to Jasper House and had set up their camp nearby. On Easter Sunday, after Mass had been celebrated, "all were regenerated in the waters of baptism, and seven marriages renewed and blessed. The number baptized amounted to forty-four, among whom was the lady of Mr. Fraser and four of his children . . ."

Fifteen days after arriving at Jasper House, Father De Smet noted in his journal: "Provisions becoming scarce at the fort, and the large Iroquois family being encamped roundabout, resolved to remain until my departure . . . we should have found ourselves in an embarrassing situation had not Mr. Fraser come to our relief by proposing that we should leave the fort and accompany himself and family to the Lake of Islands, where we would subsist partly on fish . . . We set out to the number of fifty-four persons and twenty dogs. I count the latter because we were as much obliged to provide for them as for ourselves."

They spent twenty-six days in cabins at the Lake of Islands, during which time they were well supplied with food. Hunters in the party killed "12 moose deer, 2 reindeer, 30 large mountain sheep, 2 porcupines, 210 hares, 1 beaver, 2 muskrats . . . add to this from 30 to 50 fine white fish every day and 20 trout . . . yet we heard them saying: 'How hard is living here. The country is miserably poor . . . we are obliged to fast.'"

April was nearing its end when Father De Smet and the two Cree half-breeds with whom he had traveled from Fort Edmonton set out by sled on a trail that took them toward some of the highest and most magnificent mountains on the North American Continent. It was the beginning of the season when "immense masses of snow often become loosened and roll down the mountains' sides with a terrific noise that resounds throughout these quiet solitudes like thunder . . . so irresistible is the velocity of their descent that they frequently carry with them enormous fragments of rocks, and force a passage through the dense forests. Every day . . . the noise of avalanches descending . . . breaks upon the ear . . . From these mountains the majestic rivers of the north . . . the Saskatchewan, the McKenzie, the Athabaska and Peace River, the Columbia and Frazer at the west, derive the great part of their waters."

After three days of arduous and slow travel they turned from the Athabaska at the Grand Traverse and entered the valley of the much smaller *Fourche du Trou*. They were on the route taken each year by the Hudson's Bay Brigade from the Columbia to York Factory. These were the men who traveled this great distance gathering the furs taken in remote camps and stations in the mountains. Reaching the Athabaska they pursued their long journey by water.

During the first few days of May, Father De Smet and his two companions remained camped on a small lake. Toward the evening of the 6th "we discovered at the distance of about three miles the approach of two men on snowshoes . . . They proved to be the forerunners of the English brigade."

The next day the main brigade came up, and Father De Smet was greatly pleased to find with it his good friend, Frank Ermatinger from Fort Hall. Also traveling with the brigade were the two British Army officers, Ward and Vavasseur, whom he had met with Peter Skene Ogden as he was starting on his peace mission to the Blackfeet. Nothing more was said about their orders to take over the mouth of the Columbia River for Her Britannic Majesty, Queen Victoria.

The brigade went on toward Jasper House. Father De Smet was faced with a journey of seventy miles on snowshoes. He had known that the time would come when he must undertake this ordeal if he persisted in crossing the mountains at such an early season. Rowan had talked of it with him and had bluntly expressed the opinion that he could not accomplish it because of his corpulence and lack of training. Father De Smet had thereupon cut down the size of his meals, and had taken every opportunity to practice with the unfamiliar devices.

When, during the second week of May, he started across the mountains "on sixteen feet of snow," he felt lighter, although he had no way of determining how much weight he had lost. Also, he held considerable confidence in his ability as a snowshoe traveler.

His journal of the seven days' flight to cross the mountains does not truly reveal his sufferings. His life was saved by his companions when exhaustion overcame him. He lost toenails on both feet, and his pacs were filled with frozen blood.

The greatest obstacles were encountered on the western slope, as they descended toward the valley of the Columbia. He mentioned a "great Portage River," but journal entries indicate they were going down Wood River, a stream "meandering so remarkably in this straight valley . . . that we were compelled to cross [it] not less than forty times, with the water frequently up to our shoulders."

The spring thaw was well underway, the country was flooded, and in places they were obliged to cling to each other "to prevent being carried away by the current. We marched in our wet clothes . . . The long soaking, joined to my great fatigue, swelled my limbs. All the nails of my feet came off . . . Four times I found my strength gone, and I should certainly have perished in that frightful region if the courage and strength of my companions had not roused and aided me in my distress . . . Those who have passed the Rocky Mountains at 53° of north latitude, during the melting of the snows, know whether or not we merit the title of good travelers . . . I confess I would not dare undertake it again . . . they described me as the most clumsy and awkward traveler . . ."

It was the middle of May when they reached the confluence of "three beautiful rivers—the Columbia, the Portage from the northeast, and the Canoe River from the northwest." It was a boat encampment at which traders and parties of Indians regularly stopped on their journeys through the country. Several half-breeds who had been engaged by the annual Hudson's Bay Company brigade were camped there, preparatory to returning to Fort Colville. They were well supplied with "flour, a large ham, part of a reindeer, butter, cheese, sugar and tea."

Father De Smet said farewell to the two courageous men who had seen him safely through the mountains, and departed downstream in a Hudson's Bay Company canoe. Once again his irrepressible spirit soared as he moved swiftly down the swollen river through the great mountains. Had not more serious matters taken him on, he would "willingly linger . . . the range of picturesque mountains, whose bases came to bathe in the river, whilst their summits seemed to be struggling, in the giant efforts of the avalanche, to throw off the winding sheet of winter, in order to give place to new and beautiful verdure of the month of May, with its smiling and varied flowers—the thousand fountains which we could at one view behold, leaping out with soothing music . . . Occasionally . . . would a fallow or reindeer be observed . . . peeping with uplifted ears through a thicket . . . as the strange sound of oars or the Canadian song came stealing louder and louder upon them in their quiet abode, off they bounded . . ."

On the 30th of May he stepped ashore at Fort Colville, delighted to find that during his absence the Kettle Indians, under the direction of Father Hoeken, had built a pleasant new church, to which they conducted him "as in triumph."

The factor, John Lee Lewes, arranged for him to have a seat in a company barge, and early in June he was once again enjoying all the amenities of civilization at Fort Vancouver. Not the least of these were the ministrations of the fort's physician, who assured him that with proper care his feet would be rapidly restored.

Two British ships of war were anchored off Fort Vancouver, indicating the seriousness with which England looked upon the Oregon question. They were the brig *Modeste* and the frigate

Fisgard, and they had orders to remain throughout the summer, or as long as the war clouds threatened. He was invited to dinner on the *Modeste* with the officers of both vessels and the officials of the post.

He spent some days at St. Paul's on the Willamette, noting with great pride the progress that had been made in the enlargement and development of the schools and the convent.

But if progress had been notable, the fiscal condition of the establishments in Oregon Territory were far from satisfactory, and there was no reason to believe that it would not grow rapidly worse. Nor had the personnel expected to arrive, and so badly needed, appeared, although several ships had put in at the Columbia. Gathered in council at St. Paul's, the Fathers unanimously decided that the situation warranted sending one of their number to the East. As it was only July, the trip could be made overland. Their choice of an emissary quite naturally fell upon Father De Smet, the most experienced wilderness traveler among them. Also, he had demonstrated in the past his ability to procure money, materials and recruits.

He bowed to their decision, although at the moment, so soon after his ordeal in the Canadian Rockies, the thought of making the long hard journey had no appeal to him. However, the season was not far enough advanced to prevent him from spending a few days at St. Mary's on the Bitter Root, and that prospect delighted him.

Returning to Fort Vancouver, he made preparations to take as many supplies as possible upriver for the mountain missions. As he was about to start, an accident came very near to canceling all plans and changing the course of the balance of his life.

He was almost blinded by the explosion of a powder horn. The skin was stripped from the upper part of his face and much of his hair was burned from his head. Miraculously, his eyes were not injured.

He described himself as having the appearance of a "raw-faced mountaineer."

On the Fourth of July he was in a large canoe, "well-manned
. . . during a thunderstorm in the great gap of the Cascade
Mountains through which the mighty Columbia winds its
way . . ."

On the evening of August 8th he was sitting before the hearth
in the log house he had built five years before on the Bitter Root
. . . and he had the satisfying feeling that he had once more
come home.

XXII

More than once Father De Smet had said that nothing on earth, including the western weather, was more unpredictable than the Indian. His own high intelligence, his education, training and experience, perhaps provided him with greater insight into the dark recesses of the savage mind, and greater means for discovering the sources of the red man's customs, mores and traditions, than were possessed by any other white man in all the vast territory between the Missouri and the Columbia.

Yet, he never permitted himself to entertain the idea that by virtue of his superior knowledge and understanding he could divine the events of the next moment. No man, he declared, could anticipate with any accuracy what an Indian would do next, nor state with any degree of certainty why a thing was done at all. Moreover, complicating and confusing the picture were the varying cultural and intellectual levels of the tribes, the astonishing natural contrasts between nations that bordered each other. He had been among people who were barely qualified for inclusion in the species of Homo sapiens. The next day he had sat in council with men whose mental processes, whose ability to reason and to learn, were the equal of, if not superior to, those of any so-called civilized white man who dwelt among them.

There was only one thing that all of them, the degenerate and degraded, the intelligent and the industrious, could be depended upon to do, and that was change. However, countering this aggravating characteristic was one as universally distributed, and that was the Indian's "constant desire to discover some power superior to man." It was this disposition that rendered "them attentive to the least word that seems to convey the slightest knowledge of a Supreme Being, and hence the faculty with which they believe anything that at all resembles the word of God." And it was this disposition which gave to him his greatest hope for their improvement and their redemption.

In the late summer of 1846, some eighty lodges of Flatheads and Nez Percés had joined in a buffalo hunt in the Three Forks country. It was hardly a phenomenon that a dozen lodges of friendly Blackfeet had attached themselves to them. Each year since the establishment of St. Mary's Mission, a few Blackfeet adopted the "medicine" of the Black Robes, crossed the mountains and took up residence among their historic enemies of the Bitter Root and Snake River Valleys.

When the Crows discovered that their old friends, the Flatheads, were consorting not only with the Nez Percés, with whom the Crows were estranged, but with Blackfeet, their deadliest and oldest foe, they were infuriated and declared war.

Father De Smet, accompanied by Father Point, had left St. Mary's on August 16th. He planned to travel, as he had done on previous occasions, by way of the Yellowstone to Fort Union and then down the Missouri to St. Louis. Father Point would return to St. Mary's with the Flatheads at the conclusion of the hunt. With them was a small escort of Indians, a Nez Percé guide named Charles, and Gabriel, the interpreter who had served so reliably in the past.

Reaching the Three Forks they soon picked up the trail of the Flatheads. It led them through the Bozeman Pass into the valley of the Yellowstone. After following the trail for three more days, Father De Smet sent Gabriel and Charles on ahead to overtake the Flatheads and inform them of his approach.

Gabriel and Charles rode steadily for a day and a night, then reached the scene of an impending clash between the Crows and Flatheads. Immediately they dispatched a messenger to advise Father De Smet of the serious situation and requesting him to hurry forward. Their efforts to delay hostilities were futile. The announcement that Black Robe would soon arrive and would hold a council of peace only seemed to increase the fury of the Crows.

During the night the Flatheads and their allies, the Nez Percés and Blackfeet, strengthened their position with log and brush barricades. Shortly after daylight, two hundred Crows attacked, stirring up an immense cloud of dust as they swept forward across a sagebrush flat. In the course of the next hour, the Flatheads successfully repulsed three charges, and the battlefield was strewn with Crow dead.

Victor, chief of the Flatheads, at last judged that the Crows were discouraged and their horses exhausted. He ordered an advance. Out from the barricades poured the Flatheads, Nez Percés and Blackfeet. The Crows fled in disorder, vanishing into the hills, and the battle ended.

Father De Smet reached the scene the following forenoon, and "found everything ready to repel a second attack . . . I immediately sent an express to the Crows . . . to convey to them the great desire I had to see them, especially for the purpose of effecting a reconciliation . . ."

The messenger returned with word that the Crows were moving swiftly away toward the southwest and that there was no hope of overtaking them and inducing them to return. Father De Smet was pained by the situation, but he was not surprised by it, and he expressed the opinion that the Crows had received the chastisement they deserved. The Crows had solemnly promised him they would always remain at peace with the Flatheads.

The Blackfeet, who had fought bravely in the battle, sought an audience with Father De Smet, and he invited them to his lodge fire. They were convinced that his influence had been responsible for the victory, and that when the Crows learned that Black Robe would soon face them, their courage failed. The Crows had no heart to stand before the man who spoke with the Great Spirit.

Father De Smet suddenly saw the possibility of making a second mission of peace among the Blackfeet under beneficial circumstances. With the men then before him as guides, he might succeed.

He made the proposal, and they readily agreed to conduct him to the lodges of the highest Blackfoot chiefs.

Although he was delighted, Father De Smet revealed no emotion. He simply announced that the start would be made the following morning. Much to his consternation he was informed during the night that all the Flatheads and Nez Percés had decided to join the peace march. He offered a prayer that peace would, indeed, be the will of God, but he could not refrain from a slight shudder at the thought of parading across the plains above the Yellowstone surrounded by several hundred of the most deadly enemies of the Blackfeet. Heaven be with him!

More than four hundred men, women and children, an immense horse herd, and an uncountable number of dogs, trailed the two black-robed figures in a parade a mile long that wound its way out of the valley of the Yellowstone as the month of September, 1846, began. Several of the warriors riding beside Father De Smet and Father Point had bloody Crow scalps dangling from their thighs.

For the next week the Blackfoot guides selected a trail that took them through a broken country in which little game and little water were found. The high peaks of the Crazy Range gradually vanished in the west, and far ahead toward the northwest they could see the blue eminences of the Little Belt Mountains slowly increasing in height as they advanced.

Each night Father De Smet recorded the day's events in a notebook:

September 8: The Nez Percés were troublesome. Quarrels between them and the Flatheads and the small contingent of Blackfeet were numerous.

September 10: The Nez Percés announced they would turn back, and shortly afterward rode angrily away. He shared the feeling that their departure was best for all concerned.

Two hours later the Nez Percés were seen hurrying back to

rejoin the column. They reported that signs of a large war party of Crows had been found, and they had feared they would be attacked. Angered by the return of the Nez Percés, the Blackfeet declared that henceforth they would camp away from the main body.

September 11: The Flatheads announced they would go no farther. Each of them shook his hand before departing. To the great annoyance of the Flatheads, the Nez Percés went with them.

Nicholas, the aged Blackfoot who had been the first of his nation to join the church at St. Mary's, was killed in a fall from his horse. Father De Smet wept at his grave. Since 1841, when he was baptized, Nicholas had been "a most effective missionary in preparing the way for the introduction of the gospel among his tribe . . . Happily, he leaves a son, Sata, worthy of so excellent a sire."*

They traveled through a pleasant pass between the Big Snowy Range, on their right, and the Little Belt Mountains to the left.†

September 12: Game had been scarce since leaving the Yellowstone, but this day they sighted a large herd of buffalo. A number were killed, and a feast held, followed by a dance.

September 13: (Sunday) A fine rain fell. No fuel for cooking fires except buffalo dung, and it was made unusable by the precipitation. At midday the rain turned to sleet "so sharp that one can hardly have his hands bare."

Toward evening a scout finally found wood beside a small creek, and roaring fires were built to the great comfort of all. Another scout came in to report that a large camp of Blackfeet was only a few miles away. He had met some Blackfoot hunters and had informed them of Black Robe's approach. The chief of the camp was Big Lake.

The Blackfeet with Father De Smet were excited. They in-

* Sata was to become widely known as a reliable guide. Nicholas had several wives. Sata's mother was a Flathead.
† In the area of the Judith Basin.

quired if he wished them to indicate "their happiness" as baptized Christians by painting their faces. He gave his approval, telling them: "Do your best to show your friends and brothers that your hearts are glad."

September 14: Feast of the Exaltation of the Holy Cross. Akasia, a Blackfoot, and one of his wives, arrived to see Black Robe. He was dressed in his finest raiment, including a magnificent *toque*, which "among the Blackfeet is a tail seven or eight feet long, made of horse and buffalo hair, interwoven with their own . . . Such a tail . . . is a mark of great distinction . . ."

Akasia had been captured two years before by the Flatheads, but Father Point had induced them to set him free. Since that time Akasia had made no war upon them. He and Father Point fondly embraced each other. A meeting with Big Lake was set for the next day.

Suddenly a scout came in with startling and disquieting news. The Flatheads and Nez Percés had not, after all, gone home. They were camped only nine miles back on the trail.

September 15: Tail Bearer, an aide-de-camp, appeared with the announcement that Big Lake and his warriors were approaching. Father De Smet led his company out to meet them. The two files converged on a hill and advanced together "into a lovely and very smooth plain, rending the air with our yells and songs of joy. At the discharge of all the guns we alight. Tail Bearer advances first . . . After him comes Big Lake with some of his braves. The calumet is presented, and after this symbol of peace . . . tongues are loosened as if by magic, and everybody begins telling the news. Then I addressed them . . .

"They respond with a loud voice . . . and express the satisfaction and the pleasure that it has been to them to listen to the Black Robe."

Father De Smet was greatly startled when a Blackfoot arose and said in excellent English: "Father, you have a poor interpreter. These people are deeply interested in what you have been preaching to them, but your interpreter has not put it before them in the right way."

Father De Smet asked in bewilderment where he had learned to speak the English language so well.

"In Ireland, faith," the Blackfoot replied with a laugh. He then explained that when a boy he had been taken to Dublin by a Hudson's Bay Company official. After four years in school there, during which time he had learned to speak with an Irish accent, he had rejected civilization and had returned to his people.

The meeting with Big Lake was in progress when the Flatheads appeared. For a time the situation was tense, but an appeal for amity by Father De Smet had the desired effect. ". . . the savage can open his heart, but he wishes to know to whom he is opening it. Soon the unconstrained manners of our neophytes spread to the Blackfeet . . . how touching a sight it was! What a consoling triumph for religion, to see united under the cross these warriors whose scars told of so many bloody battles with each other . . . these warriors who had never met save in mortal hatred . . .

"The headmen of both nations came together that evening in my lodge . . ."

As Father De Smet journeyed on northward toward the Missouri River, more Blackfeet joined him. By September 16, in excess of two thousand were in the train, coming from the Piegans, Bloods, Gros Ventres and other tribes. The harmony was "truly unheard of." One might have said that their ancient quarrels were "long forgotten . . . this is remarkable, because it is the duty of an Indian to cherish in his heart, even to his last breath, a desire of vengeance upon his enemies."

Apprehensively he asked: "Will this peace last?"

Only the Nez Percés remained quarrelsome and petulant, but the Flatheads were able to repress them. Once again the Nez Percés rode away, and all were glad to see them go.

A warrior appeared with news that Blackfeet from many tribes were gathering at Fort Benton to meet the Black Robes.

September 22: "Big Lake . . . continues to exert a most fortunate influence upon his people by his great natural eloquence . . . One very rare, perhaps unique, thing: he has never had but one wife, with whom he has always lived in peace . . .

"The Catholic prayers have been translated and are recited every morning and evening . . ."

September 24: Fathers De Smet and Point with a small escort set off ahead of the procession for Fort Benton, only a few miles away. En route a Piegan, Little Chief, revealed that bitter feelings existed between himself and some of the Bloods at the fort. Each side had sworn to attack the other on sight.

Father De Smet had no intention of halting his mission, or delaying it, for any reason. He declared he would act as an intermediary in the feud, and prayed that he would be able to prevent bloodshed. "When we were in sight of the fort, two Blackfeet came out in haste to meet us; they tell Little Chief that if he or any of his men come nearer, their lives are in danger. They return at once to announce our arrival. Soon the great bell of the fort is heard . . . Paying no heed to the advice we have received, we start for the fort at a gallop. The gates were opened to us at once and all the whites saluted us with the greatest cordiality . . . They are French, Spanish and Canadians . . . nearly all Catholics."

Father De Smet sought out the enemy of Little Chief and pleaded with him to drive hatred from his heart. The appeal was successful. "'All is forgotten,' the man said. 'How could my heart be bad after what the Black Robe has said?'"

The enemies were brought together. Gifts were exchanged, and they embraced. Father De Smet thought it "unnecessary to say that after the smoking all withdrew with their hearts full of joy which is easier to feel than describe."

September 25: A Grand Council was held on an island in the Missouri River. In the circle with Father De Smet were Victor of the Flatheads, and the Blackfeet Little Chief, Big Lake, White

Bull, Crow Bull, Chief's Word, Big Roller and Bruised with Blows.

The speeches were long and wearying, lasting until the sun had fallen low over the plains, but at last an accord was reached. The Flatheads might go home without fear of being attacked. No longer were the Blackfeet their enemies. Father De Smet embraced and shook hands with each councilman, then he went to his room in the post and fell upon his knees to thank God and ask Him to preserve the truce which had been achieved.

Father De Smet had completed a mission and performed a feat that was nothing less than remarkable. If he had been influential before the fall of 1846 among the Indians, he was now the most powerful "medicine man" in the West. Word of his accomplishment spread rapidly from tribe to tribe, and his name was spoken in tones of awe and veneration. If he could have remained in touch with the Blackfeet the peace might well have endured, but duty called him to other places, and without the force of his persuasiveness, his words and his personality, it was swept aside by a resurgence of the wild blood which had for so many centuries ruled that formidable nation.‡

It was with a full heart that Father De Smet took his seat in a large bateau on the morning of September 28, 1846, and started on the journey of 2300 miles down the Missouri.

He stopped at a number of trading posts on the trip to celebrate Masses, baptize children, perform marriages, and visit with old friends.

Near Council Bluffs, he met the Mormons gathering for their trek into the wilderness, and he was moved with anger and compassion when he heard of their persecution. He felt that the "atrocious sufferings endured by these unhappy people will furnish a sad page to the history of the . . . West. They had just

‡ Father Point remained at Fort Benton through the winter of 1846–47, then was sent to Canada by orders which had been more than two years reaching him from Europe. No other priest was sent to the Blackfeet until 1859, when Father Adrien Hoeken built a mission on the Teton River.

been driven out for the second time from a state of the Union. I was introduced to their president, Mr. Young, an affable and very polite gentleman. He pressed me very earnestly to remain a few days, an invitation which my limited time did not permit me to accept. They asked me a thousand questions about the regions I had explored."

At Leavenworth he had the good fortune to catch the last steamboat of the season. On December 1, he walked down the gangway at St. Louis.

His journeys of 1845 and 1846 had taken him for more than six thousand miles through the Canadian and American wilderness.

XXIII

Father De Smet spent the Christmas season of 1846 in New Orleans. He had been sent to the South soon after his return to St. Louis to confer with Jesuit and other Church officials, and the plans they outlined for him left him in a mood bordering on despondency.

He was forced to abandon any hope that he would be permitted to return to the mountains in the near future . . . perhaps for several years. His superiors felt that for the time being he could be of the greatest service as a procurator and propagandist, not only for the western missions but for the entire Church. His writings, especially such papers as his description of the human sacrifice among the Pawnees, had deeply stirred religious persons throughout the world, and had brought urgent demands for greater efforts to Christianize the American Indians.

The Church leaders had concluded that the time was opportune to send the most famous of all American missionaries to harvest the flood of contributions which appeared to be in prospect. Moreover, he was recognized in both Europe and the United States as a leading authority on the American aborigine. Therefore, he was in the best possible position to carry on a campaign in their behalf. Nor did his superiors fail to take into consideration his amazing feats of exploration, adjudging them valuable as means of inspiring the general membership to open its collective purse. He was a hero of the wilderness, the great Black Robe who had carried the cross where it had never before been seen.

In a public proclamation, Bishop John B. Purcell of Cincinnati declared: "Never, since the days of Xavier, Brebeuf, Marquette and Lallemand, has there been a missionary more clearly pointed out and called and sent for this great work . . . His plans, I sincerely believe, are all heaven-inspired . . . I beg most earnestly to recommend the Indian missions, west of the Mississippi, in behalf of which Father De Smet again is willing to risk his life, which has been too often already exposed, with a martyr's heroism . . ."

Archbishop Samuel of Baltimore wrote him: ". . . your long and perilous labors among the ferocious savages of Oregon are known to the whole Catholic world and will commend you to the veneration and charity of all . . .

"You can the more confidently appeal to the friends of religion and humanity; inasmuch as looking for no earthly reward yourself, save privations and hardships, your only wish is to 'spend and be spent' in the service of thousands of benighted and degraded souls who demand at your hands the blessings of faith and civilization."

Bishop John Hughes of New York spoke of "how greatly the bishops of the province have been consoled by the wonderful success which has attended the labors of this devoted missionary and his colleagues among the savage tribes of the Rocky Mountains . . . It would be, of course, superfluous for me to recommend to the friends of religion a missionary so well known and so justly revered as the indefatigable apostle of the Rocky Mountains, Father De Smet."

The accomplishments of the Jesuits west of the mountains since 1838 comprised an imposing list. It had been in that year that Fathers Blanchet and Demers had arrived on the Columbia from Canada. Father De Smet had reached the Flatheads in 1840. By 1847, twenty-two churches and missions had been established on the Northwest Pacific slope.

Once Father De Smet had reconciled himself to the duty before him, he plunged faithfully into the work of carrying it out. "I am like a soldier," he wrote a friend. "When I receive orders I march whither I am sent. Yet, like a soldier, I may have my preferences, and I need not tell you that these are decidedly for the Indian Country."

Early in 1847, he was ordered to make a trip through the eastern United States and then go on to Europe. After short stays in Washington, Philadelphia and New York, he crossed the Atlantic for the sixth time, landing at Liverpool. He spent the remainder of the year in England, France and Belgium.

Through the first half of 1848 he continued his quest for funds and recruits with no little success. At last he was ordered to return to America to make an extended tour. He made appeals in Albany, Troy, Niagara Falls, Buffalo and Sandusky. After going to Cincinnati by rail, he took a steamboat for St. Louis.

Trouble among the Sioux tribes stirred in him a strong desire to go among them again, and he requested permission to make the trip, giving as his main objective a wish to determine whether the time was right for establishing a mission in the Sioux Country. He was not a little surprised when he was granted the "truly consoling privilege."

Happily he set out alone in the middle of August, traveling by steamboat as far up the Missouri as Bellevue, near the Council Bluffs, some 660 miles above St. Louis. He and three French-Canadians whom he engaged as guides left there with a small group of traders journeying with a wagon to posts on the Niobrara and White Rivers, the heart of Sioux territory.

For ten days they advanced over an almost deserted plain, meeting neither Indians nor whites, and seeing only a few animals. On several occasions they could find no campfire fuel except the "dry bison dung, and three times at our camping ground water failed us. This is a hard trial for man and horse, especially after traveling all day under the burning sun of the month of August.

"Another kind of torment, still less supportable when the heat is most intense, is the appearance of fantastical rivers and lakes . . ."

Frequently the mirages seemed to invite "the weary traveler

to advance and refresh his wasted strength upon their banks. Fatigue and thirst picture in the distance verdure, shade and coolness awaiting him."

For the horses the most dreaded insect was the "gadfly, the sting of which will make the gentlest horse bound with rage. Happily for the horse in these plains, Providence has bestowed upon him a defender; the starling, unalarmed by the presence of man, which, wheeling ever about the rider, lights on the back of the horse or on his load, to dart with wonderful skill upon the malicious insect . . .

"For ourselves we were obliged to wage continual war upon swarms of mosquitoes and their allies the gnats. The latter teased us by day, the former, more cowardly, attacked us by night. These famished enemies . . . rush from their infected abodes . . . sound the trumpet of war, and darting on their tired victim, sting, harass and pursue him until . . . the unfortunate traveler, already sweltering with heat, seeks shelter under a buffalo robe or a heavy blanket."

Yet, Father De Smet would have traded places with few persons on earth: "To those who pass their days amid the quiet of domestic joys, surrounded by all the delicacies that abundance can produce, a journey through the prairies may appear a sad realization of human misery and suffering; but to the man who elevates his thoughts above earthly and passing things . . . such a one can perceive in these privations, in even greater perils and difficulties . . . only slight annoyances, which he will prefer to all the delights of indolence or the dangers of wealth."

Unaware where he might meet the Sioux, Father De Smet had planned no itinerary. He simply continued on, and when he reached the Niobrara he found himself confronted by virtually the entire Ponca nation. It was a meeting that came close to "being attended with disastrous consequences."

From a rise he could see the lodges of some thousand Poncas. As he rode on toward them, the wagon and its escort was suddenly surrounded by a howling group of young warriors. Several packets of merchandise were quickly carried off. Wisely the traders did not fire on the thieves.

Father De Smet had not yet been identified by the Indians. As he rushed back toward the surrounded wagon, several warriors called out in astonishment: "Black Robe! Black Robe!" The raiders raced away at once for the village.

Father De Smet and the traders turned upstream and made their camp four miles from the Indians. It was not long, however, before he was approached by a delegation. Then it was learned that the Poncas recently had engaged in a fight with some Pawnees, and one of them had been killed. They were in an ugly mood, and they had intended to pillage the wagon and kill one member of its escort to assuage their feelings.

After greeting Father De Smet warmly, the Ponca chief ordered the stolen goods returned. Some six hundred men and women came out to shake his hand, "a ceremony somewhat lengthy . . . I made a little distribution of tobacco."

He accepted an invitation to pass the night in the Indian village and to speak. "This was the first time that the Poncas had heard Jesus Christ preached by the mouth of his minister . . . The next day I baptized their little ones, and when the time of separation arrived they besought me with the greatest earnestness to renew my visit, and to fix my residence among them . . ."

He continued toward the northwest, crossing White River, stopping at Fort Bouis on Medicine Creek, and going on to the main Sioux post, Fort Pierre. It was his good fortune to have Colin Campbell, the trader, whom he described as "one of the best interpreters in the country," volunteer to accompany him on the balance of his journey. A circular trip to the West was planned.

While he was at Fort Pierre word was received that a band of Sioux had camped nearby, having just returned from a raid against the Omahas "with thirty-two human scalps torn from defenceless old men and from women and children whose husbands and fathers were off hunting." He set out at once to visit them.

When he rode into their camp, the wild fiendish victory celebration that was in progress quickly came to a halt. "These barbarians . . . welcomed me with open arms as a messenger from the Great Spirit. A vivid emotion, depicted in every countenance, accompanied their respectful attention to my discourse . . ."

Few Indians of the northern and western tribes needed to be convinced that Father De Smet spoke with the Great Spirit, but whether they needed it or not the Sioux at Fort Pierre were treated to a dramatic demonstration which made indisputable to them his extraordinary spiritual powers.

A band of Ogallalas came in after being disgracefully defeated at the hands of the Crows. Not only had they been driven off by the Crows they had attacked, but the Crows had pursued them armed with nothing more than rods and clubs. No greater shame could have been suffered, for a reprisal of this nature signified that the Crows thought them "worth neither the lead nor powder that would be expended in killing them."

In the affray a daughter of the Ogallala chief, Red Fish, had been taken captive by the Crows. Melancholy and humbled, he pleaded with Father De Smet to take steps to secure her freedom. As ransom he offered eighty-five buffalo robes and his best horses.

While sympathizing with the man's grief, Father De Smet offered the opinion that "without doubt the Master of Life had been offended by the unjust attack on the Crows . . . and that to himself solely he must attribute the misfortune of his child and all the other miseries which had resulted from the expedition. I exhorted him to abandon in future all unprovoked attacks upon his neighbors, and to persuade his tribe to harken to the orders of the Great Spirit . . ."

Father De Smet also promised to pray that the girl would be restored to her father.

Greatly consoled, Red Fish returned to his people and sum-

moned the headmen to tell them of Black Robe's promise to
help.

During the talk the girl was seen approaching, weary and
bruised and hungry.

She had, of course, escaped her captors, and had made her
way home alone.

"Imagine the astonishment of Red Fish and his tribe," said
Father De Smet. "Every hand was lifted to heaven to thank the
Great Spirit . . . The report flew quickly from village to village,
and this coincidence, that divine providence permitted . . . was
to them a certain proof of the great power of Christian
prayer . . ."

He added modestly that the incident contributed "much to
augment their confidence in me."

With Colin Campbell and a small company, Father De Smet
spent the next two months riding on a long, circuitous route
which passed through the Badlands above White River and along
the eastern edge of the Black Hills. It was territory he had never
seen, and although he visited numerous Sioux camps and spent
long hours, day and night, in councils, he somehow found the
time to write in detail of the flora and fauna of the country
through which he passed.

He thought the Badlands* "the most extraordinary of any I
have met in my journeys . . . The action of the rains, snow and
winds upon the argillaceous soil is scarcely credible . . . Viewed
at a distance, these lands exhibit the appearance of extensive
villages and ancient castles . . . we might consider them as appertaining to some new world, or ages far remote . . . The
industry of the settler will never succeed in cultivating and planting this fluctuating and sterile soil—no harvest ever crown its
efforts. But though it offers no interest to the farmer, and little
to the botanist, the geologist and naturalist may find abundant
material . . . for here are found curious remains of the mastodon

* Southwestern South Dakota.

. . . well-preserved skulls, horns and tortoises so large that two men could hardly raise them."

Among the Brules an idiot boy attached himself to Father De Smet, and was roughly dragged from his presence by shamed elders. He summoned the entire band to a meeting, and demanded that the boy be brought back before him. When that had been done, he baptized him, then sternly admonished them for their ill-treatment of the child. He was greatly pleased to see that his words "produced a profound impression," and that "my poor friend Paschal . . . is now treated with respect . . ."

In each camp he visited Father De Smet presented the chief with a medal bearing the likeness of Pope Pius IX. As he suspended the decoration on its ribbon about the neck of one chief the man displayed excessive signs of delight and gratitude.

"I will place it with my war manitou," he said. "It will make me as prudent in councils during peace, as the other has made me strong in battle."

"The other?" Father De Smet asked.

Opening a box the chief drew out a small packet of buckskin. Father De Smet was completely confounded when he saw a colored picture of "General Diebitsch, a distinguished Russian officer who had served in the Napoleonic Wars, in full uniform and mounted on a prancing warhorse."

How the picture had found its way into the heart of the western badlands, he was not able to learn, but he was informed, to his greater astonishment, that for some years the Russian had been "the manitou of war to the Sioux chief, and he attributed to him the success of the many victories he had gained."

As he neared the end of his journey among the Sioux, Father De Smet felt somewhat disspirited, convinced that the situation he found among them offered "little encouragement to the missionary."

He added: "There is an immense difference between them and the Flatheads and numerous other nations that occupy the regions west of the Rocky Mountains." Still he expressed the hope that in due time "something may be done in favor of these degraded Indians so long left without the aid of religion."

October had almost gone when he returned to Fort Bouis, near the mouth of Medicine Creek, and set out with two paddlers in a small skiff for the trip down the Missouri. The weather was good until they had passed the Council Bluffs, and then winter struck with snow and freezing cold. The river was soon filled with floating ice, making travel on it in their frail craft an impossibility.

He hired a farmer to drive him and his guides to St. Joseph. There he learned to his profound disappointment that the *Highland Mary,* the last steamboat of the season, had departed twenty-four hours earlier. Determined to overtake the boat, he obtained a saddle horse and set out.

"The idea of running after a high-pressure steamboat certainly does appear quite ridiculous," he admitted in his journal. "But I relied upon the numerous delays of the boat at the different sandbanks, which were more likely to take place, also, as the season was advancing. I calculated well . . ."

Twenty-four hours after leaving St. Joseph, he boarded the *Highland Mary.*

XXIV

Except in one respect, the years 1849 and 1850 were not pleasant ones for Father De Smet. Financial duties were saddled upon him in ever increasing numbers. He became a combined business manager and inspector, visiting churches, convents and colleges in Louisville, Bardstown, Cincinnati, Chicago, Chillicothe, New Orleans, Mobile and way points. His knowledge of train, boat and stage schedules would have made any veteran drummer jealous. He suffered from nightmares involving weird trial balances and fantastic bookkeeping puzzles he was unable to solve. He wrote endless reports on housekeeping problems, purchasing, supplies, real estate, and a host of other matters in which he had no interest whatsoever and which left him exhausted with *ennui*.

"Probably we shall never see each other on this side of the grave," he told a correspondent in Europe. "I hope we shall meet in heaven where all ciphering, quibbling and account-making are at an end."

The exception to the tedium was a journey he was instructed to make in the late summer and fall of 1850 to the Osage Mission on the Neosho River and to St. Mary's Mission in the valley of the Kansas. Even this trip, which let him escape for a few weeks into the Indian Country, had the odium of a business assignment. He was required to look into the finances of the establishments, ascertain their needs, report on their accomplishments and their prospects for improvement.

He took longer than was really necessary to complete the tasks, pilfering a little time to visit the Miamis, Shawanoes and several other tribes, and he was delighted that he could follow for some distance "the great Santa Fe Route." How much he would have liked to continue on the famed trail to the Southwest! How much he missed "the plains, the Indians and the wilderness with all their privations, miseries and dangers. They were treats indeed compared with the monotony with which I am surrounded."

The great migrations had been in full swing for several years, but the discovery of gold in California had swelled the onrushing western tide until it appeared that a mass exodus of the entire nation was underway. On both the Santa Fe and Oregon Trails Father De Smet saw an endless procession of caravans. People were traveling toward the promised land on horses, mules and donkeys, in wagons, carriages and stages, on foot pushing handcarts or bending under backloads. And they were dying of sickness and disease, old age and injury, and the trail sides were marked with gravestones and crosses and strewn with the whitening bones of animals.

Perhaps few men understood better than Father De Smet what effect the immense migrations would have on the Indians. He interrupted his monotonous duties to put his thoughts on paper, a task he considered an obligation.

"Imagine thousands of all countries . . . deserters, sailors, robbers, murderers, the scum of the States . . . with some honest men among them, no doubt . . . all living lawless and unbridled lives . . . The news of the abundance of gold seems to have shaken the United States to the foundation," he said.

"The facts reveal clearly the melancholy future which at no very remote epoch awaits these nations [the Indians], if efficient needs are not employed for preventing the woes with which they are threatened. My visit to several tribes, and above all that which I lately paid to the great Sioux nation, have only confirmed the sad forebodings to which my experience, during a prolonged residence among these forsaken children of the forest, had given birth.

"I have communicated these views . . . to an honorable agent of the United States Government . . .*

"It is quite a common observation . . . that the religious as well as the social condition of the Indians . . . is in no wise capable of amelioration. I am far from participating in this opinion. Let the obstacles arising from the people who style themselves civilized be removed; let all trade in ardent spirits, that deadly scourge of the Indians, be prevented; let missionaries be sent . . . with no object but the happiness of the poor souls entrusted to their care, and I am confident that in a short time we should have the consoling spectacle of a sensible improvement among them."

And he asked the question: "To put an end to the cruel wars . . . to rescue so many souls . . . to prevent the total destruction of these tribes . . . is it not an enterprise worthy of inflaming the zeal of a minister of the gospel . . . a work worthy of the efficient cooperation and assistance of a government as powerful as that of the United States?"

The introduction of agriculture among the Indians, he said, would always be difficult, and "it would prove a chimera to introduce it among them on an extensive scale in the beginning." He advocated the gradual development of agricultural programs under which their "roving habits, the wars which often spring from them, would insensibly give place to a more peaceable and domestic life. The animals which they would raise, replacing the buffalo, would erase its memory amid surrounding plenty."†

While he may have sounded sentimental at times when writing about "his Indians," Father De Smet was ever the realist. Faith and effort were not enough with which to build successful missions. His grumbling about his financial burdens did not over-

* Father De Smet's letters to the Indian Bureau have not been found, and it can only be presumed that they still exist somewhere in the voluminous and disorderly old files in Washington.
† These proposals should have a familiar ring to Americans of the present day. Since the turn of the century they have been introduced in Congress many times, and each time as something new and progressive.

shadow his understanding that money was a prerequisite. He made a strong fight to set up a channel through which it might flow in dependable quantities to the mission coffers.

He wrote to Archbishop Eccleston of Baltimore, where the Catholic prelates of the United States were assembling for the first Plenary Council. As a means of obtaining funds to maintain and increase missionary work, he proposed the creation of a new association for propagation of the faith devoted exclusively to the Indians.

He asked for action on even higher levels, appealing directly to Rome. In a letter to the Father-General of the Society of Jesus he spoke of how he had been prevented from keeping promises he had made to the Blackfeet, Crows, Poncas and other nations that Black Robes would be sent to live with them. "This year again at various times these poor unhappy tribes have gotten word to me of the pain they feel at having their hopes frustrated and their ardent desire of at least an early accomplishment," he said. "On the other hand, your Paternity is but too well aware how poor in subjects is the vice-province of Missouri, and how impossible it is for it to furnish the missions, when it has barely sufficient for itself."

Father De Smet seldom spoke of his own health, but he told the Father-General significantly that he felt "fit to undertake and endure afresh all the privations connected" with expeditions to the West. "A sign from your Paternity will make me take the road to the plains . . . where so many thousand of souls are groaning under the empire of Satan."

As another argument for the urgent establishment of new missions he cited the growing activities of "the Mormons . . . a set of fanatics . . . and the French socialists under the lead of Cabet [who] are proposing to go and form new states in the midst of the great desert. The Mormons are there already, 50,000 to 60,000 in number."

Etienne Cabet had been exiled from France for his advocacy of state control of all economy and social life, and he founded several communistic settlements in the United States. His followers were called Icarians. Father De Smet warned the Father-General that Cabet "is negotiating at this moment to go and occupy a large territory east of the Rocky Mountains. The poor simple savages will be their dupes, unless we can forestall them . . ."

Had the Father-General given the word, he would have been off to the West with all possible speed, but the statement about his good health was less than accurate. In a letter to the mountain man and historian, Charles Larpenteur, who was confined to his bed in Baltimore with rheumatism, Father De Smet said: "I am indeed sorry to hear of the continuance of your indisposition, the consequence of your many exposures, no doubt, in times past. I also begin to suffer from the same cause, with my share of provocation during several years from such attacks. In fact, disguise it as we may, old age, like the cholera, has its premonitory symptoms, and will creep slowly but persistently into our entire frame."

Father De Smet's bitterness over the failure of the federal government to protect the Indians and abide by its treaties with them, in no way adulterated the love he held for America. "What nation on earth," he asked with pride, "presents such a spectacle as the United States of a confederated government, so complicated, over such a vast extent of territory, with so many varied interests, and yet moving so harmoniously?" He wrote of a visit to Washington where he saw Congress in session, "the representatives of eight Territories and of thirty states or nations, nations in many senses, they may be called . . . that have within them all the germ and sinew to raise a greater people than many of the proud, now tottering, principalities of Europe; all speaking and learning one and the same language, all acting with one heart and all burning with the same enthusiasm—the love and glory of the Great Republic—even while parties do exist and bitter domestic quarrels now and then arise."

He wrote rapturously of his travels, revealing a remarkable

knowledge of American history, both that of communities and the nation as a whole. He bordered on the lyric in his descriptions of the Mississippi and Missouri and Ohio Rivers, of the "puff, puff, puff of the high-pressure steamboats that come sweeping in almost every hour, perhaps from a port 2000 miles off, from the then frozen winter of the North, to the full burning summer of the South . . . fleets of them as large as the world can show; with their elegant rooms, neat berths, spacious saloons and costly pianos . . . on a voyage of Atlantic distance with hogs, horses, oxen and cattle . . . corn, flour, wheat . . . all the products of the rich western lands."

He urged a nephew to come to America, expressing the belief that "You will revere the offspring of those revolutionary patriots, who not only left us such a heritage, won by their sufferings and their blood, and such a Constitution, such a government in Washington, regulating all the national concerns. . . .

"Show me a spectacle more glorious, more encouraging . . . in all the pages of history—a constellation of free states, with no public force but public opinion, moving by well-regulated law, each in its own proper orbit, around the brighter star in Washington. . . . God grant it may continue as the beautiful display of infinite wisdom that fixed the sun in the center and sent the revolving planets on their errands."

He never gave anyone reason to doubt that he was first a man of the cloth, or second a fiercely proud American.

As he had done in previous years, in 1850 he was obliged to write, not without great pain, to friends in the Indian Country of his inability to comply with their requests that he visit them. In a typical letter to Zephyr Recontre, the noted interpreter who had appealed to him to return to the Sioux, he voiced his deep sorrow at being "unable again this spring to come among my good friends in the Sioux Country; but I have so much business on my hands here, with nobody to take my place, that my superiors have put off my departure to the Indian Country to some other time; when I cannot say.

"There is nothing I have more at heart, and I feel a great desire and plenty of courage to return to a post which I regret [miss] constantly, and to spend my days in laboring for the happiness and salvation of the Indians. But I dare not make any positive promises; it depends on my superiors. I hope that before long they will be able to replace and release me.

"Tell them [the Sioux] that I often think of them; that I desire ardently to see them again; that I pray daily for their happiness; that they must take care not to offend the Great Spirit . . . Adieu!"

Despite his sadness at being held in civilization, Father De Smet's inherent ebullience and his fine sense of humor remained intact. He was delighted to receive word that his niece, Silvie, had married a young man named De Bare in Belgium, and he hastily wrote her: ". . . praise be to the Good Lord . . . my only regret is that I was not there to bless you both. . . .

"Since I now love my nephew, Mr. De Bare, as much as I love my niece, Silvie, you must be careful to give him a faithful description of your uncle, so that if I should happen in on him in your absence, he would recognize me . . .

"Uncle Pierre, tell him, is a man of medium size, with gray hair tending to white. The center of his wide face—a foot, or near it—is occupied by a nose with which a Greek or Roman would not find fault. Its nearest neighbor is a mouth of ordinary size, which hardly ever opens save to laugh or to make others laugh. It makes people love God in that manner. The rest resembles a man of fifty years, who weighs 210 pounds.

"If you ever build a new house, give the door of my chamber six inches extra width, because I don't like to be bothered getting into a room."

The end of the year 1850 found Father De Smet in New Orleans at the end of a long trip on Church business through the South.

XXV

The great western migrations had brought drastic changes in the economic, social and political structures of the United States. No longer did the East monopolize the commercial and governmental scenes. There were strong western voices and forces to be heard and heeded. Texas was a State. Oregon was a Territory. Mexico had been defeated and had ceded immense areas in which governments were being organized (to become the states of Arizona, New Mexico, California, Nevada, Utah and Colorado).

Countless thousands of men, women and children had crossed the plains, deserts and mountains to take up land. Within two years after the discovery of gold in California, more than 100,000 persons were crowded into the mining camps of the Sierra Nevadas. But not all of the emigrants had gone to the West Coast. Other uncounted thousands had gone no farther than the fertile river valleys stemming from the Missouri, on the eastern edge of the Great Plains. Father De Smet wrote of towns seeming to appear overnight, of men plowing fields where a day before red warriors had camped and hunted and fought.

Of all the problems created by the swift and drastic changes none was more complicated or presented more formidable and menacing aspects than that of the Indians. Already the tribes which had lived along the lower Missouri, the Kansas, the eastern Platte, the Arkansas, had been made destitute and homeless. Many were starving, and others had ridden away seeking the means to survive.

The relentless pressure on them continued, an impregnable force that made them helpless before its onslaught. There was no reason to believe it would abate, no hope of stopping it, except by force of arms. There was no reason to believe that the gold and land rushes to the Pacific would decrease, but there was every indication that they would continue to swell, for the western coast was a part of the United States, and agriculture and new industries were building a solid foundation for a permanent and growing society.

The Indian looked upon the mass movements not as a development, not as progress, but only as an invasion of his homeland that would obliterate him if he did not take measures to halt them. His only weapon was force, and he had begun to use it with terrible consequences.

For the federal government the only alternative to permitting a long, bloody and costly war to ensue—one in which the slaughter of civilians undoubtedly would be much greater than military fatalities—was to establish protective measures for the Indians through negotiations, that is, recognize and defend not only their just claims but their right to remain among the living peoples of the world.

It was largely through the instigation of Colonel D. D. Mitchell, the Superintendent of Indian Affairs, that the call went out from Washington for a general and conclusive council with the chiefs of every tribe east of the Rocky Mountains. The place selected for the immense conference was Fort Laramie, and the date set was mid-September 1851.

Mitchell wasted no time in asking the assistance of the man he knew could help him the most, Father De Smet. His appeal was approved by the Father-Provincial in St. Louis, and Father De Smet and Father Christian Hoeken, also a veteran Indian missionary, were instructed to place themselves at the service of the government.

Although his acquiescence to Mitchell's request involved circumventing the general custom of the Jesuits not to participate in legal and political activities and decisions that properly were the function of the authorities, the Father-Provincial, Jean Elet, found a way to ease his own conscience. Fathers De Smet and Hoeken could very easily be sent on missionary business to the tribes of the upper Missouri River, where they would be in a good position to take part in whatever events happened to transpire under the aegis of the Indian Bureau.

Father De Smet noted in his journal with diplomatic suavity that the task of himself and Father Hoeken would be that of "rendering any assistance in our power in furthering the views of the government among the tribes with whom I had become acquainted. The opportunity, at the same time, was favorable to announce the consoling word of God to the poor benighted savages of these distant regions."

The arrangement in whatever guise it was to be cloaked was highly satisfactory to Mitchell, and he wrote Father De Smet: "Understanding that you will shortly start for the upper Missouri country on your missionary labors . . . you will do me a favor by informing such of the upper tribes as you may see of the intentions of the government . . . Should your other engagements permit, I shall be rejoiced to see you at Fort Laramie. Any sketches that you can make and the outlines of maps of this prairie and mountain country will be of great importance and would be highly appreciated by the government, as well as any information with regard to the habits, history or other interesting matters appertaining to the Indians."

Father Elet's plan did not please the Father-General in Europe, and he sent an express canceling it, and ordering Fathers De Smet and Hoeken to confine themselves to their proper religious duties. Father Elet refused to change his decision, feeling that it would be unjust to break his understanding with Mitchell. Moreover, he knew that it would be no small advantage to the Church to have Father De Smet, the most influential Black Robe in the United States, in a high position at the big Indian smoke. His presence there also would be of great benefit to the Indians, for they would have by their side a staunch friend and defender of their rights. Father Elet's defiance of his superior's orders made clear, as well, his fear that the Indian Bureau might take advantage of the naïve and trusting Indians. That would not be so likely to occur with Father De Smet present.

It was on the 7th of June, 1851, that Fathers De Smet and Hoeken boarded the *St. Ange* for Fort Union "on missionary business." The owner and captain of the fine steamboat was the famous pilot Joseph La Barge, always a good friend of the Black Robes.

Father De Smet's account of his journey of 1851 and of the Grand Council itself comprised a document that created great interest and was of immense historical value.

The *St. Ange* was crowded beyond capacity with hunters, traders and emigrants . . . Irish, Swiss, Germans, Italians and "Français de France," a title given to newly arrived Frenchmen to distinguish them from French-Canadians and Franco-Americans.

"They went in quest of earthly wealth. Father Hoeken and I in search of heavenly treasure—to the conquest of souls."

That spring the entire western country had suffered late blizzards, after which excessive rains fell, and by June the river was "rolling its muddy billows from upland to upland, over a surface of eight, fifteen, and in several places of twenty miles in width. No longer knowing any bounds, the river disappeared. Beneath its waters also vanished the verdure . . . of the plains, the stately forests . . . A vast lake now covered all this space, and the immense volume of water . . . carried ruin and desolation . . . We could see the torrent descending with the violence and rapidity of an avalanche, overturning and sweeping everything with its angry waves.

". . . the whole face of the waters seemed covered with wrecks; houses, barns, stables, fences of fields and gardens, were borne away . . ."

Six days after leaving St. Louis disaster struck, not disaster to the stout steamer which was momentarily expected, but disaster to its passengers. One after another they dropped with an illness that seemed to take no definite form. Some burned with fever, others suffered severe headaches, many had dysentery, while some simply lost their strength. Father De Smet took to his bed, grievously afflicted with what he thought was a bilious attack.

". . . a mournful silence took the place of the rude shouts and boisterous conversations . . ."

Then Lewis Willcox, a clerk of the American Fur Company, suddenly became violently ill, and in a few hours was dead. His symptoms were unmistakably those of cholera.

". . . the boat resembled a floating hospital . . . in a short time thirteen fell victims to the epidemic of cholera . . . Good Father Hoeken devoted himself to the sick night and day, with a zeal at once heroic and indefatigable. He visited them; he assisted them in their sufferings; he prepared and administered remedies; he rubbed the cholera patients with camphor; he heard the confessions of the dying . . . He then went and blessed their graves on the bank of the river . . .

"This beloved Brother had naturally a hardy constitution, and was habituated to a life of privation . . . but his assiduous and fatiguing attentions to the sick completely exhausted him. In vain I warned him, begging him to spare himself . . . It gave me pain to see him fulfilling this heroic work alone, but I was in such a state of debility that I was incapable of offering him the least help . . . fears were entertained that my illness was assuming the form of cholera. I requested Father Hoeken to hear my confession and give me extreme unction, but at the very moment he was called to another sick person, who was in an extremity. He replied, going, 'I see no immediate danger for you; tomorrow we will see.'

"Father Hoeken's cabin was next to mine. Between one and two o'clock at night . . . the voice of Father Hoeken was suddenly heard. He was calling me to his assistance . . . I dragged myself to his pillow . . . He asked me to hear his confession; I at once acquiesced . . . I administered extreme unction; he responded to all the prayers with a self-possession and piety which increased the esteem that all on board had conceived for him. I could see him sinking. As I was myself in so alarming a state, and fearing that I might be taken away at any moment . . . I besought him to hear my confession, if he were yet capable of listening to me. I knelt, bathed in tears, by the couch of my dying Brother in Christ—of my faithful friend . . . Strength forsook him: soon also he lost the power of speech . . .

"Father Hoeken . . . surrendered his pure soul into the hands of the Divine Redeemer on the 19th of June . . . He was only forty-three . . . The last fifteen years of his life were passed among the Indians, who had conceived the most profound veneration for him . . . His only consolation was to be among them."

After ten days of intense suffering, Father De Smet's recovery began and soon thereafter he knew once more the surge of strength through his strong body. As the boat reached drier country, the epidemic gradually disappeared.

Thirteen years had passed since Father De Smet had first ascended the Missouri, on his way to establish the mission near the Council Bluffs. At that time one did not travel far from St. Louis before reaching Indian Country, the vast forests and plains of the game herds, the true wilderness. Now he saw "flourishing cities, fine villages and thousands of beautiful farms. This alluvial soil is probably unequaled on the earth for richness . . ."

As he traveled on up the great highway to the West, he considered the council he was to attend. Here was an unprecedented opportunity to provide the Indian with a permanent home, to give him a chance to adjust himself to the civilization that was threatening to destroy him. There still was an inconceivably enormous territory that might be set aside in perpetuity for him. Except for trails and trading posts, the map from the upper Missouri to the Rocky Mountains was largely a blank.

Perhaps it was with a feeling of futility that he asked in his letters: "Will not the President of the Republic, like some of his predecessors, pluck some plumes from the Indian eagle, once the emblem of their greatness and power, to place them in the crown composed of the trophies of his administration?"*

There was room for the red people, still plenty of room, but it was obvious that Father De Smet had little hope that it would be preserved for them. He held a vision of the President looking at a map of the northern plains country and seeing there only more stars "of the first magnitude which will enhance the luster of the galaxy of the flag of the Union. This great territory will hold an immense population, destined to form several great and flourishing states."

Father De Smet was not a true romantic. Nor did he permit dreams to carry him off. He looked upon the Indians only as people, as human beings placed upon the earth by God. He observed with a practical eye, as a scientist, a sociologist. The question of what was to become of the tribes which since time immemorial had lived in the fertile plains and valleys of the Missouri Basin awakened "gloomy ideas in the observer's mind, if he has followed the encroaching policy of the states . . .

"If they are again repelled and banished further inland, they will perish infallibly. The Indians who refuse to submit or accept the definite arrangement, alone favorable to them, would resume the wandering life of the plains, and close their sad existence as the bison and other animals on which they live vanish."

After the *St. Ange* had reached the upper river, he took every opportunity to visit Indian villages and trading posts. Often he went ahead by horseback. He celebrated Masses and baptized children among the Yankton Sioux, Arikaras, Mandans, Minnetarees, Gros Ventres. In the vicinity of the Great Bend he heard that a Sioux village nearby was suffering an epidemic of smallpox. With no regard for his own danger he hurried to it, and spent a day and night there ministering to the sick, baptizing the

---

* The President was Millard Fillmore. Father De Smet's lack of faith in him was justified, for he was an antagonist of persons of foreign birth and of the Catholic Church. He became a "Know-Nothing" Party member, its candidate for President in 1856.

little children, and giving the dying "all the consolation in my power . . . Even during this contagious disease the Indians retained their old custom of giving a last abode to the dead by placing the body, wrapped in a blanket or buffalo robe, on scaffolds raised eight or ten feet above the plain. They left them thus exposed to the burning heat of a July sun . . . The pestilential exhalations of these corpses infected the air for miles around."

Fort Union, at the junction of the Missouri and the Yellowstone Rivers, was reached July 14th. Father De Smet was deeply touched by the reception he received from a number of chiefs who, having heard from Army men that he was coming up the river, were looking forward to traveling with him to the council at Fort Laramie.

XXVI

July 31, 1851, the Feast of St. Ignatius, founder of the Society of Jesus:

Thirty chiefs of the Assiniboines, Minnetarees and Crows, and two white men, left Fort Union and set out on the trip of eight hundred miles to Fort Laramie.

They took with them two four-wheeled wagons and two carts, the first ever to be driven across "this unoccupied waste. There is not the slightest vestige of a beaten track between Fort Union and the Red Buttes, which are on the route to Oregon [Oregon Trail], and 161 miles west of Fort Laramie."

The white men were Father De Smet and Alexander Culbertson, chief factor of the American Fur Company on the upper Missouri, "a distinguished man, endowed with a mild, benevolent and charitable temper, though if need be intrepid and courageous," who was in command of the little expedition.

The route was toward the southwest, and the first destination was Fort Alexander, on the Yellowstone at the mouth of Tongue River.

August 1: At six o'clock in the morning the start was made. All through the day they watched for a sign that would warn them of the Blackfeet. The mosquitoes were an unending torment. Horses and mules were "literally covered with them." The men wore gloves and covered their heads with "sacks formed of coarse gauze." It was a "rich and beautiful country." In the lowlands and small valleys the grass was lush. There grew the wild plums, cherries, gooseberries. The "breadroot would deserve a place in a garden of choice plants." There were many "nourishing roots," and immense blankets of wild flowers.

August 3: Immense herds of buffalo were sighted. The torturous mosquitoes were gone. When Father De Smet inquired the reason for this seeming phenomenon, an Indian explained that the buffalo attracted them. As they began their perilous passage through the herds the truth of the explanation was demonstrated. They saw "these noble animals throwing the earth over their bodies by means of their horns and feet, or rolling themselves in the sand and dust, and thus filling the air with clouds, in an endeavor to rid themselves of their vexatious followers . . . During a whole week we heard their bellowings like the noise of distant thunder, or like the murmurs of ocean waves beating against the distant shore."

Father De Smet heard more about the region called Colter's Hell° by people in St. Louis, and he would have liked to go to it, but time and duty prevented the detour. He made copious notes about it, however, preparing an account that confirmed the fantastic tales the celebrated mountain man, John Colter, had told.

Colter had discovered the weird land, but no one believed his reports of seeing geysers and painted hot springs, mountains of sulphur and cliffs of obsidian. So carefully did Father De Smet question the Indians that he was able to prepare remarkably accurate maps of the region. He called it the "most extraordinary . . . and perhaps the most marvelous of all the northern half of this continent." It is "in the very heart of the Rocky Mountains, between the 43d and 45th degrees of latitude and the 109th and 111th degrees of longitude, that is, between the sources of the Madison and the Yellowstone."

His maps showed features which were not to become familiar to the world for many years: Gardiner River, Mammoth Hot Springs, Yellowstone Lake, the Great Falls of the Yellowstone and the canyon below them, Firehole River, various areas of hot springs, Jackson Lake, the Teton Mountains, Two-Ocean Pass, Atlantic and Pacific Creeks, and many other scenic and geographical wonders.

° One day to be known as Yellowstone National Park.

August 9: ". . . we were witnesses to a singularly beautiful phenomenon. The moon was surrounded by four circles; the first was of a beautiful azure, the second a rich purple, and the third white, while the fourth was obscure or black. In the midst of all these circles the queen of night shone brilliantly. The savages augured from this sign that some hostile band was near, and passed the whole night under arms, watching."

August 10: Numerous rattlesnakes were encountered, and Father De Smet learned of a remarkable antidote to the poisonous bite of them. It was called *blackroot*. "The plant has a very handsome flower, red and purple . . . It stands one or two feet above the soil; it has a long, slender, fibrous and blackish root. All that is needful is to chew the root (either fresh or dried) with the teeth, and to apply the saliva to the part bitten by the reptile. Immediately the subtile poison loses its force and the inflammation stops and subsides."

August 11: Fort Alexander on the Yellowstone was reached. About two hundred miles had been covered in twelve days. The men welcomed a rest while waiting the arrival of an American Fur Company bateau which was bringing supplies up the river to them.

August 17: The journey was resumed up the valley of Rosebud Creek.†

For four days they pushed up the twisting little stream, traveling more than a hundred miles. In the Little Wolf Mountains they came upon signs of a Blackfoot war party, and doubled their vigilance. The buffalo were less numerous, but they "perceived at every moment large troops of elk, and a great many deer and mountain sheep."

Suddenly they saw ahead a "beautiful chief's coat of scarlet cloth, trimmed with gold lace, suspended from the branch of a tree . . . waving in the air like a floating banner. There was a

† This part of the route was followed by Custer on his ride to disaster on the Little Big Horn, twenty-five years later.

race to win the prize; an Assiniboine having carried it off, it was most carefully scrutinized. The conclusion was that it had been offered only the day before by some Blackfoot chief. These Indians, when on the warpath, frequently make such offerings either to the sun or to the moon, hoping thus to render them propitious, so that through their intervention they may obtain many scalps and horses. The most precious objects which they possess . . . are often thus sacrificed. The Mandans, the Arikaras, and their neighbors go still further: they cut off fingers . . . On my last visit to the Arikaras, Minnetarees and Mandans I could not discern a single man . . . whose body was not mutilated, or who possessed his full number of fingers."

August 22: They left the headwaters of the Rosebud, crossed a chain of mountains, and descended into the valley of Tongue River. They broke a wagon trail up the Tongue, and ahead of them, toward the southwest, stood the great peaks of the Big Horn Mountains.

August 25: "We arrived quite unexpectedly on the borders of a lovely little lake about six miles long, and my traveling companions gave it my name. There our hunters killed several wild ducks."‡

August 27: Another divide was crossed, and they came into the valley of the upper Powder River, and turned up it.

With the Pumpkin Buttes in sight, landmarks visible for many miles, they met three Crow Indians from whom they received false information that brought them several days of unnecessary hardship. "These young men advised us to pursue the vale of a little river which they pointed out to us, assuring us that by taking that direction we should soon arrive in Fort Laramie. I was surprised at this counsel, for the course of the valley was southwest; however, we followed the route . . .

"This proved to be the most rugged and difficult part of our journey, hence we styled it 'the valley of a thousand miseries.'"

‡ Lake De Smet became part of an irrigation project.

The little river dried up, and two nights were spent without water.

September 2: They came in sight of the Red Buttes.§ They then understood that the route recommended by the Crows had taken them away from their destination. Had they followed their intended route, the Red Buttes would have been a considerable distance to the west of them when they reached the Oregon Trail.

Along the North Platte River ran "the Great Route to Oregon over which, like successive ocean surges, the caravans, composed of thousands of emigrants from every country and clime, have passed during these latter years to reach the rich gold mines of California, or to take possession of the new lands in the fertile plains and valleys of Utah and Oregon."

Father De Smet called it "the broadest, longest and most beautiful road in the whole world."

He was amused by the astonishment of his Indian companions at the sight of it. Having "never seen but the narrow hunting paths by which they transport themselves and their lodges . . . they were filled with admiration on seeing this noble highway, which is as smooth as a barn floor swept by the winds, and not a blade of grass can shoot on it on account of the continual passing [of the wagon trains]."

The Indians "conceived a high idea of the countless White Nation . . . They fancied that all had gone over that road, and that an immense void must exist in the land of the rising sun. Their countenances testified evident incredulity when I told them that their [the emigrants'] exit was in no wise perceived in the land of the whites. They styled the route the Great Medicine Road of the Whites.¶ They visited and examined in detail all the forsaken camping grounds on the way; they brought a great variety of objects to me to have their use and significance

§ Near the present city of Casper, Wyoming.
¶ The term "medicine" was used by Indians to describe whatever they found mysterious and incomprehensible.

explained; they filled their pouches with knives, forks, spoons, basins, coffee-pots and other cooking articles, axes, hammers, etc. With bits of earthenware which bore any figure or inscription, they fabricated some ornament for their necks and ears. How wonderful will be the accounts given of the Great Medicine Road by our unsophisticated Indians when they go back to their villages . . . !"

September 10: Approaching Fort Laramie they were surprised to see numerous large campsites which recently had been abandoned. At the fort they found only a small military contingent on guard duty. They were informed that the site of the Great Council had been moved some thirty miles eastward to Horse Creek.

The change had been ordered by Superintendent Mitchell for very good reasons. Since early in August bands of Ogallala and Brule Sioux, Cheyennes, Arapahoes, Assiniboines, Arikaras, Minnetarees, Crows and others had been arriving and had set up villages near the fort.

By September 1, more than ten thousand Indian men, women and children, some twenty thousand horses, and uncounted thousands of dogs were crowded on the plain on each side of Fort Laramie. Scores of traders had come in with their wagons heavily loaded with merchandise to take advantage of an unprecedented opportunity. Soldiers and Indian Bureau officials made strenuous efforts to prevent the sale of rotgut whiskey, but it was surreptitiously dispensed in small cups at exorbitant prices, although the traders were careful not to let an Indian have more than they thought he could handle.

Horse trading went on continuously, as did racing and wild dancing. The great babble, the neighing, the barking and the drums never ceased. The enormous herds had soon consumed the grass for miles in each direction, leaving a scarred and desolate prairie from which blew great clouds of blinding, choking dust. The foul smell which rose from the camps was becoming more than the two hundred dragoons and the civilians quartered in the fort could endure. No breeze that blew night or day could bring relief, for the filth and refuse spread in an unbroken circle around the post.

A great train of some hundred wagons carrying supplies, food-stuffs and gifts had been scheduled to arrive before the beginning of the council. It did not come. Indian tempers were growing short. Fights and quarrels were increasing in frequency. Two official interpreters, John Poisal and Blackfoot John Smith, expressed the fear that major trouble was brewing. Guard lines were strengthened.

The arrival of Superintendent Mitchell and his colleagues decreased the danger of an outbreak of uncontrollable violence. But not for long. Mitchell brought the aggravating news that the Army had bungled things, and the wagon train had been several days late in leaving Westport Landing. Thomas L. Fitzpatrick, the noted plainsman and guide, was assigned to explain the situation to the chiefs in the various camps.

The announcement was not well received, but Fitzpatrick believed he had placated the complainers, and induced them to preserve the truce to which they had agreed for at least a few more days, by which time it was believed the gifts would have arrived.

This optimistic outlook was quickly destroyed. Word was received that Jim Bridger had called together the Shoshones, enemies of virtually all tribes present, and they were approaching in force under the famed Chief Washakie. Two Shoshone warriors already had been killed en route to the council by some wandering Cheyennes. The Shoshones undoubtedly would seek revenge. A slaughter might well take place.

Interpreters, Indian agents and the military prepared for the worst. When the Shoshones were sighted, a bugle sounded, and the dragoons, augmented by a military escort which had accompanied Mitchell, wheeled into line.

This show of armed strength had the desired effect. Taunts

and insulting remarks were shouted at Washakie and his braves, hatchets were brandished, and there was some brief scuffling between agents and a few individuals who tried to start an attack. The agents won.

Washakie led his warriors, numbering less than a hundred, all of whom were arrayed in their most brilliant trappings, on a colorful parade before the line of dragoons and the frightened officials, performing several complicated maneuvers with amazing precision, then rode on to the campground assigned to them. The dangerous situation ended.

After a quick conference with other officials and the military commander, Mitchell had ordered the council moved to Horse Creek, where fresh grass was available.

September 11: Father De Smet received "a polite invitation" to ride with Robert Campbell in his fine carriage to Horse Creek. Campbell, an Irishman, had emigrated to St. Louis in 1824. He had become associated with General William Ashley in the fur trade, and had spent years in the Rocky Mountains. Returning to St. Louis he had become a leading businessman and banker. Because of his remarkable knowledge of Indians and his diplomatic talent he was frequently called upon by the federal government to participate in treaty negotiations and to handle other Indian problems.

Arriving at the Indian Bureau headquarters on Horse Creek about sunset, Father De Smet found that Mitchell had set up a large tent for him in which he might live and conduct his religious ceremonies. He was to be a guest at Mitchell's table during the council.

Although the wagon train had not arrived, the smoke was officially opened the next day, September 12th.

It was the largest gathering of Indians which had ever taken place.* Along the plain bordering Horse Creek stood the lodges of more than ten thousand red people from a dozen major na-

---

* The largest in the entire history of the West.

tions. The smoke of thousands of campfires threw a haze over the area. Following the daily talks, the deep-throated drums sounded through each night, and the chants and wild yells of dancers mocked the howls of coyotes and wolves under the prairie stars.

XXVII

Four days passed with the great smoke going on at Horse Creek, but no Army wagons appeared. Food was running out, and Fort Laramie had none to send. All game animals had vanished from the surrounding country. The stench from the campgrounds had become so terrible that troops and officials moved their camp more than two miles up the creek where, at least at night, they could escape it. The Indians were slaughtering their dogs to supplement their swiftly vanishing rations. Great hunger was imminent.

"No epoch in Indian annals," said Father De Smet, "probably, shows a greater massacre of the canine race."

The long-awaited wagon train came in sight on September 18th. As swiftly as possible the food was distributed. A catastrophe had been narrowly averted.

Even though countless lodges were without meat, and many had nothing at all to eat, there were no disorders during the distribution of the supplies. The Indians took "the respective places assigned to each particular band, thus forming an immense circle, covering several acres of land."

The gifts were passed out next, and "the great chiefs of the different nations were served first, and received suits of clothes . . . and were for the first time in their lives pantalooned . . . each was arrayed in a general's uniform, a gilt sword hanging at his side. Their long coarse hair floated above the military costume, and the whole was crowned by the burlesque solemnity of their painted faces. The conduct of this vast multitude was calm and respectful."

Throughout the council, Father De Smet worked until he

neared exhaustion. He not only attended the negotiations during the day, but spent every other available daylight hour salvaging as many souls as he could. The shadow of darkness would come soon enough for the Indians, but the light of God would shine forever. By the last day of the council he had baptized nearly a thousand children—305 Arapahoes, 253 Cheyennes, 280 Sioux, and between 60 and 80 of mixed white and red blood.

Fortunately the crude marks of the chiefs had been affixed to the treaty beside the signatures of the government negotiators when the immense camp was electrified by word that a large buffalo herd was not far away.

Pandemonium reigned as the lodges fell and preparations were made for the hunt. Government rations were all right, but nothing satisfied hunger like a buffalo tongue or a roast of hump. Across the plain streamed long lines of Indians, vanishing into the sky. Here and there could be seen a "general" brandishing a sword in the bright fall sunlight. The council had ended.

Like almost all treaties between Indians and the government of the United States, the treaty negotiated on Horse Creek in September, 1851, was ambiguous and lacking in essential provisions. It was, like those signed before it and those signed after it, only as good as the agencies allegedly obligated to carry it out. It could be beneficial only through rigid enforcement, but if any serious thought was given to this phase of the matter by responsible officials in Washington, they never revealed it.

The government got what it wanted: time. It appeared that the government thought that by getting the Indians to agree not to attack caravans and westward-moving settlers and miners for even a brief period the whole problem would somehow evaporate into the thin air of the western plains. As for the Indians, they, too, thought they had gotten what they wanted: preservation of the hunting grounds they must have to exist.

In the end, therefore, both sides left the meeting generally satisfied. The tragedies soon to come were not the product of words, nor of grandiose dreams propounded in colorful oratory.

They were the bitter fruit of reality, a reality that need not have been faced had the sovereign government kept its pledges. Washington looked upon the paper which came back to it from Horse Creek as nothing more than another worthless and meaningless document, and tossed it onto the mounting pile of other pacts and agreements signed by the people who were a nuisance to progress. Integrity and honor were, after all, relative things, not to be taken too seriously when it came to dealing with savages, and not to be permitted to interrupt political programs and the development of the American economy.

Father De Smet knew the truth of things. For two decades he had watched the Indians being destroyed in the Missouri Valley. He had witnessed the corruption and cruelty of Washington bureaucracy. He was not naïve, and he knew that to believe that the Indians of the Great Plains and mountains would receive any better treatment than those of the middle country had received would have been deluding himself, blinding himself with irresponsible reasoning.

Both his black robe and his position, however, precluded him from disclosing all the thoughts in his mind. He was a man who had dedicated his life to the service of God. He was not a politician, nor was he an official. But he was an apostle of peace, and for that cause he might work openly and without limit. That was his role as he saw it at the council, and he played it to the best of his ability, submerging his misgivings under his prayers to God to inspire both red men and white to follow the paths of righteousness.

The treaty, which had been prepared in Washington, probably by State Department lawyers who had never seen a wild Indian, was read "sentence by sentence, and distinctly explained to the different interpreters, that they might have the exact and legitimate meaning of each article."

As far as the government was concerned, the first article was the most important. Enormous territories embracing some 150,000 to 200,000 square miles of plains and mountains were designated as "Indian Country," and awarded in perpetuity to the various tribes. But Article One specified as well that the Indians recognized the right of the federal government to lay out roads and establish military posts wherever it chose in this vast area. That provision alone kept the door open for whites to invade Indian hunting grounds.

Under Article Two the Indians promised to maintain peace and to pay for losses they inflicted on white persons. How these payments were to be collected not even the schemers on the banks of the Potomac knew. But that did not matter.

As a sop to justice, the government agreed in Article Three to indemnify the Indians for damage caused in their hunting grounds by "travelers" from the States who crossed their lands— "travelers," not settlers who took their lands. A small matter, because $50,000 was to be given to the Indians at once, and that certainly would pay for all damage white travelers might cause. The whole Indian Country was hardly worth that much.

The generosity of the government would not end there, however. Under Article Four, $50,000 would be paid to the Indians annually for fifteen years.

The door to invasion was far from closed. Mitchell, Fitzpatrick and Campbell understood that, but they could do no more than present what had been given to them by Washington, and hope that even a brief period of peace might open the way to a better solution of the great problem.

Father De Smet expressed the belief that some good results would ensue, but there was little doubt that he was speaking mainly for the record, forcing himself to indulge in a bit of wishful thinking. Perhaps he thought that such a statement coming from him might have a salutary influence. Most likely he did not, for later statements he made demonstrated that he was far from convinced that a new era of peace would come to pass on the western plains. But hope was all he could do—hope and pray.

It was on the twenty-fourth of September when he set out with the government officials and their escort on the overland journey to the Middle West. At Ash Hollow the company turned from the North Platte and rode southward through a beautiful rolling country fifteen miles to the South Platte. There they met Prince Paul of Württemberg en route to hunt in the Wind River Mountains. A world-famous sportsman, the prince had wandered over a large part of the western wilderness, and he was writing an account of his adventures. *

Father De Smet was astonished to find that the prince was accompanied only by a single Prussian officer, and he thought "His Excellency must be indeed courageous, to undertake at his age so long a journey in such a wilderness, with but one man as suite, and in a wretched little open wagon . . . I learned the prince intends to choose a location suited to agriculture, for the purpose of founding a German colony."

Fort Kearney was reached October 2. With a company led by Fitzpatrick, Father De Smet turned away from the Oregon Trail and followed a route which would take him to the valley of the Kansas River.

He reached Kansas City October 15 and boarded a steamer for St. Louis, where he arrived seven days later. Sad news awaited him. Father-Provincial Jean Elet was dead.

He could look back through thirty years to the summer of 1821, when six frightened and homesick novices had started across the Atlantic to give their lives to God in an unknown wilderness. Probably no man had been a closer friend to him in all that time than Jean Elet.

As he reviewed the year of 1851, despite the deaths of Father Hoeken and Father Elet, he could feel gratified. He wrote a colleague: ". . . kind Providence has watched over me. I escaped from a dangerous illness, from the attacks of wild beasts and enemies, from the smallpox and the cholera. I passed through a

---

* A brother of King William I of Württemberg, the prince died the following year at the age of sixty-seven. At sixty-six his health and physical condition were so good that he was able to engage in the most strenuous hunting, such as the chase of the buffalo.

camp where people were dying and rottening. Alive, unhurt and untouched. I slept among the dying and dead for over a month, handling and attending on the cholera patients, and returned safe and sound. I had the happiness to place the holy waters of baptism on the foreheads of 1586 children and adults . . ."

Probably one of the most satisfying, and at the same time most saddening, events of the year was the letter he received in St. Louis from The Bear, chief of the Assiniboines. He sent translations to several friends and editors.

The letter was addressed "To the Medicine Man of the White Nation." It said:

"I was so happy as to become acquainted with you at Fort Union, in the summer of 1851; but I was then ignorant in a great degree of the motives of your visit among us, and hence I could not discover to you my inmost feelings and explain to you my thoughts.

"At Fort Union you preached to us, telling us of the Great Spirit and His law. You said you would like to come and teach us . . . I think also, that you gave us reason to expect that after two or three winters some Black-gowns would come and establish themselves among us, in order to show us how to live well and to train up our children . . . since my return from Fort Laramie I have [thought] much of the beautiful word of the Great Spirit, which you first made known to us. Now I am persuaded that this word would change our state and render us happy. At the Great Council [Colonel Mitchell] told us that some Black-gowns would come and live among us in the course of four or five years.

"Black-gown, five years are long to wait. In this long interval I and many of my children may have entered the land of spirits. Take pity on us. The Black-gowns ought not to delay their coming so long. I am growing old: before I die I should like to begin the work, and then I could depart satisfied . . .

"All my nation call loud for the Black-gown . . . [If money is needed] I will cheerfully give a portion of the annuities of my tribe to meet this deficiency.

"Do this, Black-robe, at the request of your friend."

Father De Smet's satisfaction was overshadowed by the knowledge that he could not go, nor would the plea be granted, and he wept.

XXVIII

No man in the Society had known and understood Father De Smet better than Father Elet. No man had known better his value to the Church, not only as the most successful and influential missionary to the Indians who had ever gone into the West, but as a diplomat and ambassador.

Father Elet was fully aware that Father De Smet's greatest desire in life was to spend the remainder of his years among the tribes of the mountains. Perhaps nothing would have given him more pleasure than to grant that wish for his old and dear friend, but to do it would have troubled his conscience. Father De Smet had opened the way for the mission program, and he had established for the Black Robes a foundation constructed of trust, sincerity and respect that was indestructible, and on which other capable men could and would build.

Loyalty to the Church and the Society superseded all other considerations in Father Elet, and in the last year of his life, weighing and judging the components of the matter involving Father De Smet, he found that he must reject the fondest wishes of his old brother and companion. The best interests of the Church would let him do nothing else.

He devised a plan under which Father De Smet would be sent throughout the United States and Europe—if not the whole world —for the purpose of disseminating information about the struggle of the Jesuits in the western wilderness, securing both moral and financial support for their programs, and serving as a kind of roving ambassador-at-large for the Society.

Father Elet was not merely assuming that Father De Smet would be successful as procurator of the vice-province of Missouri. He had precedents to support his decision. Father De Smet had demonstrated his talents in such work. Moreover, he was acclaimed on two continents for his feats of exploration, his religious accomplishments, and his writings about the Indians.

Father Elet had submitted his plan to the Father-General, and it had been approved. Father De Smet knew nothing of it until he returned to St. Louis in the fall of 1851. Father Elet was then in his grave.

Several of the missionaries serving among the Indians registered their disappointment when they learned that, apparently, Father De Smet's days in the mountains had been brought to an end by the decree, but Father De Smet himself displayed an attitude that gave no indication of the sadness in his heart. "Insofar as this plan regards me," he told a friend, "I will speak openly to you. I have nothing whatever to do with their choice, nor with the adoption of the plan. I affirm, nevertheless, that I am ready to execute in all things the will of my superiors. I will even admit to you, that in my secret soul, and after mature reflection and much prayer, I desire that the plan should be accomplished; and for the sole reason that I would be glad to spend the few years that remain to me, should the Lord grant me any, in the strict observance and practice of all our holy rules, and in perfect submission to the orders of my superiors. I feel the need of it, after having passed so many years in these remote American missions."

That was not, of course, an accurate statement. This truth was amply illustrated in later letters.

Father De Smet was a celebrated person, and as such he was the target, not only of enemies of the Church, but of petty and jealous men within it. He was sometimes blamed for incidents of which he had no knowledge. He was unjustly attacked, maligned without supporting evidence.

For all his courage and fearlessness, Father De Smet was a sensitive man. He was easily hurt by unfounded criticism, pained by the realization that persons for whom he harbored no ill will would attempt to injure him. Bishop Van De Velde of Baltimore had more than once counseled him not to be "too easily affected and dejected" when unfair things were said against him, but it was not his nature to dismiss such charges with a shrug, to philosophize that "the bigger the man the bigger the target."

Feeling "low, indeed," he wrote Bishop Van De Velde that he had been accused: "First. That my letters have done a great deal of harm in America. Second. That my letters are only imagination and poetry, false and untrue. Third. That I have lost the missions by overliberality to the Indians, and by promises to them, which the Fathers have been unable to fulfill."

He pointed out that letters written by a succession of missionaries in Oregon after he had left there showed the good state of the Indians, and were "sufficient to cover calumniators with shame and confusion."

He remarked that he had sent many of these letters "to Rome in the very handwriting of those Fathers, and culled others from newspapers . . . but all to which no answer has been returned."

As for his own letters, all had been "written by special requests of my superiors, chiefly the Very Reverend Father-General. I declare to have written them all with uprightness and sincerity, and that I have never exaggerated, at least not willfully . . ."

It was in a series of letters that he revealed his true feelings about being named procurator. He told Bishop Van De Velde: ". . . it will be a struggle for me to leave America, with many dear brethren and many happy recollections."

He sent a fond message to The Bear through his friend, the trader among the Assiniboines, Edwin T. Denig, speaking of the Indians as "the unfortunate race of human beings, toward the amelioration of whose sad condition I have in some measure contributed and am still anxious to contribute whatever I possibly can."

How really great was his hope that his assignment in civilization would soon terminate was disclosed in Belgium in a letter to C. D. Stas, editor of a Brussels newspaper: "Providence has supported my feeble courage . . . I saw what could be done among these wandering tribes . . . With the grace of God I hope to return next spring with Bishop Miege, the vicar-apostolic. We will be able to found missions for those nomad tribes on a soil fertile enough to support them, and thus remove occasions of war . . . let the light of faith dawn on these wastes."

To a friend in Utica, New York, he wrote: "My heart, I must acknowledge, remains still with the Indians . . . and I fervently pray, if it be God's will, to be allowed to pass the remainder of my days in the Far West."

Presents came to St. Louis for him from a trader among the Crows, and in returning his "sincere thanks" for them he asked to be remembered to his Crow friends and that they be assured "that they are not forgotten in my heart and mind and that I long to visit them once more. When this shall be I am not able, at present, to tell you. Should I receive good news in the course of this fall [1852] . . . I will let you know."

The passage of years did not diminish his great hope of returning—always in the coming spring—to the mountains. In 1854 he again wrote Denig: "Nothing . . . could come nearer to my heart than to be again employed in the midst of the Indians and to spend all my time for their spiritual and temporal welfare. The several years I passed among them I call the happiest of my life . . ."

In 1856 he wrote Joseph Rolette, the trader at Fort Union: "I have little doubt that in the course of the next spring either myself or some other Black Robe of my friends will leave St. Louis for the upper Missouri . . ."

The dream was as strong in 1858, when once more he told Denig: "If I can possibly do it I will make another trip to the plains and visit the various Indian tribes early in the spring . . . Most willingly would I spend the remainder of my days [there]."

In the years between his return from the Great Council of 1851 and the spring of 1858, Father De Smet had few idle moments. There was seldom a time when he was not traveling, or

274

preparing to travel, in the United States, France, Belgium, England, Ireland, Germany and Holland. Yet, he never failed to keep up a heavy correspondence with friends in the West, and he prepared numerous papers for publication in which he told of the customs of the Indians and described the western country. Of course, true to his prescribed duties, he never failed to stress the need for more money, more priests, more missions and more supplies for the western outposts of the Society.

"I come for alms," he told people of high and low station wherever he went. There was no reticence in his pleas, and he drove himself relentlessly in his work, but he did not hesitate to complain of the arduousness of his task nor did he attempt to conceal the frustrations he suffered.

Passing through Washington in the spring of 1853, he was received by President Franklin Pierce. The newly inaugurated Chief Executive obviously was impressed by the famed Indian missionary. Father De Smet did not say as much for Mr. Pierce, merely mentioning that "we were kindly entertained by His Excellency."

Representative Thomas Hart Benton of Missouri, the former senator, escorted Father De Smet to the White House. Secretary of State William L. Marcy also was present at the meeting. Following a talk in which Mr. Pierce asked numerous questions about the Indians, the President requested him to be the "bearer of dispatches to various Ministers" in several European capitals. Father De Smet accepted the assignment. The nature of the dispatches was not disclosed.

At the time of Father De Smet's appointment as procurator his health was far from good, and he admitted that for two or three years he had been "sensibly on the decline." His eyesight was failing, and he was troubled by afflictions which seemed to take his strength, but which the doctors he consulted were unable to diagnose.

During the next few years, however, he enjoyed a noticeable

improvement, and in 1856 he was able to state that "for years I have not been compelled to have recourse to a physician."

Once in apologizing for failing to reply promptly to a correspondent in Europe, he said bluntly: ". . . for the last few years I have been worked to death, and have had frequent and long journeys to make."

"In a temporal way," he told an Army friend, "the Fathers are sorely pinched and they sent me long lists of objects that are much needed. I am sorry that our private means in St. Louis, owing to the hard times, are in a condition that we are unable to relieve them fully."

The poverty of the vice-province of Missouri was shown by his statement that "two thousand dollars would hardly buy" what the western missionaries were requesting. "I shall do what I can," he added grimly.

"I am now in Ohio, now in Kentucky, now . . . in Missouri. Our colleges, residences and missions are far apart, and I have to go with the Father-Provincial in all his visits," he wrote a friend in 1854. ". . . one thing . . . gives me anxiety from time to time. I hold the general or common purse and have to supply all needs; *and this purse is never full; the greater part of the time it is flat . . .*"

XXIX

Having come to know the terrible slums of eastern cities into which helpless immigrants were driven after their arrival in "the promised land," Father De Smet sought to discourage poor people from coming to America. He also advised against their emigration to the Far West, because of the inescapable perils and hardships of that country. Moreover, the high plains and mountains were not places for foreigners to settle, for the destruction of the Indians' hunting grounds and the cruelties inflicted on them by both the government and American settlers were leading the nation down the road to ghastly wars between red men and white.

He received numerous letters from people he had never met requesting advice about settling in the West. "I have never taken it upon me to encourage anyone to undertake the journey," he told George Thompson of Chapel Hill, Ohio, in a reply typical of many others. "The richness of the lands in general, with all the other advantages connected with it, are much greater here [the Middlewest] than there."

Writing a nephew, Francis, he remarked that because of the failure of three St. Louis banks there "will be a great panic in the city, where thousands of inhabitants will find themselves ruined at a blow. But this will not prevent the railroad to the Pacific from being begun.

"It is a strange people in the midst of whom we live. Nothing frightens them; they will undertake anything. Sometimes they halt—stumble once in a while—but they get up and march onward.

"Several great new territories are about to be formed in the

277

Indian Country, and soon the steam engine will go out and give a shock to the buffalo and the bear . . . and the poor unhappy savages, what will become of them? They will no doubt be turned out and pushed back anew, farther into the sterile regions, where they will find only misery and death."*

The creation of the new territories brought from him some "mournful reflections." Why was it, he demanded, "that the European race refuses so obstinately to sympathize with the red race; and notwithstanding its philosophy, or love of mankind, seems rather disposed to annihilate than to civilize these poor children, offspring of the same Father? Whence springs that insurmountable barrier between the two races? Whence is it that the stronger pursues the weaker with such an animosity, and never relents until the latter is overthrown? There is involved in this, perhaps, a secret that none but the Judge Supreme can explain."

Under the administration of President Pierce, "the whole vast Indian Country within the Rocky Mountains . . . has been organized into two territories, known under the names of Kansas and Nebraska; that is to say, the Congress has decreed that this country is incorporated into the Union and open to the whites who are willing to settle there . . . Although for the moment, the new colonists have orders to respect the territories or the lands reserved to the savages, we may nevertheless say that the decree has virtually destroyed all the Indian nationalities.

"Scarcely was the law known when the emigrants, like the waters of a great river which had overflowed its banks, impetuously passed the barrier and inundated the country. Now see the poor Indians surrounded by white men, and their reserves forming little more than islets amid the ocean. The savages who before had vast countries for their hunting grounds are at present restricted within narrow limits, having naught for subsistence but

---

* Plans for a transcontinental railroad advanced by President Pierce in 1853 fell through. The Gadsden Purchase was made, but the Kansas-Nebraska Bill brought on explosive sectional difficulties.

the product of their farms, which few of them know how to culti-
vate properly. Again this state is only precarious. Unless they
hasten to divide their lands and become citizens, they are in
danger of losing all, and of being naught but vagabonds.

"How replete with difficulties is such a change! What a stormy
and tempestuous future for these unfortunate tribes! The evil is
great, but it is one that must be encountered, since there is no
remedy. The Indians, even the most advanced in civilization,
seem to us ill-prepared to meet all the exigencies of the situation."

Father De Smet believed that only Divine Providence could
prevent a catastrophe, for "imagine two societies—one represent-
ing the manners and customs of barbarians, the other all the
splendor of modern civilization—coming in contact. How many
years will elapse before there will be a perfect fusion between
the two societies, before unison will exist, before they can dwell
together in complete harmony?

"Not the first, not the second, not the third generation, notwithstanding untiring efforts, would obtain that happy result . . .

". . . the civilized society will have the advantage over the
barbarous; it will have it entirely at its mercy, to make it sub-
servient to its will and pleasure.

". . . the barbarian can no better sustain itself in the presence
of civilization than the simplicity of childhood can contest against
the malicious prudence of mature age."

He felt that it was "not difficult to descry from afar that grand
event which must engulf in one common wreck all the Indian
tribes . . . We saw the American Republic soaring, with the
rapidity of the eagle's flight, toward the plenitude of her power.
Every year she adds new countries to her limits."

Western Indians were being allotted "reservations . . . but although the letter of the treaty guarantees them such 'reservations,' you may rest assured that as soon as the supposed necessities of a thriving white population demand these lands, the
whites will find pretexts for dispossessing the Indians."

Taking Oregon as an example, he pointed out that when it

took its place as a state of the Union, "she will follow the same policy that has been hitherto followed by the other states; that is, she will subject all the inhabitants to her jurisdiction and laws.

"The policy of the United States has ever been to remove the Indians from each new state as soon as it is admitted . . . in case portions of the tribe remain on their lands, as was the case in the states of New York, Indiana, Michigan and Ohio, the situation of the Indians is extremely disagreeable, their progress very slow . . .

"When the lands of the Indians cease to be valuable, and the white can do without them, then only will the Indian enjoy the privilege of retaining them."

Father De Smet was frequently infuriated by the stupidity with which the Army and law enforcement officers bungled situations which might well have been settled by the application of a small amount of justice and a sprinkling of common sense.

The Grattan Massacre in 1854, for example, brought from him a statement excoriating the ineptness of Army officers in the handling of controversies that might easily have been amicably settled.

Two thousand Indians had assembled at the "appointed spot at the time fixed by the government agent to receive their annuities and gifts. They waited several days for the commissioner to arrive and in the meantime they ran out of provisions.

"Then a Mormon wagon train, on its way to the territory of Utah, came peaceably by the Indian camp. One of the party was dragging after him a lame cow hardly able to walk. A famished savage, out of pity for his wife and children, and perhaps, also, from compassion for the suffering animal, killed the cow and offered the Mormon double value for it in a horse or mule.

". . . the Mormon refused . . . and filed a complaint with the commandant at Fort Laramie.

". . . the illustrious commandant straightway sent out a young officer [Lieutenant Grattan] with twenty soldiers armed to the teeth and with a cannon loaded with grapeshot. He was absolutely determined to capture the so-called robber and make an example of him."

The Indians were astonished at the menacing turn, and offered the Morman three horses for the dead cow, which had been eaten. The officer was inflexible. When the Indians refused to identify the man who had shot the cow, the cannon was fired into their midst. A number of Indians were killed and wounded. They retaliated by wiping out the contingent of twenty soldiers and Grattan.

"Will you believe this tale of a cow?" Father De Smet demanded.

As a result of the unnecessary fight, "the grand and glorious Republic is going to appear on the stage of the great Indian desert to give a representation of the lovely fable of La Fontaine —always old and always new—of the wolf and the lamb. The moral is, 'The wicked and the strong always find plenty of pretexts to oppress the innocent and the weak; and when they lack good reasons they have recourse to lies and calumnies.'"

The "affair of the cow is the origin of a fresh war of extermination upon the Indians . . . An army is being got ready in Missouri . . . A very large number of whites will lose their lives without a doubt, but in the end the savages will have to yield . . ."†

Some persons thought that interbreeding, the absorption of the red by the white race, would solve the problem, but others expressed the belief that such a thing could be undertaken only after Indians had been educated in white schools, and had adopted the ways and mores of the whites.

Father De Smet thought that what such persons were really saying was that the problem would be solved after the last pure-

† Many Indians and soldiers did lose their lives in the ensuing campaign to punish Indians who had defended themselves when attacked without warning by a stupid officer . . . all because of the death of a lame cow for which triple compensation had been proffered by Indians who were hungry.

blood Indian had vanished from the earth. Neither time nor the conditions would permit the successful intermingling of the two bloods, for the Indians were surrounded "by whites who condemn them, hate them, and who will demoralize them in a very short time . . . With each successive emigration, they find their grounds restricted . . .

"Yet in all the treaties the agents promise them, on the part of the President . . . protection and privileges that are never realized."

It was not strange that the Indians gave to government agents the name of "forked tongues," or that they said the whites "walk in crooked paths to attain their objects," or that the declarations of friendship proclaimed by the whites, "all beautiful and favorable as they appear, never entered their hearts."

He cited the words of Black Hawk: "The very contact of the whites has poisoned us."

Father De Smet's tenure as procurator came at a time when the strongest and most bitter attack in American history was launched against the Catholic Church. His travels took him into the centers of the severest conflicts. It was a condition obviously which did not help him in his efforts to obtain funds for the western missions.

He wrote numerous letters about the situation, a number of which found their way to newspapers and other publications. It was apparent throughout them that his pride and faith in American democracy and freedom were dangerously shaken by the intolerance sweeping through the country.

"In a country which prides itself on its unbounded liberality and liberty," he told a friend, J. H. Conway, "we might have hoped that the Catholic religion, if not protected, would at least have been screened from persecution. This is no longer the case."

"The "Know-Nothing" Party inspired the attacks, "the principal aim of which appears to be, should they be able to reach it, to crush our holy religion throughout the land. The members of this secret society are bound by abominable oaths . . . It may

be said, in general, that the ministers of all the different Protestant sects belong to it; many have become notorious by exciting the rioters in various parts to burn churches; to insult
publicly priests and even religious ladies [Sisters]; they are
trying . . . to bring forward a code of anti-Catholic blue laws;
and threaten to establish inquisitorial tribunals . . ."

In eastern cities where Roman Catholic immigrants had con-
centrated and had been welcomed by Democrats, local nativistic
societies formed to combat "foreign" influences and uphold the
so-called "American" view. The "Native American Party" had
stemmed from the "American Republican Party," which had been
formed earlier in New York. In the 1850s many secret orders
grew up. All inquiries of supposed members were met with a
statement to the effect that they knew nothing, hence the name
"Know-Nothings." They sought to elect only native Americans
to office and to establish a twenty-five-year residence requirement
for citizenship.

As he traveled from city to city, Father De Smet heard "open
talk of murder and pillage. Every day the papers tell of attacks
on Catholics, especially on the Irish . . . a priest cannot appear
on the streets . . . without being insulted . . .

"American liberty and tolerance, so highly boasted, exist less
in this great republic than in the most oppressed country of
Europe. Catholic churches are burned and those who try to prevent it are assassinated.

"Mobs are the order of the day . . . Liberty in this country is
a perversion of the word; it is rather pure license which has
got the upper hand . . . The unhappy land is flooded with
crimes and misdeeds of every sort. Every honest man's heart
bleeds . . ."

Sad and shameful as the situation was, Father De Smet thought
it was not "without its better side."

"The American nation is a great, imitative people," he said in
his journal. "They cannot live without some or other great excitement . . . The present anti-Catholic excitement cannot pos-

sibly last long; other matters may soon present themselves that will attract their attention."

When the "Know-Nothing" movement was at its height, he had expressed the fear that it might prove disastrous to the Catholic Church. The fear became greater when fanatics burned convents and churches with impunity. Later he held the view that "instead of being injured, the Church will be benefitted by the warfare against it."

This change of opinion was in part based on the understanding that political parties were generally divided on religious questions. Recent state elections had shown that "know-nothingism is not all powerful." He thought it more than probable "that the majority of the American people will be found on the side of those principles with which Catholicity in this country has been identified."

At last he voiced the firm belief "that the result of this political agitation will be that . . . tens of thousands will have their prejudices removed, who, but for the present state of things, would remain enemies of the Church because ignorant of her claims."

He was correct. Toward the end of the 1850s the Know-Nothings began to disintegrate, their power failing. A greater, more exciting—and more sinister—issue occupied the minds of the American people. Religious intolerance and persecution became inconsequential under the darkening shadow of civil war.

XXX

The President is desirous to engage you to attend the Army for Utah to officiate as chaplain.

This message went out from Washington on May 13, 1858, over the signature of John B. Floyd, Secretary of War.

Father De Smet had been apprised that several Army officers had proposed him for the appointment. He had conferred with General W. S. Harney at the Planter's House in St. Louis, and had been assured that the commission would be approved by the President.

Privately Father De Smet doubted it. It seemed unreasonable to him that in view of the religious disorders in the country a Catholic would be named to serve in a campaign to quell the uprising of a religious sect.

President Buchanan obviously was not swayed in this case by either religious or political considerations. He had a job to be done . . . to put down the revolt of the Mormons in the sovereign territory of Utah. If he himself knew little about a priest named De Smet, his military advisers knew a great deal about the most influential man of the cloth in the West. General Harney and his staff were not interested in what denomination Father De Smet represented. They wanted the famed Black Robe whom the Indians revered with the troops so that they might benefit from his unsurpassed knowledge of the ways of the wilderness and of the tribes whose domains the Utah expedition must pass through.

It was a coldly practical measure on their part, but it was by no means the first time it had been attempted. During the six years Father De Smet had been kept away from the Indian Country every exploring party and scientific expedition going into the West had made an effort to obtain his services. His superiors had been adamant in their refusals to let him go, even rejecting the request of Isaac I. Stevens, who was charged by the government with finding a feasible railroad route across the north. Stevens wanted him to lead the surveyors and engineers through the country of the Blackfeet.

Secretary Floyd's letter to Father De Smet said that in the opinion of the President "your services would be important in many respects to the public interest, particularly in the present condition of our affairs in Utah. Having sought information as to the proper person to be thus employed his attention has been directed to you, and he has instructed me to address you on the subject, in the hope that you may consider it not incompatible with your clerical duties or your personal feelings to yield to his request.

"Should you conclude to accept this invitation you are requested to advise me of the fact, and proceed to the headquarters of General Smith at Leavenworth. . . ."

Father De Smet had recently returned from Leavenworth. He had gone there in an attempt to recover the body of Father Duerinck, who had been drowned in the Missouri. Father Duerinck's aunt had been the first wife of Father De Smet's father. The remains were not recovered.

Eager as he was to go out to the mountains, he was not enthusiastic about going under such circumstances, but his superiors felt he could not refuse a request from the President, and he accepted the appointment.

The chaplain's commission arrived on May 17 by telegraph, only four days after Secretary Floyd had written him. It had been sent before an answer from him had been received.

"It is indeed with the utmost diffidence in my own humble abilities," Father De Smet wrote Floyd on May 18th, "that I feel myself constrained by a sense of duty to accept a charge of such responsibility. Trusting, however, to the divine assistance, I shall endeavor faithfully to comply with the duties of the office assigned me.

"Allow me to beg the favor of you, Honorable Sir, to convey to the President my sincere thanks for the very distinguished honor which he had thought proper to confer upon me. I shall immediately make ready to repair to the headquarters of General Smith, as directed in your letter."

He abhorred the prospect of participating in a punitive campaign in which there would be bloodshed and death, but there were other aspects of the assignment which caused his spirits to rise, and he had some difficulty in restraining the enthusiasm which was stirred by plans taking shape in his mind. He was going back to the Indians!

He scolded himself a bit for his connivance, and decided that in all fairness he should refer at least briefly to the program he was contemplating. This would protect him from being admonished for deviousness when the time came for him to carry it out. His conscience was salved by the letter he got off to the Father-Provincial, which said in part: "It is probable that I shall proceed from Utah to the Flathead Mission to confer with the Fathers about a new establishment among the Blackfeet. There are fair prospects to bring it about. The government appears favorably disposed."

At one time Father De Smet had expressed an honest sympathy for the Mormons. They had been persecuted in Missouri and Illinois, murdered, robbed, and suffered the destruction of their homes and farms by persons far more fanatical than they. He had met Brigham Young, and had admired him as a courageous and able leader, and he had seen the "Saints" starting on their great trek across the plains and mountains in quest of a sanctuary beyond the borders of the United States. He had felt it a sad commentary on the American Government that the freedom to worship, so nobly proclaimed by the Constitution, was not defended and enforced in the case of this small minority.

This attitude had been changed by ensuing events. His sympathy for the Mormons died and was supplanted by condemnation. He spoke of them as "that terrible sect of modern fanatics . . . with hearts full of hate and bitterness." He charged them with never ceasing "to agitate the country, provoke the inhabitants, and commit acts of robbery and murder against many travelers and adventurers from the United States."

He offered a basis for his change of heart in statements he believed to be factual: "In September, 1857, 120 emigrants from Arkansas, men, women and children, are said to have been horribly massacred by the Mormons, in a place called the Mountain Meadows. These fanatics never ceased to defy the government, and announced that the day had arrived to avenge the death of their prophet Joseph Smith and his brother, and to retaliate the wrongs and acts of injustice and cruelty of which they pretended to be the victims . . .

"On two different occasions, the Governor and subaltern officers, sent by the President of the United States, had met with such strong opposition from the Mormons in the attempt to accomplish their respective duties, that they were forced to quit the territory of Utah, and return to lay their complaints before the President. Congress resolved to send a third Governor, accompanied, this time, by 2000 soldiers, who were to be followed by 2000 to 4000 others in the following spring of 1858."

Declaring that Brigham Young had brought disaster to his people by his rebellious acts, Father De Smet wrote, "he wishes to make Utah an independent state in the confederation. He has often declared that he will permit no one else to be Governor of Utah. The judges and other officers appointed by the general government for the civil administration of Utah have been expelled from the Territory . . . Young has set up tribunals of his own, and in the United States courts which he tolerated before his rebellion, the juries gave verdicts according to his direction."

After troops had been sent to Utah in 1857, Father De Smet said in published letters, ". . . the severity of the winter arrests them about 150 miles from the Mormon capital. The Mormons are not idle. They have surprised a train of seventy-six wagons, pillaged and burned them, carrying off all the animals . . . The loss is estimated at a million of dollars. The troops, ill-lodged and ill-fed, will suffer terribly if the winter is severe . . . As soon as the spring opens large reinforcements will be sent . . . I think that as the new forces approach the rebel territory, the Mormons will retire, after setting fire to their towns, and march to occupy some new district . . . Sonora [Mexico] perhaps . . . This fanatical sect will find repose only outside of all other civil jurisdiction.

"If the Mormons wish war, as they so loudly proclaim, they will have a chance this year, but they cannot long resist the troops of the United States."

Father De Smet reached Leavenworth in the last week of May 1858, and was immediately sworn in as chaplain by General Harney, who "bade me welcome to the Army, and assured me that I should be left perfectly free in the exercise of my holy ministry among the soldiers."

General Harney kept his word, and Father De Smet was to write that he "never met with the slightest obstacle in the discharge of my duties. The soldiers had always free access to my tent for confession and instruction."

Colonel Morrison, the second in command, a devout Protestant, became one of his closest friends, and expressed himself as being honored to have attached to his force "a representative of the ancient and venerable Church."

The march westward began on June 1. It had been six years since Father De Smet had seen the plains of Kansas, and he was amazed at the changes which had taken place. The grass sea had vanished, as if "suddenly arrested in its billows and converted into solid land," and on every side in the valley of the Kansas River were seemingly endless fields of "wheat, corn, barley, oats, flax, hemp, all sorts of garden stuff and all the fruits . . ." Supplanting the game herds were droves of "horned cattle, sheep and hogs, horses and mules." The Indian had taken the sunset road that led to oblivion. Not until the column had turned out of the valley of the Little Blue River, more than two hundred and fifty miles from Leavenworth, were the farms and settlements left behind.

They reached the Platte at Fort Kearney, which was "rather insignificant. It consists of three or four frame houses and several made of adobe . . ." A few miles from the fort a large band of Pawnees had made camp, and on the morning after Father De Smet's arrival they were attacked by forty Arapahoe warriors. "A combat more noisy than bloody took place. A young Pawnee chief was killed and three others were wounded. The Arapahoes lost one killed . . ."

When he had received word that the battle was underway, Father De Smet had left at once with an aide of General Harney in the hope of stopping it, but "all was over when we arrived; the Pawnees were returning with their dead and wounded and all the stolen horses . . . It was a harrowing scene."

In the Pawnee camp Father De Smet was pleased to find "two French Creoles, old acquaintances of mine from the Rocky Mountains." With the Frenchmen acting as interpreters he "delivered a sermon and baptized 208 children."

He was in his element once more, and he went on up the Platte eagerly anticipating more meetings with the people he so greatly loved. His next encounter was with thirty lodges of Ogallala Sioux at Cottonwood Springs, two days' travel from Fort Kearney. Some of the men in this village had attended the Great Council of 1851, and he enjoyed a reunion, although profoundly saddened to learn that Indians he had known well had been carried away by disease, an even greater enemy than the dangers of wilderness life and tribal warfare.

None of the eight hundred men in the ranks had served on the plains, although the commanding officers had been members of earlier western expeditions. Father De Smet was looked upon as a great authority, and he added to his religious curriculum the subjects of history, Indians, wild animals and vegetation, on which he was pleased to lecture whenever requested.

A deep impression was made on Father De Smet by the wagon trains "transporting to Utah provisions and stores of war." The government was preparing for a long and expensive conflict, and "if the journals of the day may be believed, these cost the government fifteen millions. Each train consisted of twenty-six wagons, each wagon drawn by six yoke of oxen, and containing near 5000 pounds."

The Quartermaster informed Father De Smet that if put together the supply wagons would create a train fifty miles in length. "We passed every day some wagons of this immense train. Each wagon is marked with a name as in the case of ships, and these names serve to furnish amusement . . . the caprices of the captains in this respect having imposed upon the wagons such names as *Constitution, President, Great Republic, King of Bavaria, Lola Montez, Louis Napoleon, Dan O'Connell, Old Kentuck* etc. . . . At a distance the white awning of the wagons have the effect of a fleet of vessels with all canvas spread."

The wagoners were "captains of their ships," and the "master-wagoner was the admiral of this little land fleet." Each "admiral" had command of 26 "captains and 312 oxen."

On leaving Leavenworth the "captains" and "admirals" had been models of sartorial neatness and style, "being all in new clothes, but as they advance onto the plains their good clothes become travel-stained and torn, and at last are converted into rags. The captains have hardly proceeded 200 miles, before their trail is marked with rags, scattered and flying along the route."

The filthy, littered campgrounds of the emigrants were a sad sight to one like Father De Smet, who had known the beauty of the unspoiled plains twenty years before. He could share the feelings of the Indians as they regarded "these signs of encroaching civilization . . . These rags and refuse are to them the harbingers of the approach of a dismal future for themselves . . . all that is most dear to them are about to pass into the hands of the rapacious white man.

"It is not surprising, then, that the savage seeks sometimes to revenge himself on the white man. However, it is rarely that he is the aggressor, surely not once out of ten provoking cases."

Between Fort Kearney and the crossing of the south fork of the Platte, Father De Smet counted more than a hundred families of Mormons fleeing eastward from the rebellion. He thought they "appeared delighted at being fortunate enough to leave, safe and sound . . . thanks to the presence of United States troops.

"They told us that a great number of other families would follow them . . . They confessed that they would have escaped long before, had they not been afraid of falling into the hands of the Danites, or Destroying Angels. These compose the body-guard of the Prophet; they are said . . . to carry out all his plans . . . which often involve robbery and murder. Before the arrival of United States soldiers, woe to anyone who manifested a desire to leave Utah, or abandon the sect; woe to him who dared to raise a voice against the actions of the Prophet . . ."

The various companies of General Harney's force advanced two or three days' journey apart, and "each company was followed by ambulances for the use of the superior officers, [by] a body of artillery and engineers, and a train of wagons, with six mules each, transporting provisions and baggage. Each company was also followed by an immense drove of six or seven hundred head of horned cattle, to furnish their daily food. Uncle Sam has a truly paternal heart; he provides abundantly for the wants of the defenders of the country, and will not suffer them to want their comforts."

The march suddenly ended at the South Platte crossing, some four hundred and sixty miles from Fort Leavenworth.

It was there that a military courier brought word to General Harney that the Mormons had capitulated, the rebellion was over, and troops on hand needed no support.

The companies of the Utah Expedition were dispatched to various stations on the plains to undergo further training and to patrol the western trails against Indian depredations.

Thankful that peace had been restored without more bloodshed, Father De Smet was nevertheless disappointed that he would be unable to carry out his plan to visit the Flatheads. He was ordered to return directly to Fort Leavenworth. Early in September he was back in St. Louis.

XXXI

Father De Smet had no wish to launch himself at the age of fifty-eight on a career as a chaplain, and in September 1858, soon after he had returned to St. Louis, he submitted his resignation.

The Army had no intention of letting it be accepted. General Harney had been summoned to Washington, and even before he had left Fort Leavenworth he could make a good guess as to the nature of his next assignment. Newspapers were full of reports of the uprising which had started among the tribes west of the Rocky Mountains.

Captain Alfred Pleasonton had very succinctly stated what was in the mind of Harney in a note to Father De Smet: ". . . the general is under the impression he is to be placed on service in Oregon, and in such an event, there is no one whose aid could be more valuable than your own . . . The general proposes, therefore, that you continue your commission with the Army and accompany him to Oregon in case he is sent, due notice of which he will telegraph to you . . . The general begs to assure you that every facility and encouragement will be given to the advancement of the good work you have already so successfully commenced in that country. With highest considerations of respect and esteem . . ."

The Army, and General Harney especially, understood that in Oregon Father De Smet would be more valuable and undoubtedly more effective than a regiment of soldiers. Capt. Pleasonton, whom he had known for several years, appended a "private" message to General Harney's letter: "I shall always look back upon the agreeable moments we have passed together as among the most pleasant of my life . . ."

In his journal, Father De Smet said simply: "The Secretary of War did not see fit to accept my resignation."

Orders soon came. He was to report to General Harney in New York on September 15th. The trip to the Northwest would be made via Panama.

Sadness filled Father De Smet as he studied the available reports while hurrying East. It was obvious that a general uprising was underway in the immense region in which he had been the pioneer missionary. Nine tribes already had joined forces in the revolt—the Palooses, Yakimas, Skoyelpis, Okanagans, Spokans, Coeur d'Alenes, Kalispels, Kootenais and Flatheads. "These poor savages, formerly so peaceable, the last four especially, had become uneasy over the frequent incursions made by the whites upon the lands in the southern and western portions of the territories of Washington and Oregon," he explained to a European magazine. "From uneasiness, they had soon passed to displeasure and anger, when they saw these adventurers taking possession of the most advantageous sites and settling as owners upon the most fertile parts of the country, in total contempt of their rights and without the slightest preliminary agreement."

It was the same old story. The federal government failed to enforce the law or to abide by its treaties, and when the Indians objected, the Army was sent. No thought was given to punishing the offending whites who were responsible for starting the revolt. The Indians were to be punished for defending their own homes, for attempting to preserve the resources which were legally theirs and which they must have to survive. The riff-raff, the thieves, the murderers, the low persons whose skins were white but whose hearts were black went free.

Fury seethed through Father De Smet. Those Indians with their backs to the wall through no fault of their own were his friends. They were decent, law-abiding, intelligent, religious people. They wanted only the right to maintain homes, rear and supply their families, acquire educations and worship God. What manner of persons were the white men who would deprive them of these simple things to which they were entitled?

Despite his great anger, however, he retained his dignity as he informed various publications how the mountain tribes, among whom he had spent so much time, had at last concluded they had no alternative but to "drive back the whites, or at least to make resistance to their progressive encroachments . . . Their first blow was a victory for them, and in their eyes a complete one, for they had not only driven off the enemy [a military contingent] but had besides captured his train and provisions. The precipitate retreat of the Americans even seemed to them a shameful flight. It was, however, a perfectly natural thing, since the brave Colonel Steptoe, having no suspicion of the [general] rising, had with him only one company of 120 men, on their way to maintain order at Colville. Intoxicated with their first success, the Indians thought themselves invincible and able to meet the whole United States Army.

"On the other hand, the government thought the affair of sufficient gravity to make it prudent to put it in the hands of General Harney. This officer had won glory on many occasions in the famous Indian wars . . . He wished to have me with him on this distant expedition . . .

"I hoped to be of some service in that capacity to the men, but above all to the Indian tribes of the mountains; I desired greatly also to be in touch with my missionary brethren in the difficulties which the war would doubtless bring upon them."

The railroad had reached the Mississippi, and in only fifty hours Father De Smet traveled the eleven hundred miles to New York. On September 20th, he boarded the steamer *Star of the West* with General Harney and his staff for the voyage to Panama.

The Isthmus also was crossed by railroad. The trip northward by ship began October 2nd, and five days later a stop was made at Acapulco, where "you will find but a single church, and a very poor one at that. Look at the houses, how wretched they are and what an indolent and lazy air the inhabitants have. Poor people! They live chiefly on fish, do a little business in fruit and vegetables and a little pearl fishing . . ."

He wrote at length of the changes which had taken place in California, Oregon and Washington since he had first seen them. San Francisco, which a dozen years before had been nothing but a small village on a magnificent bay, was now "a marvel, and the port *par excellence* of the whole Pacific Ocean. A population of at least 60,000 souls has sprung up, gathered from all the corners of the earth. There are 4000 Chinese, preserving faithfully the manners and customs of their fatherland, including the long queue . . . in this modern Babel one's ears are continually rent by strange sounds and cries . . .

"But what consoles and reconciles one with all this uproar . . . is the sweet thought that our holy religion has its share . . . besides a fair cathedral, there are five churches, four convents, a college directed by our Fathers and several schools . . .

"The markets were covered with the most beautiful fruit . . ."

He spoke of the rich agricultural lands, the giant redwood trees and the great sugar pines, "the soft climate of this lovely land . . . its fine mountains, its rich valleys . . ."

A "large and handsome lighthouse" stood now on Cape Disappointment to guide vessels over the dangerous bar at the mouth of the Columbia, where his ship had been so close to disaster in 1844. The Indians, "formerly so numerous along the coast and the river, have almost entirely disappeared. Every approach of the whites thrusts them back by force or otherwise; they go upon reservations, in a strange land, far removed from their hunting and fishing grounds, and where drink, misery and disease of every sort mow them down by hundreds." New towns stood on each side of the great river, and he hardly recognized the Willamette Valley, where there were "a great number of towns and villages, rich and beautiful farms . . ."

Settlers were still pouring into the Oregon country. The juggernaut of civilization could not be stopped, nor could it be made to change course. As Father De Smet understood his own role, he had only a single mission to perform, and that was to convince the Indians of the futility of fighting. Perhaps through peaceful means he might win for them some concessions that would put off the day of their entrance into oblivion. Bloodshed and violence would only hasten that day. The sooner he could embark on his mission among them the better for all.

General Harney agreed, and late in October, Captain Pleasonton, now the assistant adjutant general of the Second Dragoons, informed Father De Smet that "The general commanding instructs me to say, that he most cordially approves of your proposition to visit the Coeur d'Alene Mission this winter; for he conceives the happiest results from your presence among the Indian tribes of that vicinity . . . The general desires you to impress upon the Indians . . . the strong necessity existing for them to live up to the conditions to which they have so lately subscribed in the treaties they have made, more especially in the surrender of such persons as were demanded of them. Two of these persons, Kamiakin and Schloom, it is reported, have gone away among the Flatheads, but that circumstance must not prevent the tribes concerned from using every endeavor to obtain possession of them . . .

"While informing the Indians that the government is always generous to a fallen foe, state to them that it is, at the same time, determined to protect its citizens in every part of its territory; and that they can only expect to exist by implicitly obeying the commands they receive."

Troops, Pleasonton reminded Father De Smet, "will most assuredly be placed upon their trail in the spring with instructions to give no quarter, should they again turn a deaf ear to what has been told them." He ordered Army contingents to aid Father De Smet in every way possible and to furnish him with any supplies and men he requested.

Nothing was said in the orders about warning white persons to stop shooting Indians, stealing their lands and burning their homes. Father De Smet found it necessary to remind himself often that he was no longer only a Black Robe, free to move as he pleased among the Indians and to carry out whatever program he deemed most advantageous for them. He was now a soldier. He was obliged to take orders. His prerogatives were curtailed. He had to struggle to keep from adding to the general's instructions that the situation would be greatly helped if the white people . . . not to mention the government and the Army . . . also were ordered to live up to the treaties signed with the Indians. He made no such comments in an official capacity, but they were made by him in time in the capacity of a priest. He felt that nothing would be gained by disclosing the thoughts in his head as he started for the interior.

At Fort Walla Walla he found Coeur d'Alene and Spokan families who were being held as hostages by the military. Among them were Indians he had known eleven years before, and "these people were greatly surprised at my arrival . . . they appeared delighted . . . I learned with pleasure that all of them, and especially the Coeur d'Alenes, had managed during their captivity to gain the good will of the officers and soldiers of the fort by exemplary and Christianlike conduct." The Army men had been astonished to hear the captives reciting Catholic prayers and singing canticles.

Father De Smet at once arranged to have them freed and to take them with him, assuring the commandant that there need be no fear they would rejoin the revolt as long as he was with them. Then with the released prisoners, he started for the Coeur d'Alene Country, where the Army would make no attempt to go until the advent of spring. He rode a horse on toward the mountains, the Indians surrounding him, eager to please him and anxious to be of help. He rode, a lone white man, into the camps of Indians who had sworn to let no more white men into their country, to kill all who attempted to enter it. They would not kill him. They would welcome him into their lodges, and they would listen to his words, and they would weigh them in their minds, for they respected and trusted him, and they knew he spoke from his heart.

He went on across the Snake at the Traverse, on into the valley of the little river called Two Canyons, and there came upon the main camp of the Palooses. These were Indians who had taken part in the attack on Colonel Steptoe's troops. From them he learned that for the past two years unidentified white men had told the mountain tribes that soldiers were coming to drive them out. These white men obviously had been trying to start trouble. If the Indians could be incited to revolt, then troops would come and they would be imprisoned or killed, and whites could move into their lands. Believing that this result would occur, whites had formed companies and had been planning to sell the stolen Indian lands to settlers.

In camp after camp Father De Smet expounded his theme: violence would only make the situation worse. Violence would only bring death and destruction, suffering and hunger.

On November 21st he reached the Sacred Heart Mission near Lake Coeur d'Alene. The mountain passes ahead were blocked by snow. In the lower valleys heavy rains were falling. Winter had begun, and further attempts to travel would be inadvisable.

He set up his winter quarters at the mission, and sent out word of his presence. Leaders of the revolt soon came in to talk with him, and often the fire in his hearth burned through the night while a smoke was in session. The Masses he celebrated were crowded, and he could speak in high praise of the work which had been carried on by the Black Robes who had followed the spiritual trails he had broken.

He located Kamiakin and his brother, Schloom, especially wanted by the military, and he "held several talks with them . . . and acquainted them with the general's orders . . . they invariably listened with attention and respect. Kamiakin made an open avowal of all he had done in his wars against the government, particularly in the attack on Colonel Steptoe, and in the war against Colonel Wright."*

Father De Smet believed Kamiakin's statement that he had advised his people against joining the revolt, but had at last been forced to enter it by a personal attack on him from "the deceitful Telgawax" made before a full council of chiefs.

In his reports he expressed the conviction that should Kamiakin be pardoned and permitted to live in freedom with his people, "it will have the happiest and most salutary effect among the upper Indian tribes, and facilitate greatly all future transactions . . ."

Kamiakin's people, he declared, "were living in great poverty and misery . . . Kamiakin, the once powerful chieftain, who possessed thousands of horses and a large number of cattle, has lost all . . .

"His brother, Schloom, if he lives, will come in in the course of the summer. I left him at Clark's Fork sickly and almost blind . . ."

He had no sympathy for the Paloose leader, Telgawax, whom he charged with being not only dishonest but "the prime mover" in the fighting against Steptoe and Wright.

He thought Telgawax was hiding "among the Buffalo Nez Percés . . . His influence is not great, but he remains unceasing in his endeavors to create bitter feelings against the whites, whenever he can meet with an opportunity."

Father De Smet told General Harney he believed the revolt had been broken, not so much by the military forces as by the good sense of the Indian leaders. A few recalcitrants were holding out, but there was every reason to believe they could be brought into submission.

Captain Pleasonton replied: "The confidence you feel in the peaceful desires of the Indians toward the whites is shared by the general . . .

* Who led the troops in the successful campaign in the preceding summer, 1858.

"The general approves your proposition of permitting some of the chiefs of the various nations to accompany you to this place to pay him their respects. He will be glad to see them and to explain to them the intentions of the government as far as they are concerned. Their expenses and food will be provided them during the journey to and from their homes, but they must not expect presents for the general has none to give.

"It would be well that you return as early in the spring as practicable . . ."

Although Pleasonton's letter had been written January 1, 1859, couriers could not break through deep snows and cross raging rivers with it until the middle of March. By that time Father De Smet was among the tribes of territory that was soon to become western Montana.

He had left the Sacred Heart Mission on February 18th with Father Joset. They had arranged to meet Father Hoeken on Clark's Fork. "The ice, snow, rain and winds impeded very much our course, in our frail canoes of bark . . . We met with several camps of Indians in winter quarters . . . They received us everywhere with great kindness, and, notwithstanding their extreme poverty, willingly shared with us their small rations . . ."

The Mission of St. Ignatius, among the Pend d'Oreilles, was reached on March 11th. While he planned to visit as many tribes as possible, Father De Smet had one uppermost thought. He wanted to go "home." Home was the valley of the Bitter Root and St. Mary's Mission for the Flatheads.

The Jesuits had seen fit to close St. Mary's in the spring of 1851. Father De Smet had always thought that "the why and how" he could "pretty easily guess at." He had "left it in a flourishing condition in 1846; the testimonials and letters of Fathers Joset, Mengarini, Ravalli, Point and Acolti bear testimony to my assertion. It is abandoned five years later and I am accused of being the cause of this, 'by my liberalities and promises to the Indians, which they [the Society] have been unable to sustain.'

Liberal in what? Promises of what? I am at a loss to imagine . . ."†

On the 18th of March, traveling through deep snow, Father De Smet, with tears welling in his eyes, stopped before the door of the church he had built at St. Mary's. From the surrounding forests came the Flatheads, and many of the old men and women threw their arms about him, weeping in their joy at seeing him again. Black Robe had come back to them. Never had they forgotten him. During the eight years the mission had been closed, they had continued to assemble periodically to say the prayers he had taught them.

As soon as he received General Harney's approval of his plan for a council at Fort Vancouver, he dispatched messages to the tribes asking that their head chiefs meet him early in April at St. Ignatius. When he returned there about the middle of April he found awaiting him "Alexander Temglagketzin (Man-Without-A-Horse), chief of the Pend d'Oreilles; Victor Alamikin (Happy Man) . . . he deserves his name, for he is a saintly man . . . chief of the Kalispels; Adolphus Kwilkweschape (Red Feather), chief of the Flatheads; Francis Saxa (Iroquois), another Flathead chief; Denis Zenemtietze (Thunder Robe), chief of the Skoyelpi or Chaudières; Andrew and Bonaventure, chiefs of the Coeur d'Alenes; Kamiakin, chief of the Yakimas, and Gerry, chief of the Spokans. The last two are still pagans, though their children have been baptized."

The gathering of the leaders demonstrated the unlimited trust which the mountain tribes held in Black Robe. They were willing to follow him into the headquarters of the military men whom a few months before they had engaged on the field of battle. They went without fear.

The start for Fort Vancouver was made April 16th, and all "suffered much and ran many dangers on the route, on account

† The mission was not re-established until 1866. It was permanently closed in 1891, when the remnants of the Flatheads in the area were moved to the Jocko Reservation.

of the high stage of the rivers and the heavy snow. For ten days we had to clear a way through thick forests, where thousands of trees, thrown down by storms, lay across one another, and were covered with four, six, and eight feet of snow; several horses perished in this dangerous passage."

A month was required for the trip. On May 18th, the group assembled with General Harney and representatives of the Indian Department.

Father De Smet arranged to have the chiefs taken on sightseeing trips, at the cost of the government, "to the principal cities and towns of the state of Oregon and Washington Territory, with everything remarkable in the way of industrial establishments, steam engines, forges, manufactories and printing establishments—of all which the poor Indians can make nothing or very little."

It was his opinion that they were impressed the most by their trip to the "prison at Portland and its wretched inmates, whom they found chained within its cells. They were particularly interested in the causes, motives, and duration of their imprisonment."

The entire conference, Father De Smet thought, "produced most happy results on both sides."

This was a gross understatement. The conference brought peace to the Northwest, and to him must be given the credit.

General Harney wasn't accurate when he reported to Army headquarters in New York City that the chiefs had come to Fort Vancouver at the suggestion "of myself through the kind offices of Reverend Father De Smet." But that was not an important matter. The results were the important thing, and they were far-reaching.

The general credited Father De Smet with counseling the chiefs during the previous winter, "both as an agent of the government and in his clerical capacity, as to the advantages accruing to them by preserving peaceable and friendly relations with the whites at all times . . . All these chiefs assert there will be no difficulty for the future as regards the whites traveling through their country, *or in occupation of it.*"

That statement was accurate as far as it went, but it was incomplete. The Indian chiefs did promise to stop fighting, but they asked in return that an adequate reservation be set aside for them, and it was promised to them. All Harney said was that "They request the government to secure a reservation to their people, upon which they desire to live and be protected. I am convinced that with proper care, another Indian war of any magnitude cannot soon occur in this department."

It gave him great pleasure, Harney told the General-in-Chief of the Army, to commend "the able and efficient services the Reverend Father De Smet has rendered."

During the winter when he had been isolated in his lonely mountain headquarters, Father De Smet had spent hours considering a program which might save his beloved savages of the mountains from extinction. At Fort Vancouver he organized his notes and prepared a report. General Harney submitted it to New York as being "valuable from the rare advantages Father De Smet possessed for many years, in his position as missionary among the tribes, to obtain accurate information of the country; and his purity of character will always give respect and importance to his statements."

Father De Smet had known what he was doing when he selected a site for a reservation in the area of the "upper Clark's Fork," for, as General Harney told his superiors, this country "will not be occupied by the whites for twenty years; it is difficult of access, and does not offer the same inducements to the settler that are everywhere presented to him on the coast . . . The plan proposed by Father De Smet . . . places the Indians in a country abounding in fish and game, with sufficient arable land to encourage them in its gradual cultivation; and by the aid of the missionaries at present with them, that confidence and influence will be established over their minds, by degrees, as will induce them to submit to the restraints of civilization, *when the inevi- table decree of time causes it to pass over them.*"

The proposed reservation area would "*not be occupied by the whites for twenty years.*" Of course, after that the whites might want it, and then the Indians would be driven out again, and God alone knew what would become of them. Anyway, they would be permitted to live for twenty years.

It was to his credit that General Harney seemed to recognize the weaknesses of a military regime. He disclosed the conviction that the missionaries among the Indians of the Oregon Depart- ment of the Army "possess a power of the greatest consequence in their proper government, and one which cannot be acquired by any other influence. They control the Indian by training his superstitions and fears to revere the religion they possess, by associating the benefits they confer with the guardianship and protection of the Great Spirit of the whites.

"The history of the Indian race on this continent has shown that the missionary succeeded where the soldier and civilian have failed; it would be well for us to profit by the lessons its experience teaches, in an instance which offers so many advan- tages to the white as well as to the red man, and adopt the wise and humane suggestion of Father De Smet."

There is, perhaps, no instance in western history when a man of the sword and a man of the cloth were in closer accord on such a vital issue. General Harney and Father De Smet con- sidered conditions in the light of truth. Each was experienced, each was honest and each was wise, but even more important, each was striving to reach a solution that would be fair to both races. Had the federal government heeded their words and adopted their proposals, much of the tragedy and bloodshed that occurred in the next few years would have been averted.

The Administration, the War Department and the Indian Bureau ignored them.

Father De Smet requested that he be permitted to return home by way of the Missouri River. This meant crossing the mountains and making the dangerous trip down the far western trails, but he held a great desire to visit tribes he had not seen for several years.

Once more he submitted his resignation.

General Harney was agreeable to his plan, and June 1, 1859, issued Special Order No. 59 approving it. Father De Smet received the order while still at Fort Vancouver. To it was appended a letter in which both Harney and Pleasonton expressed profound appreciation for his services.

"The general is anxious," Pleasonton said, "that I should communicate to you the deep regret with which he feels your separation from the service, and in making the announcement he is assured the same feeling extends to all those who have in any way been associated with you."

The tribute of the veteran Indian fighter reached its height with the words: "By the campaign of last summer submission had been conquered, but the embittered feelings of the two races, excited by war, still existed, and it remained for you to supply that which was wanting to the sword. It was necessary to exercise the strong faith which the red man possessed in your purity and holiness of character, to enable the general to evince successfully toward them the kind intentions of the government, and to restore confidence and repose to their minds.

"This has been done; *the victory is yours,* and the general will take great pleasure in recording your services at the War Department . . ."

With the chiefs he had brought out of the mountains, Father De Smet left Fort Vancouver on June 15, 1859, on the long overland journey to St. Louis. Perhaps he felt that he was making his last trip through the wilderness, for he planned to travel the entire distance by horseback so that he might more easily reach remote villages.

Through the latter half of June and the month of July he worked his way gradually over the great divide of the Rocky

Mountains. In countless camps he held services and spent hours smoking with old friends.

On July 29th he arrived at Fort Benton, after having held a council with Blackfeet Indians at the Great Falls of the Missouri. It became apparent that he would have to abandon his plan to travel farther by horseback, "for my six horses were entirely worn out, and unfit for making so long a journey; they were all more or less saddle-galled, and, not being shod, their hoofs were worn in crossing . . . the rough, rocky mountain roads."

In that journal entry Father De Smet was concealing the facts of his situation. It would have been no trouble for him to have obtained all the fresh horses he required, and he could have charged the cost to the Army, for he had with him orders to the commanders of posts along his route "to afford him every facility and assistance," and his traveling expenses were to be paid in full by the War Department.

The truth was that he was not well. All the time he had been on the Oregon campaign he had suffered from a strange soreness in his throat. At times he had been close to complete exhaustion. It was apparent that as he stood on the bank of the Missouri River and watched it rolling away into the eastern sky, he felt that he did not have the strength to make the trip of more than two thousand miles, which remained ahead of him, in a saddle. The river would carry him swiftly to his destination . . . "I ordered a little skiff to be made . . . Mr. Dawson, superintendent of the Fur Company, had the very great kindness to procure me three oarsmen and a pilot . . ."

On the 5th of August he waved farewell as the craft moved rapidly down the Missouri from Fort Benton.

It was in a way a homecoming journey. He saw "thousands of Indians of different tribes . . . I always stopped a day or two with them. I received the greatest marks of respect and affection . . . they listened to my words with the utmost attention."

It was a journey, as well, which brought to him a depthless sadness. He saw the great good he and other Black Robes had done, and he saw, written across the boundless western sky, the signs of doom for the Indians of the vast northern plains. Nothing, he told himself, could save them from oblivion.

In their little "cockleshell" they often made "fifty, sixty, and sometimes, when the wind favored us, eighty miles a day." They took the first steamboat they met at Omaha City. The steamer made about 700 miles in six days, and on the 23rd of September they entered the port of St. Louis.

FATHER DE SMET'S EXPENSE ACCOUNT IN OREGON AND FOR HIS TRIP TO ST. LOUIS

With Indian Chiefs to Council at Fort Vancouver:

Private traveling expenses from Champoeg to Portland	$ 10.00
Expenses for Indians, clothing, saddles etc.	35.50
To hire and use of Indian horses from Dalles, Oregon, to Fort Benton, Nebraska Territory, in June and July, at two blankets or $10 a month	120.00
Private servant and assistant from Coeur d'Alene Lake (Washington Territory) till St. Louis, during the months of July, August, and up to the 23rd of September, 1859	65.00
To Indian guides and canoemen from Coeur d'Alene Mission to St. Ignatius Mission, near Flathead Lake	72.00
To four Indian guides, assistants, and guard from St. Ignatius Mission to Fort Benton, twenty days going and coming	60.00
To hire of two Canadian boatmen from Fort Benton to St. Louis, at rate of $45 each	90.00
To pilots and interpreters from 3d of August till 9th of September, from Fort Benton to Fort Randall	30.00
To tobacco etc., during my intercourse with Indians, east and west of the Mountains	20.00
To provisions for attendants in July, August and September to skiff, etc.	59.50
To steamer (for self) from Omaha City to St. Louis	18.00
To drayage for baggage in Omaha and St. Louis	2.50
	$582.50

XXXII

Father De Smet's resignation from the Army was accepted, and the Society wasted no time getting him back to the duties he had performed before he became a chaplain. He spent the last three months of 1859 and the first eight months of 1860 in his St. Louis office, with the exception of brief trips to Chicago and other midwestern cities. In September 1860, he was directed to go once again to Europe. He sailed from New York on the SS *Fulton* for Havre. It was his twelfth trip across the Atlantic.

He left the United States as the shadow of war clouds was growing rapidly darker, his heart sick with the thought of the tragedies it would bring. The disruption, devastation and destruction which he could imagine would occur in the settled portions of the United States were terrible to contemplate, but not only there would the horrors of the conflict be known. Beyond the frontier, under the shadows of the mountains and on the great plains, the warfare would be no less fierce and terrible. With the white men fighting each other there would be little hope of maintaining any form of peace among the Indians. All the good work of the past in preventing intertribal conflicts would be destroyed. Once again the drums would sound for the war dance, and the cries for blood and glory would be heard from the Red River of the North to the Columbia.

Actually, the government of the Union would have two major wars to fight, the war against the South and the war against the Indian hordes that would sweep upon western settlements to burn, maim, destroy and kill. Any withdrawal of military forces west of the Missouri would open the gates to the red legions, already seething with hate and bitterness because of the treatment they had received.

Until April 1861, Father De Smet was held by his work in Belgium, Holland and France. Then once again he took passage on the SS *Fulton* for the United States. He had with him three young novices going out to follow in his footsteps in the Far West.

The vessel reached New York on the night of April 14, only a few hours after the "great American metropolis had been thrown into the utmost confusion and consternation by the news that Fort Sumter, in South Carolina, had been captured and the great star-spangled banner of the Union lowered and torn to pieces by the Southern rebels—an irremedial and ineffaceable insult in the eyes of all America."

If Father De Smet was not what he termed "a man for war," he was a loyal citizen, and he had no hesitancy in letting it be known that his sympathies were with the North. He was unalterably opposed to any form of human bondage, and he felt that on the question of slavery "there was and is no room for compromise." He thought it evident "that according to the Constitution . . . no state has the right to secede from the Union. The Union was intended to be perpetual." Firmly he declared that "either slavery or freedom must triumph in this gigantic contest . . . The friends of the human race everywhere must feel a deep interest in the fate of the Great Republic . . ."

From New York in the spring of 1861, he hurried on to St. Louis, while "throughout the 1000-mile journey nothing was heard save the rattle of arms and the cries of war." He was there only a few weeks when he found it necessary to return to the East. He was in Washington at the time of the first Battle of Bull Run, and he "witnessed its fatal consequences."

The trip was a severe hardship for him, for he was suffering from recurring attacks of dyspepsia. While this condition gradually disappeared, it was followed in the fall by erysipelas, which kept him in bed much of the time.

As the year drew to an end he was so seriously ill that it was feared his life was in danger. The cause of the infection was not determined . . . indeed, doctors knew very little about the causes of erysipelas, although it had been known to afflict mankind since ancient times. Patches of his skin became highly inflamed. He grew weak. The remedy that was resorted to was rest, nourishing food and the drinking of large amounts of water. It was obviously beneficial. In December he was well on the way to a full recovery.

He made no mention of his illness in the letters he wrote to his family shortly before Christmas in which he told them that the feelings of bitterness engendered by the war in Missouri "seemed deeper than elsewhere.

"You have heard of the horrors of the first French Revolution, in histories of civil war in various ages and countries, where everything was turmoil and confusion and robbers and assassins had free and open field for murder and devastation of property.

"All this will give you but a faint idea of the horrible situation to which Missouri finds herself reduced. Her own children, divided . . . between North [Union] and the South [Confederacy], are dipping their hands in blood and cutting one another's throats, burning and sacking one another's dwellings; while enemies from outside enter the State to glut their insatiable vengeance . . ."

January, 1862, found Father De Smet hurrying once more to Washington. His trip this time had to do with the delinquency of the government in its allotments to the Jesuit Indian missions. As he explained the matter in a letter to the Father-General, since "the outbreak of the war and the great expenditures which it occasions, the government is necessarily delayed in the payments of its contracts with the Indian tribes, the motto for today being 'the expenses of the war before everything else.'"

A sum in excess of $18,000 was due the missions among the Potawatomies and Osages alone, and Father De Smet presented his request for the money to the Superintendent of Indian Affairs "with the remark that a refusal or delay on the part of the government, of its debt and promise, would singularly disarrange the ideas of our Indians, who have thus far been loyal and attached to the Union side." He expressed the further view that "if we were obliged by lack of means to send some 400 children back to their poor parents, they would conclude that their Great Father, President Lincoln, had taken the money that ought to have gone to the support of their children, and used it for other purposes, and that they might be led in consequence to lend a favorable ear to the secessionists."

This "all but *casus belli*" seemed to please the superintendent, and he promised to "do his utmost to satisfy our good savages." He enlisted the aid of "several influential persons," and Father De Smet could report that he had got $11,000 and felt that he had done "very well in the settlement of my business."

The presence of the famed missionary in the capital was duly noted by the White House, and despite his great burdens President Lincoln asked that he call for a talk. The President was well aware of the seriousness of the situation on the western plains, with the garrisons badly depleted in manpower. He questioned Father De Smet intently, and Father De Smet found the Great Emancipator "very affable and well disposed toward us, and promised me that he would favor and aid us in our efforts to ameliorate the unhappy lot of the Indians. The Secretaries of the Interior and Treasury and the Attorney- and Postmaster-General were likewise very favorable to me."

Who presented him to the cabinet officers, he did not record, but it was apparent that the doors of Washington were opened to him. This was true as well of the foreign embassies.

The Belgian Ambassador, Edward Blondeel, gave a dinner in his honor which was attended by the Ambassadors of France, Russia and Spain. "They all had their *grands cordons*," he said, "and I had a frock coat well worn and with two buttons gone. However, it all went off agreeably."

He felt that he had done the best he could "among these great personages; but I remain of the opinion that I shall always be more at my ease sitting on the grass and surrounded by savages, each one making his jokes and at the same time eating with good appetite a fair rib or roasting piece of buffalo or fat dog."

Altogether, in 1862 Father De Smet went three times to Washington. In September he "heard the roar of cannon at the Battle of Antietam."

He wrote the Father-General that "The secession movement is evidently on the decline."

Despite the many ecclesiastical concerns which occupied him, he managed to make the long trip by steamboat from St. Louis to Fort Benton and back during the summer of 1862.

His conferences with high officials in Washington for the most part had been held behind closed doors, and there were no documentary records of them. Yet it was obvious that the swiftly deteriorating conditions on the frontier—especially in the Sioux Country—caused Administration leaders to urge him to use his good offices in any way he could to halt the uprisings. Under the demands of the great conflict, the War Department found it impossible to send sufficient troops to control the Indians and stop the massacres that were taking place in virtually all areas penetrated by settlers. Moreover, the discovery of precious metals in the mountains had launched stampedes. White men, crazed by the dream of riches, cared no more for the rights of Indians than they did about the laws.

"Thousands must be on their way to these mines at present," Father De Smet had written a friend in March 1862, and he mentioned again how he had long known of the existence of great lodes of gold and silver in several sections of the West, but in the hope of protecting the Indians "I have kept my secret for twenty years past."

When he returned to St. Louis from his spring trip to Washington, his superiors acquiesced in his proposal, apparently first suggested by the War Department, that he go up the river to observe the dire situation and make what efforts he could to relieve it. He wrote to Frank P. Blair, the noted publisher, politician and adviser to President Lincoln, advising him of his intention to make the trip.

Numerous letters from Father De Smet reveal his close friendship and his familiarity with men of prominence and high position. The letter to Blair was a good example of this. In it he expressed his "most sincere thanks for the many favors and kind services you have so often rendered me," and asked that his kindest respects be presented to "Mrs. Blair and her mother."

The records are vague and inconclusive, but they indicate that Blair was one of the persons with whom he had discussed his mission of observation to the upper Missouri territory, for he spoke of it casually in his letter and without the introduction which would have been necessary had it been a matter not previously mentioned.

"Feeling, as ever, much attached to the Union of my adopted country, I shall do all I can to promote it among the Indians . . ." he told Blair. "The thought came to my mind, that if I could go in some official capacity from the government (I ask for no emoluments) my object might be strengthened by it and be more efficacious."

What official status he was given is not known to history, but from the nature of his actions and his subsequent letters it may be assumed that the trip was officially sanctioned and expenses such as transportation were paid by the War Department.

He left St. Louis early in May on the steamboat *Spread Eagle*. The only account of the trip—and it is very brief—is found in a letter to Father Boone [otherwise unidentified] in which he mentions that the boat captain "had a little chapel prepared on board" for him, enabling him to offer "the holy sacrifice of the Mass every day . . . We were six weeks making the trip."

Although the boat was crowded with miners destined for Fort Benton, where they would start overland for the gold fields, it obviously was engaged as well in government business, for it stopped frequently to "distribute among the savages the government gifts and annuities." He seized "all these precious moments to visit them in their buffalo-skin dwellings or cabins . . . I was welcomed everywhere . . . they met me most eagerly, with the calumet of peace in their hands . . ."

He held councils with Blackfeet, Crows, Assiniboines, Minnetarees, Arikaras, Mandans and Sioux, but "circumstances did not allow me to penetrate very far into the interior of the Sioux Country, on account of the great uprising or warfare made upon the whites . . ."

The determination of the Sioux to defend their country to the death was graphically illustrated shortly before he reached Fort Pierre, when "the head chief of the Sioux was killed by his own people" because he had indicated a willingness to negotiate for peace. Father De Smet was unable to find an interpreter or guide who would accompany him into the interior, "and for that reason I have put off this visit and mission to next spring."

He made the round trip on the *Spread Eagle,* returning deeply grieved and alarmed by the situation on the upper river. There could be no doubt that terrible events were to take place, and the entire Indian Country would run red with blood.

His conclusion was correct. In August 1862, the horrible Minnesota Massacre occurred. Nearly a thousand white people were slain by Sioux raiders. The intelligence reports he had received on his trip perhaps gave him greater knowledge than that possessed by either western officials or those in Washington. Settlers and authorities in Minnesota had treated the Sioux so brutally, robbing them of their lands, and destroying their possessions and homes, and wantonly murdering them, that they were driven to desperate acts to survive. Moreover, the Sioux had been led to believe that the Civil War had so crippled the federal government that it could neither protect them nor effectively resist their attacks. England was siding with the South, and British agents had circulated among the Sioux encouraging them to raid the settlements, to pillage and kill.

War or no war, the government had no alternative but to put

down the uprising, and a force under General H. H. Sibley was rushed into the area. While Father De Smet was traveling during the fall of 1862 in the East, Sibley defeated the Sioux in several engagements. Some three hundred were taken prisoners.

Father De Smet returned to St. Louis from the East early in December. Newspapers reported that thirty-nine of the captured Sioux raiders were to be executed. He at once proposed a plan which he thought would be more effective than the death penalties imposed by the court. "While the Sioux murderers deserve no better lot," he told the Indian Department, it should not be forgotten that captive white men, women and children "were still held alive by several Sioux bands, and the thought makes me shudder."

He proposed that instead of being executed, the convicted Sioux warriors "be kept as hostages; let it be known to the whole [Sioux] nation that for every white man they kill one of the prisoners shall atone for the murder. The murderers would thus become answerable before their own people."

The plan was rejected without comment. The executions were carried out. In Sioux camps white prisoners were tortured to death.

For many years Father De Smet had dreamed of establishing a mission among the Sioux. Various bands of the (Sioux) nation had repeatedly requested it, and he was convinced that the residence of Black Robes in the Sioux Country would contribute greatly to the maintenance of peace, not only between them and the federal government, but between them and other tribes. The Jesuits had never felt that they could afford the mission on the scale necessary to insure its success, and the plan had been held in abeyance from year to year.

The outbreaks of 1862, of course, made the project totally unfeasible, even though the necessary funds might have been obtained. Yet, Father De Smet defiantly announced that he had not abandoned the plan, and that he intended to make every effort to carry it out in the face of the adverse conditions.

"How it will be this spring [in the Sioux Country] it is hard telling," he wrote Father Hoeken. "It may be worse than last year . . . Harney will go out against them with a large force. I will leave in all probability by the 1st of May . . . I would be happy indeed if arrangements could be made of your going . . . We might pick upon a spot where a mission might be commenced in the course of the summer of 1864 . . . means and men might be obtained in Europe."

In his travels to Washington and in New York State he had become a good friend of the politically powerful Thurlow Weed and the Weed family in Albany. He was fully aware that in all probability no man was more in the confidence of Secretary of State William H. Seward. And through Seward's office ran a direct path to the White House.

If he were not much of a politician, as he maintained, Father De Smet understood how to get the attention and hold the interest of the highest men of the Administration, as well as the powerful individuals behind the scenes, and he was not hesitant to call on them for assistance if he thought the circumstances demanded it.

The Civil War Draft Law, which made no exceptions of the clergy, was one of the most troublesome problems facing the Jesuits. They were few in number. Nearly all of them were teachers. The priests, of course, were penniless, and the Society had no money to hire substitutes to take the places of members who were called. Moreover, the Jesuits were opposed to war and sworn not to participate in it. Father De Smet's service as a chaplain had not been considered a war service. He had gone with General Harney only as an emissary of peace to the revolting tribes.

The difficult task of obtaining exemptions from the draft for the Jesuits was given to Father De Smet. It weighed heavily upon him as he prepared to depart on his journey to the Indian Country in the spring of 1863, and he took the step he concluded would have more favorable results than another personal visit to Washington. He wrote to Thurlow Weed.

His letter was an outstanding illustration not only of his thorough knowledge of the machinery of government but of his skill as a diplomat.

First he informed Weed of his pending journey among the various tribes, including the Sioux "to promote among all religion and friendly dispositions toward the government."

Next he indulged in a bit of flag waving and patriotic oratory, declaring that "My adopted country, for these forty years I have lived in it, has always been truly dear to me. Its welfare has been the constant and uppermost wish of my heart and the end of my poor prayers. I have sworn obedience to it and from this sacred duty I have never and shall never swerve."

These preliminaries dispensed with, he mentioned casually to Weed that there was an important matter on which he wished his advice. "You are aware," he said, "that the Jesuits are a body of priests and Brothers, devoted, by solemn vows, exclusively to the service of God and the spiritual good of their fellow men. In the West here we number about 200 members, some of whom would fall within the limits of the conscription law lately passed by Congress . . .

"These vows . . . separate us from the world . . . and subject us to the canon law of the Church, which strictly forbids priests and religious men, who have taken these vows, from taking up arms in any cause whatsoever. We are ministers of peace . . . this law binds our consciences. We cannot violate it without doing violence to our duty to God; therefore we cannot obey any law which would require us to violate that duty.

"You perceive the predicament in which this places us at the present moment, and from which I desire your advice to enable us to extricate ourselves.

"As to the remedy of paying $300 for each member that may be subject to the draft, I must say that it is scarcely fair to require this of us, who are really not subject to military service, by reason of the life we have embraced . . . And besides this, such a sum paid for all those who might be called upon among us would prostrate all our establishments and leave us destitute of the means for carrying on the works we have undertaken for the good of our countrymen . . . the war has inflicted severe losses upon us, as upon many others; and if we cannot escape the conscription . . . I do not see how we shall be able to continue our exertions . . . we have here a conflict of duties; we desire as far as possible to comply with both, but we cannot sacrifice our conscience . . ."

When he had passed through Albany the previous year, a daughter of Weed had asked him for his photograph "to place in her beautiful album," he reminded the politician. Considering the request a great honor, he had left the only picture he had, "bearing but a small resemblance." With the letter about the draft he sent a better one for her, "with my best respects to your kind and good daughter."

Who Thurlow Weed talked to in Washington about the matter was not disclosed, but his representations in behalf of the Jesuits were highly successful. Father De Smet learned in time that verbal orders had gone out from the White House that the Fathers were not to be conscripted.

The instructions apparently had not reached Kentucky in time to prevent two Jesuit priests there from being taken off to war. When Father De Smet was informed of the unfortunate occurrence, he promptly got in touch with Secretary of War Edwin M. Stanton, appealing for their release.

He was somewhat astonished at the ease with which he was "able to obtain their liberty . . . In order to evade the law, the Secretary ordered our conscripts to stay at their homes until he calls them, and this call, according to his promise, shall not be issued as long as the war lasts."

Father De Smet was unwilling to attribute the exemption of the Jesuits to his political influence, protesting that he had none whatsoever, for politics was something he had studiously avoided all his life. He reported to the Father-General that his success had been accomplished only "by the Lord's favor, through the intercession of the Holy Virgin and the prayers of my Brothers."

On May 9, 1863, he left St. Louis on the steamboat *Nellie Rogers* for the upper river. Once again he went with renewed hope that he might find the means of interceding in the Sioux revolt and help to bring about a truce. There had been, he noted in his journal, "a great outcry in the United States against the execution of these [Sioux] prisoners of war, who seemed to be given over to the vengeance of the whites on the frontier . . . Indians are often wronged, insulted and outraged beyond measure by the whites, and there is no recourse open to them for the obtaining of justice."

The inability of Indians, either as individuals or as tribes, to carry the fight for their rights into the courts long had been a situation which Father De Smet had demanded be corrected. Indian thieves or marauders were quickly tried and sentenced, but Indians had no means of bringing actions against white persons who stole from them or murdered them.

Although Father De Smet was precluded by his black gown and his oaths from entering openly into a fight to have this evil eliminated, there was nothing to stop him from writing his views in letters. He did so frequently, and his sentiments paralleled the more public denouncements of Governor Horatio Seymour of New York.

A staunch friend of the Indian, Seymour proclaimed: "Every human being born upon our continent, or who came here from any quarter of the world, whether savage or civilized, can go to our courts for protection—except those who belong to the tribes who once owned this country. The cannibal from the islands of the Pacific, the worst criminals from Europe, Asia, or Africa can appeal to the law and the courts for their rights of person and property—all save our native Indians, who, above all, should be protected from wrong."

But in the summer of 1863, when Father De Smet was on the

upper Missouri, conditions had deteriorated beyond the point where the enforcement of any law could have brought peace. No court of justice could have halted the bloodshed and terror. Only the united forces of guns and death could do that, and they were present, both taking their toll.

A joint campaign under Generals Sibley and Sully in the field, and directed by General Pope, commander of the Department of Dakota, was underway. Sibley, after defeating the Indians in three battles, reached the Missouri late in July. Sully was to drive up the river and form a junction with him, but he failed to connect. However, he also was victorious in several actions.

In a letter to a colleague, Father De Smet unhesitantly placed the blame for the conflict on the "numerous injustices and misdeeds on the part of the whites, and even of agents of the government. For years and years they have deceived the Indians with impunity in the sale of their holdings of land, and afterward by the embezzlement, or rather the open theft, of immense sums paid them by the government in exchange therefor. The Indians, driven to extremity . . . and without being able to obtain any justice against their oppressors, utter at last their terrible war cry . . .

"The speculators, contractors and *enjusdem generis* of the region will do what they are able to protract this unlucky war, because it is so much money in their pockets."

The heat of the summer of 1863 in the upper Missouri Valley was extraordinarily intense and lasted for unusually long periods without relief. Under drought conditions, which occupied the entire region of the northern plains, the river continued to fall until there was not enough water to carry a steamboat. At the mouth of Milk River, the *Nellie Rogers* was stopped by an immense bar. On June 29th, "the captain found himself under the hard necessity of putting all his ninety passengers and all his cargo (200 tons) ashore . . ." They were still more than three hundred miles from Fort Benton, and there was little hope that the water would rise before the season had advanced too far for them to proceed to their destination and return in safety to St. Louis.

Messengers were sent to Fort Benton in a canoe and on horseback, asking for help. Meanwhile "every passenger chose a spot for himself in the forest and bestowed himself as best he could. General Harney had made me a present of his big camp tent before I left St. Louis; I had my little chapel, my little kitchen, the necessary bedding and provisions . . ." With Father De Smet were two Italian Brothers assigned to mountain missions, and "we were properly established under the shade of some big cottonwoods."

The voyage of the *Nellie Rogers* from St. Louis to Milk River had been without serious incident, although war raged in the country through which she had passed, and stops had been made at numerous Indian camps. Most of the passengers were willing to attribute their escape from attack simply to good fortune, but some of the veteran plainsmen and scouts aboard had another explanation. They knew of the respect which the Indians held for Father De Smet, and they maintained that it was his presence on the boat which had kept the Indians from firing at it or attempting depredations.

Perhaps they were right. The *Nellie Rogers* was the only steamboat to pass unscathed up the river that summer.

Speaking of this, Father De Smet was to write that "Other travelers were less fortunate than we." That was all he said of the matter, but he might well have added that several boats had been forced to turn back, and none were able to get as far as Milk River. Passengers and crewmen on other crafts were wounded and killed by shots from shore. A Mackinaw boat carrying twenty-one men and three women was attacked at the mouth of Apple Creek, only a short time before Sibley's troops arrived there, and all were slain.

After being unloaded, the *Nellie Rogers* turned back downstream. For four weeks the stranded passengers waited in their camp to be rescued. They were visited "by a great number of savages . . ." These Indians manifested no unfriendly desires, but defenses were erected and a constant vigilance maintained in the fear that a Sioux war party might attack.

The Sioux came. Scouts for a war party of six hundred braves were sighted while the camp was preparing to hold a Fourth of July ceremony. Suddenly arrows tore into tents. Two men were wounded. One received arrows in the arm and thigh. The other was struck in the side with an arrow that went in as far as the feather. Wild staccato yelps were heard as the main body of the raiders appeared.

In the terrorized camp men ran about in confusion, crying out their fear, and some fired wildly at the sky or in the general direction of the encircling Sioux. Father De Smet stared toward the naked horsemen. Any attempt at defense against such a formidable force would be futile. In the first charge the Sioux would sweep through the camp, and no passenger would be left alive. He called out a command to fire no more shots. Then he walked slowly out toward a group of Indians which had moved nearer the camp in advance of the main body. Men cried out to him to come back, that he was going to his death. He kept on.

Suddenly the Indians began to gesture wildly, as if sending signals to each other. Several more raced forward from the line of warriors, staring toward Father De Smet in obvious astonishment.

He was recognized. He heard his name shouted: "Black Robe!" As he came up to the first horsemen, several dismounted and made a sign of welcome. The first Sioux to shake his hand was Red Fish, whose daughter had been captured by Crows and had been miraculously returned after Father De Smet had spoken to the Great Spirit in her behalf. Red Fish had not forgotten.

Father De Smet's account of his bravery and the perilous situation was ridiculously modest. He simply called the meeting with Red Fish "truly providential." He "talked with him and his companions for about an hour. On leaving them I made a little present of coffee, sugar and crackers, and I saw them depart with no further thought of attacking . . ."

Men in the camp wept unashamedly as they sought to thank Father De Smet and marveled at his courage. He advised them to fall upon their knees and thank not him but God. And many of them did.

For another twenty-five days the passengers, their fears diminished but far from ended, waited to be rescued. On July 30th help arrived. A long train of wagons drawn by oxen moved toward them across the burning plain. Father De Smet was in a weakened condition, for his body had been "poisoned and bloated by a plant, commonly called *l'herbe à la puce* (the *Rhus Toxicodendron* of the botanists) . . ." Luckily the "good Fathers of the Mission of St. Peter, among the Blackfeet, sent me a comfortable conveyance for the journey . . ."

The trip to Fort Benton was slow and difficult, "through the midst of a wilderness where grass had almost entirely disappeared, by reason of the great drought of the spring and summer —for not a drop of water had fallen for months—where all rivers were dry, leaving only here and there a little pool . . ."

Camp was made each night beside one of the "water holes," in which fish were crowded, starving, suffocating and dying, "and the horses and cattle scattered over a vast expanse to graze on the dry and scanty herbage. The hunters, however, were able to find enough wild game to furnish the caravan with some fresh meat each day. Fort Benton was reached August 15.

Father De Smet was a weary and disappointed man, for, as he wrote, "When I left St. Louis, I had intended to see a very large number of Indians during the summer and fall, but local conditions and the dangers of the cruel Sioux war had absolutely blocked my plan."

At Fort Benton he learned that "the contagion of this war had spread to the upper tribes of the Sioux, who had hitherto been at peace with the whites. The reports that reach us every day of robberies and massacres committed by the Indians of the plains on one hand—and on the Salt Lake route by marauders and murderers of another species, the [white] off-scourings of civilization, living by robbery and assassination on the unhappy travelers whom they meet . . ." brought to him the realization that he was trapped in the Far North.

Getting through to St. Louis by horseback was probably impossible. Attempting to descend the river in an open skiff would have been suicidal. Moreover, he could find no one willing to attempt the trip, either by land or water, with him.

He had only one alternative to spending a long winter at Fort Benton, and that was to travel across the mountains to the Columbia and take ship to Panama.

With a small contingent of Indians and half-breeds, and the two Italian Brothers, he set out by horseback on August 25, 1863, for the Mission of St. Peter at the Great Falls of the Missouri. From there he would follow a new road which had been surveyed by government engineers—one of them his old and good friend, Captain John Mullen.

He was unaware, of course, that he was starting on his last journey to the mountains.

XXXIII

As he traveled westward in the late summer and fall of 1863, Father De Smet found the Jesuit missions "prosperous and flourishing," a condition attributable not so much to his pioneering in the remote areas as to his competency as a business manager and procurator. For years, with tireless zeal and determination, he had begged and borrowed and implored throughout the United States and Europe to obtain the supplies and equipment, the manpower and money, to keep the mountain establishments going.

If he did not know that he was making his last journey through the wilderness he had first seen more than twenty years before, he would, when he looked back on it, recall that it was the most pleasurable he had made, that it was a triumphal march as well as a farewell visit. Everywhere he went he was overwhelmed with friendliness, received with shouts of joy and accorded unlimited reverence and respect. He preached and he celebrated Masses, and he saw the "edifying spectacle" of Indian men, women and children reciting prayers and singing canticles and asking God for the privilege of living in peace.

Beyond the mountains he no longer had to face the peril of a canoe trip down the raging Columbia or endure the hardships of a journey by horseback, for at Walla Walla he met the wave of civilization that was sweeping up the Columbia Valley from the Pacific Coast. Walla Walla had been "barely a town of yesterday, but already it has over 2000 inhabitants . . . All the places adapted to agriculture are covered with vast farms, for thirty to forty miles around . . ."

From Walla Walla he took a scheduled stage to Wallula,

thirty miles distant, and early on the morning of "the 7th [of October] I embarked upon the steamboat which makes regular trips to the Dalles." Where steamboats were halted by rapids, there were "little railroads" to speed the travelers on their way, and below each rapid another steamboat waited to take them on.

He sailed from Portland on October 13th and reached San Francisco on the 21st. After visiting the College of Santa Clara, he went to San José. There in the establishment of the Sisters of Notre Dame de Namur he found the five nuns whom he had conducted to America in 1843. They had been the first Sisters to cross the Columbia bar, the first to enter the Oregon wilderness, and although their years of hardship and sacrifice were registered in their bent bodies and lined faces, he was delighted to find them "still in good health."

He left San Francisco by steamer on November 3. A stop was made at Acapulco to take on coal and mail, and Panama was reached on the 17th. The SS *North Star* took him north in the Atlantic, and on November 26th sailed into New York Harbor.

Early in December he was in Washington to report on his journey, and "I also had an errand—matters to bring before the government in favor of our missions among the Indians." Six months had passed since the Battle of Gettysburg, and the war was going well for the Union, but he could make no such claim for the bloody conflict raging across the Great Plains on either side of the Missouri River.

There seems little doubt that he had another audience with President Lincoln. Subsequent letters he wrote indicate he was at the White House, but he made no mention of a meeting with the President. If he was not received by Mr. Lincoln there is ample evidence to show that Mr. Lincoln was aware of his presence in the capital.

He was requested to go once more to the Sioux Country in the coming spring, this time in the official capacity of a representative of the President, and he was offered compensation and expenses for the mission. His status would be that of a diplomatic emissary. It seems unlikely that such an assignment would have been proffered him without Mr. Lincoln's knowledge.

He reached St. Louis shortly before Christmas. Chiefly for two reasons, he had made no commitment regarding the proposed peace mission.

The first reason was that he was not well. His physician in St. Louis considered him seriously ill, and kept him in bed as much as possible. He also ordered him to let his beard grow, for what therapeutic purpose, if any, was not revealed.

Father De Smet's irrepressible sense of humor prompted him to have his photograph made with the growth, and he sent it off to his family in Europe. He thought he might be called upon to play the role of Santa Claus—he had the proper girth, as well —but in the letter accompanying the picture he admitted that he was "broken down with all sorts of troubles." Among these was a growing deafness in one ear.

"I cannot hide from you, dear Silvie," he told his niece, "that my health has been wavering for some months past, and begins to be threatening . . . I suffer particularly with my head; it is seldom that I can leave my room. In case my health should permit, I will have to make an effort to take the road again, to undertake a very long and dangerous journey among the Indian tribes."

He showed even greater concern for his health in a letter to a nephew, written about the same time in the early part of 1864: "Insensibly the years pass on. I find myself already in my sixty-fourth year, and I feel a conviction that my end is near—*fiat voluntas Dei.*"

On another occasion he told a friend, Gustave: "Like a regular old man, I am full of infirmities . . . my greatest privation is to be unable even to celebrate Holy Mass. It is the first time since I was ordained priest in 1827 that I have been prevented by sickness from celebrating at the altar. I can see that the doctors are not without some uneasiness . . . I am conscious of a wish to be able to renew and continue my missions and travels among the Indians . . . The government desires me to go thither as a pacificator, and I will do so gladly if in any way my health allows it . . . As for myself, I am not without hope . . . we are in the Lord's hands."

The second reason which gave him pause in considering another journey among the Sioux was that it had been suggested he travel with military forces. On each previous journey the only banner he had carried was that of the Church, his only insignia the cross. No weapon of war had every accompanied him when he entered an Indian village.

He feared that if he went to the Sioux supported by soldiers or under the American flag he would not only be compromising his influence but he might be looked upon as a traitor, at least as an agent of the power which the Indians believed had only one motive—to destroy them.

On several occasions he wrote friends and colleagues that the request to make the peace trip had been made to him by Secretary of State Seward and Secretary of the Interior John P. Usher. In other letters he said he had been asked to go by the "government," and by the "Indian Department."

He told a colleague in March of the request by the "Commissioner of the Indian Department . . . to bring about, if possible, a peace among the hostile Sioux, acting in concert with the general troops and the appointed agents.

"They offer to pay all my expenses, with a handsome remuneration for myself. Not being well as yet I have not accepted their request. I fear I would lose all caste among the Indians. They have hitherto looked upon me as the bearer to them of the word of the Great Spirit . . . Should I present myself in their midst as the bearer of the word of the Big Chief of the Big Knives in Washington, no longer their Great Father, but now their greatest and bitterest enemy, it would place me in rather an awkward situation.

"I have written to the commissioner that if I can go, I will go on my own hook, without pay or remuneration . . ."

He wrote a friend that his reception by the Sioux "would be very different if I presented myself in company with the General of the American Army and the agents of the government. Surely my black robe would then cease to be a passport for me into the Indian Country. I tried to make the Commissioner of Indian Affairs see this."

Despite his grave illness and his misgivings about the plan for the peace mission, he must have suspected all along that he would go, for as early as February, 1864, he had informed the Father-General that he had "written to two Sioux interpreters, trusty men, raised among these tribes, to consult them and obtain information regarding the present state of the Sioux Country with respect to the war, as to the disposition of the Indians in regard to peace, and whether my presence among them could be of any use . . . I propose to visit those warlike tribes in the course of the coming summer . . . I have not compromised nor engaged myself in any way with those high [government] officials."

Commissioner of Indian Affairs W. P. Dole's eagerness to have Father De Smet make the trip prompted him to make a compromise. While Father De Smet need not always remain with troops, he insisted that Indian agents go up the river at the same time, and that "an expedition under orders from the War Department will either accompany you or be in the country during your stay so that you may be able . . . to confer and cooperate with the commander of said expedition as to the best course to be pursued . . ."

Dole's insistence on these arrangements was understandable. Should Father De Smet be successful in negotiating an agreement of peace, he wanted both his own agents and the military available to carry it out for the government. Father De Smet would be in no position, and would have no authority, to conduct such actions.

But Dole expressed the belief that Father De Smet could by

himself "safely visit them [the hostiles] in their camps and convey to them any message that the government may wish to send them for either the Interior or War Departments."

Dole, thereupon, proposed the message he thought should be delivered: "Tell them how good it is to be at peace with the government, whereas their utter extermination will be the result if they continue in hostility to the white people."

As if in an afterthought, Dole added: "I have very great confidence in your prudence and capacity for this mission and therefore forbear to give you specific instructions for your guidance."

Father De Smet did not know whether to laugh or cry. The Sioux had learned long ago how "good" it was to be at peace with the government. That was not the kind of a peace they wanted again. Dole's letter, in addition to being stupid, was gratuitous and patronizing, if not insulting. Prudence, indeed! Yes, he would be prudent, and that would mean above all else that he would not follow Dole's advice. Threats of extermination would have no effect at all. The Sioux had already concluded they were facing death, and they were determined to fight until it came, unless . . . unless they could be convinced that the forked tongue of the federal government had ceased to wag. Prudence! His words would be the words of the Great Spirit, for whom he was the recognized spokesman in the minds of the Indians. If they would no longer listen to those words, there could be no peace.

He believed they would. He believed, as well, that the greatest problem was not getting the Indians to leave the warpath, but was getting the government to live up to its promises, to be honest.

Early in April 1864, Father De Smet's health had begun to show a marked improvement, and he made his decision: he would go on the mission to the Sioux.

XXXIV

If he had been a man of less fortitude, of less resolution, Father De Smet might well have left the steamboat *Yellowstone* as it fought its way up the Missouri in the spring of 1864, and have made his way by any means possible back to St. Louis.

When he heard the story of the Winnebagos, he was tempted to throw up his hands in disgust and abandon his mission to the Sioux as hopeless. How, he asked himself, would it be possible to plead for peace in the name of a government that could not be trusted, a government that had displayed unmistakably its evil characteristics of dishonesty and improbity?

He went on, but with an aching heart he dispatched to a European magazine a story which indicted the American Government throughout the civilized world.

The reservation of the Winnebagos was in the upper Mississippi country. It had been guaranteed to them in perpetuity. They had developed good farms, built good homes, and were completely peaceful. Because of the Sioux War, in which they had taken no part and to which they were opposed, they were forced by the federal government to abandon their property. It was immediately invaded and taken over by white settlers.

The Winnebagos, numbering two thousand, presented no threat whatsoever to anyone. Their forceful expatriation actually was the result of a diabolical and inhumane scheme, condoned by the Indian Department, to steal their valuable lands. Its cruelty was augmented by the inconceivably absurd manner in which it was carried out. They were taken from Mankato down the St. Peters to Fort Snelling, loaded on steamboats, thence down the Mississippi to the Missouri, and up the Missouri

333

to the new reservation assigned them. It was below the Big Bend of the Missouri, 1363 miles from its mouth, but only about 300 miles by land from their old dwelling place. Men, women and children jammed like animals on the boats were carried more than 2000 miles, when they might have reached their destination easily and without hardship by wagon caravans on an overland journey of only 300 miles.

They had been promised good homes and good lands. They got neither. They were unceremoniously put ashore on raw land, and there was no housing. Only a little food was given to them. They had no farm implements. They starved and died by scores, while soldiers patrolled the area to keep them from leaving to obtain food. Men who attempted to hunt game for their starving families were shot down. Women were raped by drunken soldiers.

Similar conditions prevailed at other places along the river. From Yankton in Dakota Territory, Father De Smet wrote an editor friend: ". . . peace is rendered almost impossible by the recent occurrences . . . and inflames the hatred of the whites in every Indian heart . . . I am sent out under the auspices of the government, in the capacity of 'messenger of the word of peace.'

"Still it is impossible to deceive one's self . . ."

The news that Black Robe was coming up the river went ahead of the boat. The Kettles and the Yanktonnais left the warpath and came fearlessly into Fort Sully to talk with him, bringing their little children to be baptized. He gave them 164 images of patron saints and numerous medals of the Holy Virgin.

Casually he brought into the council the subject of the war, citing its tragedies and warning of its futility. The Kettle and Yanktonnais chiefs were irresolute, but they listened thoughtfully to his words.

The situation was both ironic and tragic. Here was a lone Black Robe moving without danger among the Sioux, smoking at ease with them, eating wild game with them. Not far distant,

soldiers armed with the most modern weapons of war were dying
while they fought to capture ghosts.

Systems and tactics developed at West Point were of no value.
The Sioux were "here today and somewhere else tomorrow." Suddenly one night they are stampeding the horses and mules and
cattle of the emigrants and settlers. Suddenly they are attacking
the caravans, and vanishing like wraiths into the shadows. Suddenly they are pouring a deadly fire into a passing steamboat
and leaving its deck red with blood.

"The Indian," said Father De Smet, "has the gift of being
everywhere without being anywhere."

They gathered for battle, and they scattered if the fortunes of
war turned against them. Most of the time they left their wives
and children in concealment, like animals going forth to hunt
food for their young. The Indian "has neither towns, forts nor
magazines to defend, nor line of retreat to cover. He is embar-
rassed with neither baggage nor packhorses. He goes into action
when a favorable occasion is presented, and never risks himself
without having the advantage of numbers and position on his
side."

There was not a nation on earth more ambitious for military
renown than the Sioux, not a nation that held in higher estima-
tion the conduct of a valiant warrior, and not a savage people
alive with finer physiques, greater courage or superior intellects.

Fort Berthold had been built as a trading post in 1845. In the
summer of 1864, when Father De Smet reached it, it had been
converted into a military station. He arrived on June 9th, and at
once sent out an express by Indian courier to advise the Sioux of
his presence there and his wish to smoke with them.

For reasons of economy and war the Gros Ventres, Arikaras
and Mandans had united and were residing at the old Mandan
villages adjacent to the fort. Father De Smet called them together and "made known to them the motives of my visit."

He gave these as: (a) to announce the word of the Great
Spirit; (b) to baptize children; (c) to penetrate among their

enemy, the Sioux; and (d) to deliver to all tribes a message of peace from the President of the United States.

He erected an altar in a room of the trading post, and performed religious services and devotions while he waited for an answer from the Sioux tribes who were in the forefront of the fighting.

Nearly a month passed. No reply from the Sioux came. Then suddenly the Sioux themselves were there. The ghosts appeared on the bank of the Missouri opposite Fort Berthold.*

Father De Smet gave careful attention to the invitation from the Santee Sioux. His conclusion was that it would be unwise for him to visit them as an emissary of peace, in the name of Mr. Lincoln, without some assurance that the military would not violate the terms of any truce he might secure. He had no intention of making promises, only to have the Army break them. If he secured a peace pact, he wanted the unequivocal word of the government that it would be respected to the letter and carried out in all its provisions.

In accordance with this decision, he set out down the river with a small military escort to meet General Sully and discuss the matter with him. He found the main body of troops, some five thousand in number, two hundred miles below Fort Berthold.

General Sully unhesitantly rejected his request. He had, the general declared, been sent out to find and punish the Sioux, and he felt it incumbent upon him to perform the duty to the fullest success possible. He would make no agreement to respect the terms of any surrender or agreement for a cessation of hostilities that Father De Smet might effect. The Sioux hostiles would be captured and punished, or they would be annihilated.

Father De Smet knew there could be no peace that year.

When the next steamboat went down the river, he was aboard. His notation on the issue said simply:

* See the Prologue.

"In consequence of the general's declaration, and the circumstances of the case, my errand of peace, though sanctioned by the government, became bootless and could only serve to place me in a false position; namely, that of being face to face with the Indians without being able to do them the least service."

He reached St. Louis late in August and left there for Washington on September 3rd, to report "to the government all that had passed . . ."

Not only in the year 1864 would there be no peace in the Sioux Country. Unless the policies and the behavior of the government underwent drastic revisions, there would be no peace for years to come.

XXXV

It was the decision of the Father-General of the Society of Jesus that Father De Smet had served the American Government to the fullest extent that might reasonably be expected of him—at least for the time being. Affairs of the Jesuits which Father De Smet was particularly well equipped to handle had been neglected during his absences. The Father-General directed the Father-Provincial in St. Louis to instruct the great missionary and peace envoy to report to Rome.

Father De Smet found the order waiting for him when he returned from Washington in the fall of 1864. In October he sailed from New York on his fourteenth crossing of the Atlantic.

During the next eight months, he traveled on Society business throughout the Continent. He was received at least three times by Pope Gregory XVI. From the Belgian King he received the decoration of Chevalier of the Order of Leopold. Throughout Europe he was honored at countless dinners and was a guest in the mansions of illustrious persons.

It was for the most part a thoroughly enjoyable trip, and he met with great success in obtaining money and recruits for the Indian missions, yet he knew a sense of relief and a feeling of gratitude when, on June 7, 1865, he sailed for the United States on the SS *City of New York*.

In his journal he made no mention of a premonition of death, but his entries made it clear that he feared his days on earth were drawing to a close.

"I leave anew my native country, my family, my friends, my benefactors, my brothers in religion," he said. "*Adieu, adieu* to all—and who knows? it may be forever, until the supreme reunion in heaven.

"This separation gives me no small heartache; but I hope to be able to work yet a little for the glory of God and the salvation of souls; this is the supernatural magnet which draws me so far away from dear Belgium and the affection that I have found here.

"I always miss something when I am not among my good Indians . . . I am conscious of a certain void wherever I go, until I come again to my dear Rocky Mountains. Then calm comes back to me; then only am I happy. *Haec requies mea* . . . after having passed a good share of my life among the Indians, it is among them that I desire to spend the few years that are left me still; it is among them also, if it be the will of God, that I desire to die."

The black crepe of mourning for Abraham Lincoln hung in the bright light of peace, and Father De Smet hoped "that President Johnson will remove from his side the vengeful agitators, and then the return to the Union will render this land more beautiful, prosperous and great than it has ever been. But the more violent and widespread the fire, the longer time will it take to extinguish it. The American torment has been disastrous in its effects, but the wisdom of the people will avail to heal it in the end . . . at least we must hope so."

He could not show the same confidence with respect to the Indian question. There was sarcasm in his tone when he said that Congress was "investigating" the terrible Sand Creek Massacre, in which troops led by Colonel J. M. Chivington butchered several hundred helpless Cheyennes who had arrived at Fort Lyon, Colorado, after being guaranteed protection by the government.

The newspapers announced that the war against the upper Missouri tribes was being pushed at full speed. General P. E. Connor, in command, had ordered his men to pursue the enemy "without rest, never stopping to parley with them and never leaving their trail before coming up with and chastising them.

They must be severely punished to begin with, and then we will see whether, by good behavior, they show themselves worthy to escape complete extermination."

Sadly Father De Smet sighed: "The same atrocious policy."

Reaching St. Louis on June 30, 1865 he found conditions in a grave state. A new state constitution and a number of ordinances had been forced through the legislature by the Radical Republicans, who had won control of the state government, which subjugated religious freedom and civil rights to political beliefs and affiliations. The constitutional provisions and the stringent laws were designed to perpetuate the control of the Radical Republicans, but their fanatical and bigoted authors made no secret of their hope to cripple the Catholic Church more than any other denomination.

Discriminatory taxes were imposed. "According to the Constitution of the State," Father De Smet wrote a friend, "all our churches, cemeteries, charitable institutions, have to support enormous taxes, while all sectarian establishments, including those of the Jews, are exempt from taxation."

The new constitution also provided that no person could vote, hold public office, preach, teach, practice law, solemnize marriages or serve as a juror who could not swear under oath that he had never sympathized with the Confederate cause and who would not proclaim loyalty to the Radical Republican Party and uphold its political tenets.

Father De Smet openly condemned the new constitution and ordinances because, like many others, he believed they abrogated basic rights and freedoms guaranteed all citizens under the American Constitution. He maintained that not only would priests and nuns be forced by them to engage in partisan politics, but they could be prevented from teaching in schools and be denied the right to worship in accordance with their beliefs.

It was the first time in his life that he had refused to obey the law, and he was greatly troubled, but he declared firmly that "no Catholic priest in Missouri will take the oath."

He thought it "curious that a land so proud and jealous of its liberty can hatch so many tyrants of the lowest and most detestable kind," but he expressed the belief that the laws were so absurd that they would soon "be smothered and expire."

Perhaps because of his prominence, no effort was made by the authorities to force him to abide by the noxious statutes, but several priests and nuns were arrested for continuing to teach without taking the oath.

"We pray and keep our patience under the wings of the American Eagle," Father De Smet said.*

Father De Smet had been directed to remain in St. Louis through the winter of 1865–66 and direct the defiance of the Catholic clergy. He did that, but he also busied himself at other tasks. In letters to his family he disclosed that he was writing histories of both the Potawatomies and of Missouri.

By the spring of 1866, Father De Smet's health had so improved that he felt himself able to undertake a trip up the Missouri to Fort Benton. Oddly enough, the journey had been suggested by his superiors. There were plans being considered to open new missions, especially among the Sioux, if possible, and there were several matters involving old establishments that should be dealt with at first hand—such mundane things as accounts to be rectified, drawings for new buildings to be approved, transfers to be effected, supplies and money to be budgeted for the coming year, needs for churches and schools to be estimated.

There was, of course, always a chance that he could be of some assistance in inaugurating peaceful relations between the government and warring tribes, or even between Indian nations fighting each other, but that work would be secondary. He would travel primarily on business for the Jesuits. Anyway, there was little hope of his succeeding as an emissary of peace as long as the government persisted in the current Indian policies, as

---

* His contentions were upheld. The Supreme Court of the United States found the Missouri Constitution unconstitutional in January 1867.

long as dishonest officials, unscrupulous politicians, thieves, swindlers and corrupt bureaucrats were giving orders.

The Army did not make Indian policy. It only attempted to carry it out. Nevertheless, although government plans and programs were diametrically opposed to those advocated by Father De Smet, the Army was always glad to have him in the Indian Country. Whatever he did, even though it be inconclusive, was beneficial to both sides, not to mention mankind in general.

When the Army learned that he was planning a trip up the river in the spring of 1866 on "church business," it promptly issued him a "passport." This was, of course, merely a gesture of good will. Yet, one could never tell when the occasion might arise on which he could be of some specific service.

Father De Smet needed nothing less than a piece of government paper. The cause of peace might have been aided immeasurably if the situation had been reversed, if a passport had been given by him to the Army. He could go alone where a military force would be obliged to fight for every step it advanced.

"Headquarters Military Division of the Mississippi," the Army passport said. "All officers of the Army within this Military Division are required, and all citizens are requested to extend to the bearer of this letter, the Reverend Father De Smet, a Catholic priest who has heretofore traveled much among the Rocky Mountains and is now en route for missions under his control, all the assistance and protection they can to enable him to fulfill his benevolent and humane purposes.

"He has always been noted for his strict fidelity to the interests of our government, for indefatigable industry and an enthusiastic love for the Indians under his charge."

The signature was that of Major General William Tecumseh Sherman.

Father De Smet's 1866 trip was notable mainly for the writings he produced during it and as a result of it. His journal, the articles he prepared for publication in periodicals, and his letters to friends comprised a valuable contribution to the history of the time. He wrote detailed descriptions of the country, of the river, of the economic conditions, the military scene, of the people he met and with whom he traveled.

Upon entering the Sioux Country, the *Ontario,* on which he was traveling, "was put in fighting trim. The pilot house was planked over and made safe against bullets or arrows, the cannon was mounted in the bow, all the carbines, guns and pistols were inspected and loaded, and above all, sentinels were posted by night to keep guard against any surprise by the enemy."

But once again a steamer on which Father De Smet was a passenger passed without violence through the Sioux. War parties were sighted, but they kept "at a respectful distance from the boat, without the least hostile demonstration." When the *Ontario's* destination, Fort Benton, was reached, Father De Smet was "glad to say our firearms have served only to slay the timid animals . . . which were at once cut up for the kitchen and dinner table . . ."

He took every opportunity as usual to visit Indian camps. He talked with the Yanktons, Yanktonnais, Brules, Ogallalas, Two-Kettles, Santees and Sioux-Blackfeet. The Indians had just "emerged from a long and severe winter; the new grass was barely beginning to show, and the leaves of the willows and cottonwoods that fringe the river to develop. For several months the Indians had existed on the flesh of their lean dogs and horses, together with a pittance of wild roots. A great mortality, especially of the children, had brought desolation and mourning to most of the families; scarlet fever and other maladies were still continuing their devastation."

For hours he listened to headmen pouring out their troubles, relating the sufferings of their people, and "In my quality of Black Robe I did my best to give them salutary counsels, as well as to console them."

His heart was sick. The "vengeances which they on their side provoke are often most cruel and frightful. Nevertheless, one is compelled to admit that they are less guilty than the whites. Nine times out of ten, the provocations come from the latter—that is to say, from the scum of civilization, who bring to them the lowest and grossest vices, and none of the virtues, of civilized men."

His writings of 1866 on the religion of the Indians were acclaimed by theologians as critical, historical and psychological studies of great merit. They revealed a remarkable knowledge of Indian beliefs, and, perhaps more important, a profound understanding and appreciation of those beliefs.

It was his opinion that there were "no people amongst whom the Christian religion has yet been attempted more various and obstinate in their superstitions . . . By most persons the capacity of the Indians has been greatly underrated. They are generally considered as low in intellect, wild men thirsting after blood, debased in their habits and groveling in their ideas.

"Quite the contrary is the case. They show order in their national government, order and dignity in the management of their domestic affairs, zeal in what they believe to be their religious duties, sagacity and shrewdness in their dealings and often a display of reasoning powers far above the medium of uneducated white men . . ."

A letter was received by Father De Smet from J. B. Chardon, an Indian trader at Greenwood, Dakota Territory. It said: "I send you a few lines from the chiefs of the Yanktons. They say when they were at Washington their Great Father promised them a school and teachers, and now it is seven years and they have seen nothing as yet . . . What we want is to learn the American language and their ways.

"I am now very old and before I die I want to see a school and the children learn how to read and write in the American language, and if you will try and get with us, I will be very happy . . . I think that the Great Spirit will take pity on us and grant all our requests. Hoping that we may hear and see you soon, we remain, ever yours."

After each signature on the letter, which Chardon wrote, there was an X. The names were:

> The Man That Strikes the Ree
> Little Swan
> Feather in the Ear
> Medicine Cow
> Jumping Thunder

Tears stained Father De Smet's browned face as he wrote the Commissioner of Indian Affairs: "Should our Board of Missions agree to grant a Catholic missionary establishment, as expressly desired by the chiefs of the Yanktons, will it meet with the approbation of the Indian Bureau in Washington?"

He reminded the Bureau of the promises made to the Yanktons and diplomatically inquired as to the stipulations—as if he did not know what they were—of the treaty which the government had signed with these Indians. He enclosed a copy of the letter from the chiefs, but he had little hope that anything would come of the matter.

The river journey of 1866 took a heavy toll of his strength. He suffered severe physical hardship, to which his experience of one night in a Sioux camp attested.

Worn by the heat of the day and the strain of a long horseback ride, "I expected to enjoy a good sleep. I had reckoned without my hosts. I had been perhaps ten minutes in bed and was almost asleep, when I was awakened with a start. The dugout was swarming with famished rats; they came and laughed in my very face . . . They carried on at a shocking rate. They were rummaging all my bags of provisions, and were about in earnest the transportation of such of their contents as suited their purposes to their caves, when I stopped them short . . . I hung my sacks on the posts of my mansard out of reach . . . of these highwaymen.

"During this labor I felt myself assailed by another enemy, the flea. If he is not so formidable as the rat, he is more importunate

and he attaches himself to his prey in a most tenacious manner
. . . I was awake and up all night, making play with my hands,
fingers and nails to defend myself . . ." not only against the rats
and fleas, but "their comrades in evildoing, the mosquitoes, the
bedbugs, the ants, the spiders, *et omne genus muscarum.*"

Father De Smet spent the last five months of 1866 in St. Louis.
At the age of sixty-six, he found he could not recover his strength
as swiftly as he once had been able to do. It felt good to lie for a
little time in his clean and comfortable bed after waking in the
morning.

XXXVI

The years 1867 and 1868 in several ways were the most important in Father De Smet's life. They were active years, devoted almost entirely to an attempt to bring about a cessation of the disastrous Indian wars of the northern plains.

Once again—and this time with unprecedented forcefulness and drama—it was demonstrated that he was without a peer both as a spiritual leader and a secular mentor in all the immense territory between the Missouri and the Columbia.

Indian tribes were still considered foreign nations by the government. Thus, negotiations with them could be carried on legally only through diplomatic channels. The absurdity of this reasoning, and the injustices which were the fruit of it, were without equal in history.

If the tribes were foreign nations, then the American Government was guilty of invading foreign countries. The government was demanding that people whose property, rights and lives were being destroyed by American citizens stop defending themselves. It was asking that the Indians agree to treaties which gave Americans the privilege of continuing to invade their lands and devastate their holdings.

It was as if America had invaded Canada, then asked the Canadians to sign a treaty of peace which would sanction the invasion and permit them—if they were able to find enough to eat—to continue to exist in their own country.*

---

* It was not until 1871 that the Congress, perhaps ashamed of making treaties only to break them, or grudging the time, money and parchment wasted, decided that Indian tribes were not foreign nations but simply residents of certain areas, and most of all damn nuisances. Treaties were

There was more than met the eyes of newspaper readers in the stories which came out of Washington in March 1867, reporting that Father De Smet had been asked to serve once more as a government peace negotiator in the Indian Country. The request ostensibly had been made by Secretary of the Interior O. H. Browning, but as it was a matter involving foreign nations the sanction of the State Department had been obtained, and the White House had been informed of the plan. Placing a man of Father De Smet's distinction, capability and integrity in such a role could result in nothing harmful to the Administration. Even if his mission was a total failure, it would indicate that the government was making every humane effort to secure peace. Moreover, if a man of his influence could not induce the Indians to abandon the warpath, nothing could do it, that is, nothing but extermination.

The politicians knew what they were doing. They would appoint Father De Smet an "envoy extraordinary"—impressive title —and they would give him big pay and all the expense money he needed.

Father De Smet had other ideas. He was too shrewd and too experienced to be hoodwinked in such a manner. He would accept the mission, and if they wanted to call him by a fancy name, and pay his traveling expenses, that was all right, but he would go only as Black Robe, in the name of God, humanity and justice. The Indians would think of him as Black Robe, and as nothing else. He would go "with the distinct understanding that I shall not accept any remuneration for my personal services. I prefer to be altogether independent in money matters and my only object is to be of use to the white and still more to the poor Indians."

The government accepted his terms, but the politicians were

---

thereafter to be called *conventions*. The only difference was in the name, and by any name the pacts could be broken. The government continued to ignore the *conventions* as fast as they were signed.

annoyed by his pronouncement that the Indians "are for the most part the victims of the misdeeds of the whites.

"I do not hesitate to say that the depredations of the Indians are in general the result of incessant provocations and injustices on the part of the whites. When the savages raise the hatchet to go on the warpath, it is because they are pushed to the limit of endurance, and then the blows that they deal are hard, cruel and terrible. That is their nature.

"It is always true that if the savages sin against the whites it is because the whites have greatly sinned against them."

The depredations against them and the failure of the government to keep its word had driven the Indians to form what Father De Smet termed a "formidable coalition which seems from recent information to be growing from day to day."

In the coalition were "Cheyennes, Arapahoes, Sans-arcs, Hunkpapas, Blackfeet, Bloods, Brules and a great many other tribes. Will they receive me among them? . . . all hatchets are raised against the white . . . hundreds of scalps dangle and flutter from the tips of their lances . . . Eagle feathers are in great demand . . . their horses' manes and tails are covered with them—each plume denoting a scalp taken from the enemy.

"I have a very large and difficult task, and all that encourages me is the prayers that accompany me."

His good friend, Pananniapapi, the Yankton chief, and twenty-eight headmen of the tribe had been taken to Washington shortly after the first of the year for a conference with the Secretary of the Interior. When Father De Smet heard they were en route home and would arrive by railroad in Omaha about the middle of April, he quickly made plans to go there with the hope that he might travel up the river with them to the Yankton Agency.

He left his wagon, two mules, a saddle horse, his trunks, camping equipment and supplies to be sent up the river to him, and at three o'clock on the afternoon of April 12th, he took the night train for Chicago. The trip of two hundred and eighty miles from St. Louis was made in *only fourteen hours*. The train stopped at fifty-three stations on the way.

At eight-thirty on the morning of April 13th, he boarded a North Western Railroad train in Chicago for Omaha, where it was scheduled to arrive on the afternoon of the 14th. The age of speed had come to the midwestern prairies, but if distance could be accomplished with astonishing rapidity man had not yet been able successfully to defy the elements. Spring rains washed out numerous bridges. At the little village of Denison, Iowa, the train halted, the line being "rendered impracticable by a continued series of washouts and other breaks caused by the flood."

After waiting several days for repairs to be made, Father De Smet and five other travelers engaged a wagon to take them the hundred miles to Sioux City. The first leg of the journey, however, ended at the Little Sioux River. No way could be found to get the vehicle and team across the raging stream. The travelers at last made a precarious crossing in a tipsy skiff, and on the opposite side found a farmer who agreed to take them on to their destination.

As good fortune would have it, Chief Pananniapapi and his colleagues arrived in Sioux City in mud-spattered rigs the next day, April 23rd. He and Father De Smet shared an affectionate reunion.

Father De Smet and the Yanktons embarked on the steamboat *Guidon* on April 30th. The boat "was crowded with passengers and merchandise for the new territories of Montana and Idaho. It was number 15 of the immense fleet of steamboats that were going this year to Benton, a distance of 3160 miles."

At the Yankton Agency, some two hundred and sixty miles above Sioux City, the Indians who had been to Washington were "received with open arms by their families and friends . . . I too shared, in my capacity of Black Robe, in their friendly demonstrations. They were all delighted to see us again in such good health."

Father De Smet found lodging in the house of the "excellent

interpreter of the nation, Mr. Alexis Giou." In a little attic, "my altar, bed and all my things were straightway arranged, and in a few minutes I found myself in a real little *chez moi,* glad and happy to have escaped from the noise and tumult of the boat."

For more than two weeks he waited for his outfit to arrive from St. Louis. On May 17th he noted in his journal: "The steamboat *Bighorn,* thirty-three days out from St. Louis . . . landed in good order my wagon, my little traveling necessities, my two mules and my saddle horse.

"These three animals, on coming ashore after so long an imprisonment, performed capers without end. The attractive perfume of the fresh grass caused them a delirium of joy; they threw themselves down with all four feet in the air, rolled right and left on the sod, jumped and skipped, and carried on at such a rate that they were near playing the mischief with the spectators, assembled to admire their leaps and exploits. Still, these four-legged humorists did not forget the matter of refreshments; in a short time each was going around with a rounded paunch, looking like a bag of hay."

On the trip up the river, the saddle horse had slipped from its tether and had gone overboard so quietly and skillfully that its absence was not discovered until an hour later. The boat was turned about, and at last the animal was "found safe and sound at the foot of a bluff too steep for him to climb; otherwise he would have got to the woods and that would have been the last of him. The deckhands brought him on board again."

On the 21st of May, Father De Smet set out on the journey that would take him through the heart of the Sioux Country. Chief Pananniapapi and some of the Yankton warriors would accompany him for a time, but would drop out as they reached their respective homes. Otherwise, the "little caravan was composed of a Sioux interpreter, a guide, a horse herder and a hunter."

Spring was in full bloom. The grasslands reaching to the sky were like a rolling emerald sea. Game was plentiful, and they enjoyed roasts of young venison and antelope. Birds were thick in the bottomlands, and prairie chickens, grouse and pheasants were flushed from the thickets.

"Everything seems to call me to be going . . ."

The journey to old Fort Pierre and Fort Sully, near the mouth of Teton River, was a succession of daily councils with moving bands.

May 24: The chief of the Brule tribe, Ghost Bull, "joined us on the road, and we camped together at the foot of the hills at Bijou."

May 27: More than a hundred lodges were found in the vicinity of Fort Thompson, belonging to the "Brules, Two-Kettles and Yanktonnais." The object of his mission for the government was already known to them. He was welcomed by "Iron Nation, Iron Eyes, Two Lances, White Hawk, Hunting Bear, Knuckle-Bone-Collar and White Bear . . . I opened the session with a solemn prayer . . ."

The chiefs laid before him "quite simply, their delicate and critical position."

Iron Nation spoke: "Commissioners and agents of the government come to us every year. What is the reason that so many fine words and pompous promises always come to nothing, nothing, nothing?"

May 30: "I found myself among 220 lodges . . ."

May 31: I convoked the chiefs and braves in a grand council —Chief Ghost, Yellow Hawk, Man-Who-Soars-above-the-Bird, Killed-the-First-One, Dispersed-the-Bears, Took-the-Enemy, Big Mandan, Serves-as-a-Shield, Iron Heart, Iron Horn, Red Tail Eagle . . . They complained bitterly of the bad faith of the whites, of the commissioners and agents of the government . . . This conduct sticks in their minds . . . They declared themselves favorable to peace—and ready to call on their young warriors to bury the hatchet . . ."

June 1: (Near Fort Sully) "I spent the whole day with the principal chiefs in conversation concerning religion and the . . . dangerous situation of the plains tribes . . . After the example of the whites, the Indians have proclaimed a sort of martial law; the war chiefs have assumed sole command."

June 2 to 5: These four days were occupied principally with conferences with Indians . . . "The coming and going is without end. Little Soldier has joined the camp; his tribe reckons more than 400 lodges . . . In the evening of the 5th a terrible hurricane . . ."

June 6 and 7: Generals H. H. Sully and E. S. Parker joined Father De Smet.

June 8: The generals called a grand council. They asked Father De Smet to speak first to the chiefs and braves, "to draw their attention and inspire confidence."

The chiefs had heard generals before, and they knew the emptiness of their promises. Father De Smet held their trust, and they knew he did not speak with a "forked tongue."

If Father De Smet disliked to appear in the company of military men, he did not feel that on this occasion he was being improperly used or that the generals were taking unfair advantage of him. He believed the officers to be men of integrity who would live up to their words to the best of their ability. It was not the Army that was at fault, but the system. Actually, a general had no more authority than an Indian agent. The men in Washington made the final decisions.

Each chief in turn "showed all his mind." Father De Smet thought the Indian speeches were "models of good sense and eloquence."

June 9: Chief Iron Shell, with several of his braves, presented himself. He proffered a plan that would bring peace to the plains, "but to establish it, three conditions appeared to him absolutely necessary. First, he said, send all your soldiers out of the country; close all your public roads through the Black Hills; prevent steamboats coming up the Missouri, so that the buffalo and other animals may not be disturbed. This was the *conditio sine qua non* of Iron Shell."

General Sully told Iron Shell "that the soldiers had been

brought into the country by the massacres that had taken place in Minnesota and on the plains of the Missouri; that if these murders and massacres continued, the number of soldiers would be increased, until they would cover the country as the grasshoppers cover the fields. Bury the hatchet, and the soldiers will return whence they came."

The two statements clearly illustrated the stalemate.

On July 10th, Father De Smet left Fort Sully for Fort Buford at the mouth of the Yellowstone, some seven hundred miles upstream, on the *Graham,* ". . . a floating palace, and the largest boat that has ever come up the Missouri. [It] is 249 feet in length."

On board were "five companies of soldiers destined for the different forts. My quality of envoy-extraordinary of the government carries with it the title of 'major,' strangely mated, it must be owned, with that of Jesuit. Still . . . it gives me readier access among the soldiers, a great many of whom are Catholics. I gave them, not as a major, but as a priest, all my spare moments."

On June 16th, the *Graham* reached Fort Rice, and "on both sides of the river were about 530 lodges encamped and waiting for our coming." Another "grand council," lasting through the 17th and 18th was held.

The next stop was Fort Berthold, 175 miles farther on, where a talk was held with the chiefs of the Mandans, Arikaras and Minnetarees, almost all of them old friends of Father De Smet. "They complained bitterly of the government agents and the soldiers. They deceive and rob them in the distribution of their annuities . . . All last winter they were the slaves and playthings of a hard, tyrannical captain, who seemed to make it his business to torment the poor wretches. When the women with their starving babies came up to the fort to pick up the filthy refuse thrown out by the soldiers' kitchen, they were pitilessly driven off with scalding water . . ."

June 28: Fort Buford was reached. There "a good number of chiefs and braves belonging to . . . the Assiniboines were waiting . . . A council was held with them and chiefs of the Crow and Santee tribes."

Late in July Father De Smet started back down the river, stopping wherever possible to smoke with Indians he had not met on the upbound trip. He got off the boat at Leavenworth when he was informed that a new peace commission named by President Johnson had gathered there. Immediately he was requested to accompany the commission on their trip of observation to the Indian Country. Although extremely weary after nearly four months on the upper river, he accepted the invitation.

His personal effects had gone on down the river to St. Louis on the boat which he had left at Leavenworth. It was necessary that he recover them before starting out again for the upper Missouri posts, and he left for St. Louis, promising to return at once and join the commissioners.

Descending the river, he had begun to prepare the report he would send to Washington. "All that I have observed and been able to learn among the different bands of Indians," he wrote, "makes me augur favorably of their good dispositions to live at peace . . . They ask, and have a right to demand, to have justice done them; that the annuities granted them by treaty should come to them; that the practice of putting them off with fine words should cease at once for all; that they be protected against the whites who come to sow iniquity and misery in their country; and in conclusion they humbly beg their Great Father the President to grant them agricultural implements, seeds, plows and oxen to till the soil. I repeat it, if our Indians become enraged against the whites, it is because the whites have made them suffer for a long time."

He kept a "strict list" of all the complaints made to him, and transmitted it to the Interior Department.

Regarding proposals to place all tribes on one or two large reservations, he declared: "It is not possible to change the nature of any race of men in a moment. The Indians were born to be hunters . . . It will take patience to transform them into cultivators; the thing will necessarily require some years. The Indians whom we visited are disposed to choose reservations suitable for agriculture . . . In every band a good number of families showed a favorable disposition to go to work without delay . . . If they succeed for the first three years in their noble efforts, the example of that industrious portion would soon be followed by the mass . . ."

On his journey of 1867, Father De Smet had sat in council with more than 15,000 Indians, and "they gave dilligent attention to all my religious instructions, and listened favorably to the words I brought them from the government."

Bluntly he told the President in his report that he was convinced "a general peace could be brought about, if honest agents were employed . . ."

Terrible summer heat prevailed in St. Louis as he prepared, late in August 1867, to rejoin the peace commission up the river. He knew a growing exhaustion. Suddenly fever struck him down.

His physician was alarmed when he found that Father De Smet's weight had decreased from 200 to 167 pounds. Examinations disclosed that he had for some time been suffering from Bright's disease.

There would be no second trip up the river for him that year.

"Let the Indians know, particularly the hostile bands . . ." he wrote his friend, C. E. Galpin, the trader at Fort Rice. "I shall try my best to be there next spring . . ."

XXXVII

Even though confined by his illness during the fall of 1867 and the following winter, Father De Smet kept up a heavy correspondence, striving to reply to all the letters he received. The hours at his table—sometimes he wrote on a board while in bed —taxed his limited strength, but he felt the work worthy and mandatory upon him.

It was not all pleasant correspondence by any means. In addition to the deplorable state of the government's relations with the Indians, upon which he felt obliged to speak, he was faced with the strongest personal attack of his life. For some time past he had been aware that it was being carried on against him, but he had refrained from commenting on it in the hope that it would die out and could be forgotten. At last it had become so virulent that he decided it was necessary for him to defend himself.

He was being charged, more or less surreptitiously, with permitting his name to be signed to letters, articles, reports and other documents which he had not himself prepared or written. The implication was disseminated that the writings which carried his signature, and which had brought him fame in both Europe and the United States, were not authentic, the information in them was not founded upon fact, and the descriptions of the country and the Indians, as well as the scientific data, were not reliable.

The accusations, as far as he could learn, had originated in Germany. German Jesuits coming to serve in western America had spread them, believing them to be true.

Father De Smet took the matter up with his superiors, and he wrote letters of protest to supervising Fathers in Europe. These were passed from hand to hand, and some of them found their way into print.*

In objecting to the malevolent criticism, he spoke forthrightly and did not hesitate to name the men he believed to be guilty.

"For some years past," he said in a letter to the German Jesuit, Father Roder, "several German priests are saying in America, on the testimony of one or several Fathers in your province, that my name is only an assumed name in the letters which are printed and the books that are published afterward bearing my name.

"The reverend and good Father Hasard, after his arrival at St. Louis, declared that it was the opinion in his province that I merely lent my name to the letters that were published.

". . . during my mission among the savages [in 1867] I met the Reverend Joseph Anthony Maria Gaes [from Freiburg, Germany] . . . I read him copies of three long letters upon the mission among the Indians in which I was then engaged. The reverend gentleman expressed his gratitude, accompanied by an admission . . . that the reading of my letters had rid him of the unfavorable impression concerning me which he had received from the Reverend Father Rothenflue before his departure for America. That this reverend [Rothenflue] . . . had assured him in confidence that I was not the author of the letters . . ."

Father De Smet recalled in his dissents that when he first went among the Indians he had been encouraged by his superiors "to write very fully in regard to them and to enter into minute details upon everything that concerned the Indian missions, the diverse countries inhabited by the Indians, the manners, customs, beliefs, etc. of these strange and unfortunate tribes."

The Father-General of the Jesuits had urged him "to give details of my missionary labors year after year. All the superiors and provincials of Missouri have also called for them . . ." He thought the volumes of his writings already published bore "witness that I have at least endeavored to discharge the duty laid upon me."

* At this time, five volumes of Father De Smet's collected letters had been published in French and English.

Father De Smet admitted to being sensitive to personal attack "which I have in no wise deserved," but he felt that more harm had been done by the accusations to the Jesuit province of Missouri, which had been "more or less compromised," and "would not permit such a fraud or imposture."

In a categorical denial of the charges, which was approved by his superiors, he declared that "the printed letters bearing my name are due to no other person, and permit me to protest to Your Reverence against those of your province who advance the contrary."

The campaign of slander halted.

Father De Smet prayed daily that he would recover his health enough to be able to join the peace commission in the spring of 1868. All the disappointments and frustrations of the past were not strong enough to kill in him the feeling that some beneficial results might follow the commission's efforts, and he wanted to use all the influence he possessed, perhaps his last ounce of strength, as well, to help bring about that end.

As in the past, however, he did not permit hope to deceive him from the realities of the situation. He was aware of the confusion which reigned in official circles. The Administration and several departments each had what were called "Indian policies." The people of the West had one of their own, as did the organized Protestant churches, powerful commercial and financial interests, and the United States Army. No single policy conformed with any of the others.

Even if reconciliation of the policies had been possible, which it was not, it would bring little progress to a solution of the troubles. Direction in any case—honest, forceful, competent direction—was mandatory. Without it nothing could be achieved. But where was it to come from? Needed was an overriding power that was not attainable by any group, bureau or even the Administration itself.

As for the Indian Department, it was composed of two camps. Over them both waved a hybrid emblem woven of many kinds of thread, its colors suffering from the admixture of ineradicable, adulterous shadings. In general, the Indian Bureau advocated a policy of peace and good will to the "noble red man," as the hypocrites in it spoke of the Indian. This attitude won it the affection of a great many nice old ladies and sentimental and sanctimonious Easterners who closed their eyes the better to see the world as they wanted it to be. In those who kept their eyes open and saw something of the truth of things, the Bureau's policy caused a sickening of the stomach. Those with stronger anatomies covered their faces with a hand to conceal their smirks and evil smiles.

Father De Smet did not quarrel with any attempt to bring peace and good will to the peoples of the earth. He used the same words in a letter to General Sherman in January 1868, but his application of them was different from that of the Indian Bureau. It was not so much peace and good will on the part of the bureaucrats that were needed. The immediate problem was to "instill peace and good will into the minds of the Indians." Once the Indians had them. They had not arbitrarily destroyed them. The white men had done that.

He had learned from sad experience that the Indian Bureau's contingent of starry-eyed idealists was the largest, but it was not the strongest. By comparison, the contingent of grafters, swindlers and venal adventurers, the hard-minded and unconscionable, although fewer in number, wielded far more power.

Practicality seldom disturbed the dreamers, reality never. They wanted decent treatment for the Indians, they wanted justice, but most of all they wanted peace, and in the hope of obtaining it they argued that it was cheaper to furnish the hostiles with the necessities of life—which included arms and ammunition—than to engage them in warfare.

The situation was hardly a credit to the reasoning powers of the officials. The Indians were being furnished with weapons, and then being condemned to death for using them.

But peace at any price was the doctrine of the idiotic tub-thumpers who confused absence of turmoil with godliness in government, and they dressed it in fine phrases and predicated it on lofty principles which were difficult for any stupid-but-honest person to question.

As for the thieves in the Indian Bureau, they had every reason to give such a policy tacit support. It was made to order for them, for peace on the plains meant an even larger pork barrel than war. You couldn't furnish Indians with the necessities of life if you couldn't find them, or if you had to fight them. No one had devised a scheme for supplying dead Indians with anything but graves. As it was, even a mildly enterprising agent could save ten to twenty thousand dollars a year on an annual salary of twelve hundred, and comparable thriftiness could bring a clever manufacturer or wholesaler even greater returns on a modest investment. These were not insignificant rewards, but they would be inconsequential in the face of those to be gained if all Indians could be induced to abandon their historic way of life and take residence in permanent establishments. Under such circumstances the number of wards to whom the government would be obligated to furnish the necessities of life would be immeasurably increased. The possibilities for theft were delightful to contemplate.

Father De Smet was too intelligent not to realize that continued railing at the government would do little good—no more good than damning an Indian for not surrendering when his means of living had been taken from him, when his wife and children were ragged, cold and starving, when his own belly was empty.

His duty was to get there, to participate in any negotiations and councils, to gain for the Indians any measure of improvement possible, to stand by their side. Condemnation and criticism would secure no benefits under the present conditions. Action was the important thing. Let the government think that his sole "object in offering my services in this affair proceeds merely from a feeling for the general welfare." That was what he told General

Sherman. It was not a dishonest statement. He believed that if the government saw him in that light, he might be able to use his influence to a greater advantage than he could if he was thought of only as defense counsel for the Indians.

In considering the members of the peace commission with which he hoped to travel in the summer of 1868, Father De Smet said of the Army officers on it: "I hesitate not to say, that the gentlemen . . . are all animated with the best of feelings toward the Indian tribes and to provide for their future welfare."

He was speaking specifically of Lieutenant General Sherman; General Alfred Terry, a Civil War hero; General Christopher C. Auger, whose military record was highly commendable; and his old friend, General Harney, who knew more about Indian fighting than any of his colleagues.

He made no public comment on the other members of the commission, no doubt because he was well aware that the corruptors had been on hand to protect themselves as much as they could when the commissioners were named. Certainly the Indians had no reason to feel comfortable about the civilian members. They were Senator John B. Henderson of Missouri, chairman of the Senate Committee on Indian Affairs, but whose main affiliations were with Eastern industrialists; N. G. Taylor, the Commissioner of Indian Affairs, a former minister to whom, one committeeman observed, sanctity still clung like a well-fitted coat; General [political] J. B. Sanborn, a Minnesota lawyer, party hack, and self-appointed court jester; and Colonel [political] S. F. Tappan, who rarely spoke and maintained a position in Taylor's shadow.

General Sherman was in St. Louis in February 1868. He brought cheering news from Washington. Congress had adopted a resolution which might go far toward halting corruption in the Indian Department. Father De Smet hastened to write Gerard at Fort Berthold that Sherman "assured me . . . that the distribution of annuities, henceforth, will be made under the special supervision of an officer of the Army, whose special duty will be to prevent all frauds. An Indian Department, independent of all others, is to be instituted, very different in many points from the old Indian Bureau."

He added, as if he felt it necessary to provide himself with an escape hatch: "I have not as yet seen its laws and regulations. When received I shall forward them to you."

The commissioners would assemble at Omaha on April 2. Some would go to New Mexico to hold meetings with tribes in that area of the country. A second group would go to Cheyenne to talk with any Indians who might be on the southern perimeter of the northern plains.

After that the movements of the Cheyenne contingent would necessarily depend upon the location of the hostile tribes operating in the Sioux Country. Final strategy would have to be formulated after Cheyenne had been reached and all available intelligence studied. Sherman would lead the northern group, and he expressed the hope that Father De Smet would be well enough to accompany him.

As the winter of 1867–68 neared an end, Father De Smet's physical condition was steadily improving. Some weeks had passed since he had suffered a hemorrhage. His strength was returning, and his weight was increasing. His physicians would have preferred to have him remain in St. Louis for the next several months, but at last consented to let him join the peace commission. His growing restlessness and the fear that profound disappointment might cause more of a setback than the exertion of traveling were factors which influenced their decision.

As Father De Smet packed his luggage he had the feeling—and history was soon to know the accuracy of it—that he was going on the most important journey of his many years in the West.

XXXVIII

Rolling westward across the Nebraska plains in a new palace car of the Union Pacific Railroad early in April, 1868, were Generals Sherman, Harney, Sanborn, Terry and Phil Sheridan, a group of staff aides and clerks, and Father De Smet.

Alongside the tracks ran the Platte River, and as Father De Smet gazed out at the ocean of greening grass and the thin lines of cottonwoods, he could only shake his head in wonder. His thoughts went back nearly thirty years, when he had made that same journey for the first time with the long caravan that was taking him to the mountains.

He abruptly halted the suggestion that he had developed wings before his time.

Word that Black Robe was traveling with the commissioners had gone ahead by telegraph. If the Indians did not comprehend the method of communication, they were willing to accept the information it brought. At North Platte City, where the river divided into its two great forks, Spotted Tail, head chief of the Brules, and his principal warriors were awaiting the train, eager for a smoke with the white man in whom their trust was unqualified.

"The council," Father De Smet reported, "terminated favorably, and was followed by a rich distribution of presents—victuals, garments, weapons—which made the hearts of our savages melt with joy."

Spotted Tail indicated that he was agreeable to meeting at a later time in the summer to negotiate a treaty which would provide his people with adequate hunting grounds and protection from white invaders. These things were solemnly promised to him by General Sherman.

If the conference with the Brules was encouraging, the information received from them, and from other Indian leaders at Fort Laramie, was not. The hostile bands of Sioux which the commissioners were most anxious to meet had lost themselves in the vast territory of the upper Missouri and the Yellowstone . . . no one could say where they might be. One thing, however, could be said with confidence: they would not be easy to find, and they would be even harder to draw into a council.

As Sherman viewed the situation, he concluded there was only one step to be taken. Someone had to go in search of them and induce them to come out of hiding for a conference at a place of their own selection.

There was unquestionably only one man who could undertake such a mission and have a reasonable chance of remaining alive.

A few days later, Father De Smet was speeding back to Omaha.

On April 21st, when the *Columbia* started up the Missouri River he was aboard, his "little chapel" set up in a stateroom, his destination Fort Rice in the heart of the Sioux Country, six miles above the mouth of the Cannonball River.

No one is capable of explaining adequately the functioning of the "wilderness telegraph." It was known, of course, that Father De Smet had gone to Cheyenne with the peace commission. That information had gone up the river in letters, in newspapers, and with civilian and military messengers. But how it became known that he was aboard the *Columbia*, and that he intended to go into the interior to find the hostile Sioux bands, must always remain a mystery.

Somehow the word had gone ahead of the boat, for at every landing Indians were waiting for him, and "I often had occasion to exercise the holy ministry among the inhabitants . . . who came to the woodyard or wharf, marrying couples who were awaiting the presence of a priest . . . and regenerating in the holy water of baptism a great number of children and several adults."

The water of the Missouri was unusually low, and the *Columbia* was in a "constant struggle with the current, sand bars and snags." The trip to Fort Rice consumed thirty-three days.

Father De Smet stepped ashore "in the midst of a great number of Indians, who were waiting for me and overwhelmed me with friendship . . . I had to pass first through a numerous file . . . In all their fantastic accoutrements they made a truly picturesque and, for the kind, admirable spectacle; their heads were adorned with feathers and silk ribbons . . . and their faces were daubed with the most varied colors. I received a good grip from each one . . . all the great chiefs of the different tribes were waiting for me to hear the important news . . ."

His simple statement that "I had my hands full at Rice" fell far short of portraying the situation.

He saw to it that all religious ceremonies were completed and all spiritual requests fulfilled before giving any attention to temporal obligations. For the first four days after his arrival he was kept busy with ecclesiastical duties, in that period baptizing more than six hundred children, celebrating Masses, and devoting himself for hours to the Catholic soldiers of the garrison.

On June 1st and 2nd he sat in council with the headmen and discussed his plans. They appeared to be astonished "and they hardly concealed from me the dangers that were involved —even touching the security of my scalp."

To those who advised him not to attempt such a perilous journey he replied that six lamps would burn for him before the altar in St. Louis all during the time of the expedition, and that many persons, perhaps thousands, would implore every day "before these burning lamps, the favor and protection of heaven upon all the band who accompany me."

Suddenly the councilors, "as by one impulse," cried out: "We will go with you! When shall we start?"

"Tomorrow at sunrise," he told them.

There were a hundred riders in the column that camped on the bank of the Cannonball River, twenty-two miles southwest of Fort Rice, Dakota Territory, at sundown on June 3, 1868.

Two of them were white men. One was old C. E. Galpin, who for thirty years had been a trader among the Sioux. He had with him his aging Sioux wife, a descendant of illustrious leaders, and influential throughout the immense domain over which her people roamed. The other white man was Black Robe, and though he was surrounded by chiefs he was the real commander of the expedition, he was the voice on earth of the Great Spirit, and among mortals no man could hold higher office.

"Galpin, a man of honesty and great experience, had generously offered to accompany me in the capacity of interpreter," Father De Smet told his journal.

Among the other volunteers were Two Bears of the Yanktonnais, "a very remarkable man, from his zeal for peace, his valor and his eloquence. He has solemnly adopted me as a brother"; and Running Antelope of the Hunkpapas, "renowned for his deeds of arms against his enemies, more especially against the whites"; and there were Bear's Rib, The Log, All Over Black, Returning Ghost, Red Cloud, Little Dog and Sitting Crow, chiefs with many lodges among the Santees, Sissetons, Ogallalas, Minneconjous, Blackfeet-Sioux, Yanktons.

"All of them offered themselves generously and freely in my service, with the sole object of persuading their hostile brethren to lend me an attentive and favorable ear, and if need were to protect me." Each had brought with him a number of carefully chosen warriors, experienced men who had known the terror and bloodshed of battle. In two wagons were provisions, the tent and blankets of Father De Smet, and the trunk containing his portable altar and other treasured religious articles.

It was June, the lovely month, The Moon When The Ponies Shed, and the great rolling plains were "covered with a rich carpet of verdure . . . with a great variety of flowers . . . all

seemed animated and enchanted . . . the hunters came in with
four fine antelope . . ."

The mission was grim, the business to be conducted full of
unknown quantities, but the days and nights were a succession
of bright sun and deep-blue sky and smoking silver stars.

When the stop was made at the end of the day's ride, and the
horses were turned out to graze on the fine buffalo grass, some at
once "busied themselves about the arrangements of their beds,
composed of small branches of willows and cottonwoods, others
hastened to kindle fires, fill the kettles and coffee-pots and arrange
rows of roasts on sharpened sticks, to content the inner man . . .
Every Indian is the owner of an excellent stomach, and . . . a
large capacity. For digestion's sake they dance around a few
times . . . accompanied with joyful songs . . . Then they sit
down, while the inseparable calumet goes its slow rounds from
mouth to mouth, they talk and argue on the affairs of the day,
tell stories, give their experiences in the chase or in their exploits
in war, laugh and joke until sleep overcomes them . . ."

The dawn was scarcely breaking each morning when the camp
would be aroused, and "We quickly light the fires again, prepare
the kettles and hot water, say the morning prayers, take in haste
our cup of coffee, our slice of meat and our biscuit . . . by five
o'clock we were on the road."

The country rose steadily toward the west, and as they neared
the Little Missouri it became rough and tortured. Great buttes
lifted their angular crests against the immaculate sky. Water became scarce, and often that found was unfit to drink.

On the 9th of June, four scouts—The Log, Red Cloud, Little
Dog and Sitting Crow—had gone ahead. Each of them carried
"a small charge of tobacco" sent by Father De Smet to be given
to whomever they might meet. The tobacco was a "formal invitation, or the announcement of a desire to confer upon important affairs."

No word had been received from the scouts when camp was
made on June 16th near the source of Beaver Creek. As the sun

sank, the ever watchful eyes of a horse herder picked up a group of riders in the far distance. Field glasses soon told Father De Smet that the scouts were returning, and "they came in at the head of a deputation of eighteen warriors . . . all came and shook hands with me with special eagerness, and after we had smoked the pipe, they announced in the name of the head chief of their camp that my tobacco had been favorably received . . ."

They declined, however, to reveal the exact location of their camp, although they were willing to escort Father De Smet to it, but only if he first agreed to certain conditions. He would not disclose their location, and he would promise to make no attempt to bring Big Knives [Army officers] into contact with them. The country was closed to all other white men.

It was an honor as well as an ultimatum. Father De Smet agreed to the terms. His word was all the hostiles wished. The understanding reached, the feasting and the singing and the smoking and the dancing began, and dawn was in the sky when it ended.

The trail taken on June 17th led directly into high hills, "a most arid and desolate region." Camp was made on Poplar Creek that night. The water was poor but there was an abundance of wood. "All the following day was occupied in crossing high rolling plains, in which cactus predominated . . . and we camped on the Big Sandy."

Twelve miles were traversed across a high plateau on June 19th, and then the valley of the Powder River "lay before us . . . [and a] lovely landscape was presented to our sight."

Now Father De Smet looked upon a spectacle that was as frightening as it was colorful. Five hundred warriors, every one with blood on his hands and scalps dangling from his horse, were riding up the valley of the Powder toward him.

He took from a saddlebag a banner, and it was attached to a slender pole and given to the breeze. It was "my standard of peace—with the holy name of Jesus on one side and on the other the image of the holy Virgin Mary, surrounded with gilt stars."

The cavalcade of horsemen halted, as if uncertain of the meaning of the strange flag. Presently four men advanced. Father De Smet and his company stopped and waited, sitting in silence. The investigators stared at the banner. Then, as if at some mysteriously given signal, they surrounded Black Robe and each in turn shook his hand.

Five thousand warriors were camped beside the Powder. They formed a long line to receive their distinguished visitor. As Father De Smet shook hands with the chiefs he was "touched even to tears . . . It was the fairest spectacle in which I have ever had the happiness of taking part, and, against all expectation, it was filled with manifestation of the profoundest respect. Everything was wild and noisy, but at the same time everything was carried out in admirable order."

The warriors had donned their finest raiment for the occasion, and "plumes of eagles and other birds adorned their long hair, and even their steeds had them in their manes and tails, mingled with silk ribbons of various colors and scalps . . .

"By the penal code in force among the savages, every Indian who has lost a member of his family at the hands of the white is obliged to avenge himself on the first white man he meets. Well, there were a good many of them in this position . . .

"Nevertheless, my heart was tranquil and my mind calm . . ."

Around him were thousands of Indians who had broken out of the tethers by which the Great White Father, whom they had been taught through suffering and death could not be trusted, had sought to imprison them. They were the wild ones, the hostiles. They were the people dedicated to fight to the death for their country.

But for one white man they had prepared a large lodge, and they had mounted guards around it, not so that he could not escape but so that he would be protected, and they awaited with all solemnity and respect the words he would speak.

Father De Smet was too weary to speak then. His body was wracked with pain, and he was on the verge of exhaustion. He asked for food, and when he had eaten, he asked that he be allowed to rest, and when he stretched out on his bed he fell quickly into a deep sleep.

Father De Smet's eyes opened an hour or two later to rest at once upon the broad, muscular, copper face of a heavy man, naked except for a breechcloth, who sat nearby. A few feet away were three other men whose feathers denoted their high rank, and beside them was Galpin.

The man closest to him was the great Sitting Bull. The others were Four Horns, Black Moon and No Neck.

Father De Smet uttered a word of welcome. The men nodded in appreciation, and their eyes moved to the famed medicine chief, whose privilege it was to speak first.

Sitting Bull's words came slowly and with precision, and his obsidian eyes held steadily to Father De Smet's face. What he said was interpreted by Galpin with equal slowness and precision.

"Black Robe, I hardly sustain myself beneath the weight of white man's blood that I have shed.* The whites provoked the war; their injustices, their indignities to our families, the cruel, unheard-of and wholly unprovoked massacre at Fort Lyon of 600 or 700 women, children and old men, shook all the veins which bind and support me.† I rose, tomahawk in hand, and I have done all the hurt to the whites I could. Today you are here, and in your presence my arms stretch to the ground as if dead. I will listen to your good words, and as bad as I have been to the whites, just so good am I ready to become toward them."

It was agreed that a full council would be held the following day. As Father De Smet prepared to retire for the night, a "venerable old man, of remarkable stature but bowed beneath the weight of age, supporting himself on a staff tipped with an

---

* Father De Smet and Galpin recorded the speech later, as they remembered it.

† This was the Sand Creek Massacre in November 1864, committed by troops under the command of a sadistic, barbaric colonel of the Colorado militia, John Chivington.

old bayonet, came to offer me his hand and express his happiness at seeing me again. He wore upon his breast a copper cross, old and worn."

Father De Smet could not remember meeting the aged warrior, and asked who had given him the cross.

"It was you, Black Robe. I have never laid it aside for twenty-six snows."

The council began with songs and dances, and then came the smoking. Beyond the circle of the chiefs and headmen hundreds of Indians watched and listened in respectful silence. Two hours of ceremonies had passed before Four Horns said: "Speak, Black Robe."

Father De Smet rose and stood with his hands to heaven, and he "made a prayer to the Great Spirit, imploring light and blessing from him and his help in this great meeting. Then, for almost an hour, I laid before them the disinterested motives that had brought me among them . . ."

He talked of the dangers with which the hostile bands were surrounded, and he told them of their weakness before the incomparable strength of the United States Army. He spoke of the great harm which had been done by the war, of the atrocious crimes committed by both sides. Now the Great White Father had given him a message for them. Washington desired that all should be forgotten and buried. Washington wanted to aid them, to give them farms and agricultural implements, domestic animals, men to teach them field work and teachers for their children, and they would not have to surrender their lands. They were engaged in a war of attrition. Halt it while there was still a chance to salvage some of their rights, before all was destroyed and there were none left to fight. Let there be a grand council, a great smoke, at Fort Rice. Send delegates to receive gifts and sign a treaty of peace. The alternative was death and oblivion. He spoke not as a man of the sword, but as a man of God, and as their friend.

Sitting Bull, Two Bears and Running Antelope replied with

eloquence, but of all the speeches made, Father De Smet considered that of Black Moon the most significant, and he and Galpin took pains to put it on paper as they believed it had been delivered.

"Lend an ear to my words," Black Moon said. "The Black Robe has made a long journey to come to us; his presence among us makes me very glad, and with all my heart I wish him welcome to my country. I can understand all the words that Black Robe has just said to us; they are good and filled with truth. I shall lay them up in my memory.

"Still, our hearts are sore, they have received deep wounds. These wounds have yet to be healed. A cruel war has desolated and impoverished our country . . . not kindled by us; it was the Sioux east of us and the Cheyennes south of us who raised the war first, to revenge themselves for the white man's cruelties and injustice. We have been forced to take part, for we too have been victims of their wrongdoing.

"Today we ride over our plains, we find them spotted here and there with blood; these are not the bloodstains of buffalo and deer . . . but those of our own comrades or of white men, sacrificed to vengeance.

"The buffalo . . . have quitted our immense plains; we hardly find them anymore, except at intervals, and always less numerous. May it not be the odor of human blood that puts them to flight? I will say further—against our will the whites are interlacing our country with their highways of transportation and emigration; they build forts at various points and mount thunders on them. They kill our animals, and more than they need. They are cruel to our people—massacre them without reason—even when we are searching for food . . . They cut down our forests in spite of us, and without paying us for their value. They are ruining our land. We are opposed to having these big roads which drive the buffalo away from our country. The soil is ours, and we are determined not to yield an inch of it. Here our fathers were born and buried. We desire, like them, to live here . . .

"We have been forced to hate the whites. Let them treat us like brothers and the war will cease.

"You, Messenger of Peace, have given us a glimpse of a better future. Very well . . . Let us throw a veil over the past, and let it be forgotten.

"We accept your tobacco. Some of our warriors will go with you to Fort Rice to hear the words and the propositions of the Great Father's commissioners. If their words are acceptible, peace will be made."

Father De Smet estimated that the camp on the Powder was some three hundred and fifty miles from Fort Rice.‡ When the return trip was begun, shortly after dawn on the morning of June 21st, he gave the guides instructions to take the most direct line possible to their destination. He was fully aware that he had accomplished an extraordinary feat—more than he could have hoped for—and he understood the need for haste. The variableness of the Indian—always subject to influence by all manner of ghosts—was no mystery to him.

Nearly three hundred persons were in the column when it left Powder River. The wagons were abandoned, so that they might travel faster.§

"We traveled thirty-five to forty-five miles every day; the weather was fine . . ."

On June 25, at Box Elder Creek, Father De Smet dispatched a courier, All Over Black, with a letter advising the commissioners of his success and his position. He estimated his arrival at the fort "in about five days." Galpin also sent a message.

A courier with a reply from Major General Terry reached Father De Smet on June 29. ". . . not only ourselves but the nation owes you a debt of gratitude . . ." Terry said. "Generals Harney and Sanborn arrived here on the twenty-first and they will remain until a treaty can be consummated."

‡ It was probably 300 miles by air line.
§ Unfortunately, with the exception of the famous chief, Gall, Father De Smet did not name the delegates.

Terry had learned from Galpin's message that Father De Smet was "quite unwell," and he expressed the hope that "the rest and quiet which will follow your return will speedily restore you to health."

Nine days after he had left Powder River, Father De Smet rode into Fort Rice. Behind him came a long column of Sioux, feathered lances held aloft in salute. Awaiting him were three generals of the United States Army and several thousand Indians from many tribes who had traveled hundreds of miles, not alone to attend the peace council, but to see and hear the words of the great man they called Black Robe.

The "Peace Council took place on the 2nd of July [1868]. Fifty thousand Indians were there represented. It was the greatest council that had been held on the Missouri . . ."

A treaty was signed, and "on the 4th of July the distribution of presents was made . . . I left the same day . . ."

XXXIX

Before they left Fort Rice, Generals Harney, Sanborn and Terry wrote a joint letter to Father De Smet. In keeping with Army regulations, copies went with their other reports and papers to their superior, General Sherman, to the War Department, to the Indian Department, and through one or more of these channels reached the newspapers.

". . . but for your long and painful journey into the heart of the hostile country, and but for the influence over even the most hostile of the tribes . . . the results which we have reached here could not have been accomplished," the letter said.

"We are well aware that our thanks can be but of little worth to you, and that you will find your true reward for your labors—in the consciousness that you have done much to promote peace on earth—but we should do injustice to our own feelings were we not to render to you our thanks and express our deep sense of obligation under which you have laid us."

Major General David S. Stanley sent a copy of the letter to "H. G. Monseigneur Archbishop John B. Purcell, Bishop of Cincinnati," seeking to make sure that the one superior of Father De Smet he knew was apprised of his feat. Stanley added more than a few words of his own:

"He is the only man for whom I have ever seen Indians evince a real affection . . .

"It is the most complete and the wisest of all the treaties thus far concluded . . . the Indians are to be abundantly provided with victuals, clothing and agricultural and mechanical implements."

Stanley's next words were an indictment of the government

which employed him: "No money payments have been stipulated [in the treaty]," he said, "as unfortunately money excites the covetousness of more than one and often converts commissioners, governors of territories, superintendents, agents and traders into a band of thieves."

Whatever the future was to bring, said Stanley, "we can never forget nor shall we ever cease to admire . . . Father De Smet, who, at the age of sixty-eight years, did not hesitate in the midst of summer to undertake a long and perilous journey, across the burning plains—constantly exposed—and this without seeking either honors or remuneration . . . but solely to arrest the shedding of blood . . ."

General Stanley was a capable and sincere officer, but he was a poor prophet.

On his way down the Missouri from Fort Rice, Father De Smet paused for a few days at Fort Sully to perform religious duties. He went on to Leavenworth, thence to St. Mary's Mission on the Kansas River. He reached St. Louis August 20th, his strength hardly great enough to sustain him until he could drop into his bed at St. Louis University.

For several days the doctors despaired of saving him, but miraculously he rallied, and at last he was able to sit at a table to eat and write a few letters.

To the editor of the *Précis Historiques* in Antwerp, he said: "This letter may well be my last. My health is very much undermined in consequence of the fatigues of my late painful journey . . . but still more by the shocking heat . . . In proportion as I advance in age, heat becomes more and more insupportable to me. Very often anyone would say that I resemble a man whose end is at hand."

He had finished an account of the peace mission for the magazine while traveling down the river, but he felt it rather an unsatisfactory piece of work, and he begged the editor "to pay no attention to the disconnectedness of my narrative."

The historian Chittenden said that Father De Smet "looked

with deep dread upon the prospect of Grant's election in 1868. He felt that the great general shared the Protestant antagonism to his Church, and that he [Grant] could not withstand the more radical element in his party who would use his great authority among the people to further their extreme measures."

That was true, but Father De Smet also feared Grant for another and perhaps more important reason. He had every confidence that the Church could weather the anticipated storm, but he did not believe the Indians could survive the blows he expected to be struck against them by the Grant administration.

He was to live long enough to find that every apprehension he had held had been fully justified. It was during President Grant's tenure that corruption in the Indian Bureau rose to its greatest height, that Indians of all tribes received the most cruel treatment in history.

By the late fall of 1868, Father De Smet's health had once again improved to the extent that he talked of going up the Missouri in the spring to establish a mission among the Sioux, a project that had been postponed for so many years and which was so dear to him. In alarm his doctors and his superiors put their heads together to find a means of changing his mind, for they knew that another journey to the Indian Country would bring the end of his life.

In November he was ordered to make a trip to Europe, assertedly on Jesuit business. He went without complaint, but he understood that the voyage was nothing more than a scheme to make his last days on earth as comfortable as possible in his own country and among the members of his family.

He spent most of the next eight months in Belgium. When he returned to St. Louis in the summer of 1869, he was more determined than ever to carry on with the project of the Sioux mission, and he proposed that he go at once up the river to select a site.

"I have just made a little test of my strength and have succeeded so well that I have hopes, *Deodante,* of being able to accomplish my visit and mission to the Indians of the upper Missouri," he wrote a nephew in October 1869.

The doctors stood firm in their refusal to sanction the plan until June of the next year, and then gave in. Father De Smet traveled up the Missouri as far as the mouth of Grand River,* spending most of the time en route in his stateroom. He talked with many Indians and traders, and he found what he considered a suitable place for the new establishment. It was on the Grand River Reservation, where bottomlands adjacent to the agency were "susceptible of cultivation, with plenty of timber and good grazing ground."

The trip was his last to the Indian Country.

Early in August he was back in St. Louis. In a letter to E. S. Parker, Commissioner of Indian Affairs, he admitted that his health had been "feeble for some time past." He attributed this condition to "the excessive summer heat of the upper country."

The doctors knew better.

Throughout the winter of 1870–71, he spent as many hours as his strength would permit at his desk. He carried on a heavy correspondence, and he began to write a book that had always been close to his heart, a history of the province of Missouri. When spring came again he began to chafe over the slowness of the Society to approve the location he had selected for the Sioux mission, and he talked again of going up the river.

Once more arrangements were made for him to go to Europe where, it was hoped, his concern over Indian affairs would be interrupted by other matters, and he would be assured of comfort and good medical care.

In July 1871, he sailed from New York. If the doctors thought that he would remain idle in his family home in Termonde, they were very much mistaken. He continued his voluminous correspondence, and he prepared for publication some of his most outstanding papers.

* Opposite the present city of Mobridge, South Dakota.

During January and February of 1872, he was gravely ill. Hemorrhages again occurred, but neither the serious affliction nor pleas by his doctors and colleagues could prevent him from planning his return to the United States.

The pain of his body was not to be compared with the pain he was suffering in his mind. The Treaty of 1868 had been violated in a dozen ways by the government. Hordes of settlers and miners continued to pour into the Black Hills, into Dakota and Montana, driving the Indians from lands pledged to them, robbing them, cheating them, murdering them. President Grant not only condoned the outrages, but declared the treaty inoperative and worthless. Plans were announced to build a railroad through the heart of the Sioux Country.

In 1870, while en route East, Father De Smet had attended briefly a conference on Indian missions called by the government. Later he was informed that of forty-three missions to be authorized for reservations in all parts of the West, "only four are assigned to the Catholics." The other thirty-nine would be awarded to Protestant denominations.

In several letters to superiors and friends he italicized the words: "In the whole of this affair the Indians have not been consulted as to the religion they desired to belong to."

Indeed, his fears of President Grant had been justified.

Again and again from the Indian Country the appeal had been sent to the White House: "We want Black Robe to visit us. We want Black Robe, our friend, to live among us."

The appeal was ignored.

Bright's disease was ravaging his body, but the knowledge that all the good he had done in the years spent trying to help the Indians was being swept away, forever destroyed by a few evil, bigoted politicians in Washington, was breaking his heart.

Father De Smet crossed the Atlantic for the nineteenth time in April 1872.

He never left St. Louis again.

On the 23rd of May 1873, he fell asleep in the sparsely furnished room at St. Louis University that was his home, and he did not waken.

The city of St. Louis mourned that day. Church bells tolled, and the thousands of men and women—the great, the rich, the famous, the humble, the poor, the red and the white and the black—wept as they passed his bier.

Far out on the Great Plains that washed their gold and brown waves against the shores of the mountains, a banner waved before the lodge of a chief named Gall. It had been given to him on the Powder River by Black Robe one day in 1868, and he had tenderly cared for it. Gall the bloody, Gall the Sioux murderer, the soldiers and settlers called him.

In the graveyard of the Jesuit novitiate at Florissant a cross marked the resting place of the body of a man who had given his life to people of lesser privilege and greater need, a man who, almost to the day, in a May fifty years before had walked for the first time on that bit of earth, then far in the wilderness of the West.